100 MILES TO FREEDOM

THE EPIC STORY OF THE RESCUE OF SANTO TOMAS
AND THE LIBERATION OF MANILA: 1943-1945

100 MILES TO FREEDOM

THE EPIC STORY OF THE RESCUE OF SANTO TOMAS AND THE LIBERATION OF MANILA: 1943-1945

ROBERT B. HOLLAND

TURNER

Turner Publishing Company
4507 Charlotte Avenue, Suite 100
Nashville, TN 37209
Phone: (615)255-2665   Fax: (615)255-5081

www.turnerpublishing.com

100 Miles to Freedom: The Epic Story of the Rescue of Santo Tomas and the Liberation of Manila: 1943-1945

Library of Congress Cataloging-in-Publication Data

Holland, Robert B.
  100 miles to freedom : the epic story of the rescue of Santo Tomas and the liberation of
Manila, 1943-1945 / Robert B. Holland.
      p. cm.
  Includes bibliographical references and index.
  ISBN 978-1-59652-775-1
  1. Santo Tomas Internment Camp (Manila, Philippines) 2. World War, 1939-1945--Con-
centration camps--Liberation--Philippines--Manila. 3. World War, 1939-1945--Prisoners
and prisons, Japanese. 4. Prisoners of war--Philippines--Manila--Biography. 5. Prisoners
of war--United States--Biography. 6. Holland, Robert B. 7. Marines--United States--Bi-
ography. 8. United States. Army. Cavalry, 1st--History--World War, 1939-1945. 9. World
War, 1939-1945--Personal narratives, American. 10. World War, 1939-1945--Campaigns-
-Philippines--Manila. I. Title. II. Title: One hundred miles to freedom. III. Title: Hundred
miles to freedom.
  D805.5.S28H64 2011
  940.54'259916--dc22
                              2010050854

Printed in the United States of America

I dedicate this book to the memory of the three most wonder-ful women in my life: my wife, Jeanette, who devoted herself to our family and spoiled all of us for thirty-eight years; my loving mother, Sadie Holland, who raised five boys after our father died when I was three years old; and my mother-in-law, Jane Pevy Ashby, who was like a mother to me.

Contents

Contents

Foreword

For more than fifty years, we heard very little about "the Greatest Generation," as Tom Brokaw calls us. We were the loyal Americans who lived through World War II. In our lifetime, we have never known such love, honor, and respect for our great United States of America as during this time, 1941–1945. Men and women, boys and girls, Americans in the true sense, worked and sacrificed for their country to turn around the horrible nightmare of war. The war deeply affected every family, every person in some life-changing way. Yet it was a great time, because literally everyone pulled together to create a better and safer country for all of us.

This book is a story told by one U.S. Marine, who like many other millions of Americans, accepted the challenge that had been thrust on him, putting his life and future on hold until the job that had to be done was finished. Bob Holland tells the story of his part in the release of 3,700 American civilian prisoners of the Japanese at Santo Tomas University Internment Camp in Manila, the Philippines. Until their miraculous rescue on February 3, 1945, these civilians had been interned for more than three and one-half years.

This is also the story of the tactics used in achieving this rescue. We had developed Close Air Support in the Pacific early in World War II. It was carried out by Marine planes, mostly to support ground troops as they landed on beachheads such as Guadalcanal and the other Pacific islands. The campaign in the Philippines carried air support one step further by providing cover for ground troops inland. The Marines' use of the old reliable SBD dive-bombers, which could pinpoint a target, turned out to be very effective.

Army commanders were at first reluctant to utilize Marine air support, fearing "friendly fire" on our own troops, but after seeing what this support could accomplish safely, they made effective use of it. This was an excellent example of the team spirit that existed among the various military services as they worked together closely in combat.

Before Bob volunteered for the U.S. Marines, he had a secure government job at San Antonio Air Depot in San Antonio, Texas, repairing radio and radar equipment for U.S. Army Air Corps military aircraft. One day Bob walked into the Marine Recruiting Station in San Antonio. Later, he would walk out a Marine. Though not knowing what lay ahead, this was a proud moment for him—knowing he was serving his country as best he could.

Many veterans of World War II have waited a long time to tell their own stories. There are many stories like this one that need to be heard, but will soon be lost with a dying age of American patriots. Through this and other books, we can know and better appreciate what our proud and dedicated generation of true Americans did for our country.

—B. Gen. Robert Edward Galer, USMC

Robert Edward Galer was a student at the University of Washington and a Marine Cadet in the NROTC unit there. On graduation day, June 1, 1935, he became an aviation cadet in the United States Marine Corps. He volunteered to join the Marine Corps. From there he went to Pensacola and received his wings in the Corps as a Second Lieutenant. His first assignment was at the Marine Corps Air Station in Quantico, Virginia. After his exemplary service in Guadalcanal and the Solomon Islands, for which he received the Medal of Honor, he made the landings at Iwo Jima, Luzon, the Philippines, and Okinawa. Later, after World War II, he served in Korea and retired as a brigadier general, U.S. Marine Corps, in 1957. Brigadier General Galer received the Medal of Honor from President Franklin D. Roosevelt at the White House on 23 March 1943, which reads:

GALER, ROBERT EDWARD, Major, U.S. Marine Corps, Marine Fighter Squadron 244. Solomon Islands Area. Entered service 1 June 1935, Seattle, Washington. Other Navy Awards: Navy Cross, Distinguished Flying Cross. Citation: For conspicuous heroism and courage above and beyond the call of duty as leader of a Marine fighter squadron in aerial combat with enemy Japanese forces in the Solomon Islands area. Leading his squadron repeatedly in daring and aggressive raids against Japanese aerial forces, vastly superior in numbers, Major Galer availed himself of every favorable attack opportunity, individually shooting down 11 enemy bomber and fighter air-craft over a period of 29 days. Though suffering the extreme physical strain attendant upon protracted fighter operations at an altitude above 25,000 feet, the squadron under his zealous and inspiring leadership shot down a total of 27 Japanese planes. His superb airmanship, his outstanding skill and personal valor reflect great credit upon Major Galer's gallant fighting spirit and upon the U.S. Naval Service.

Preface

The decision to write about my experience in World War II first came about rather casually. In September 1998, I was visiting Dallas. While having dinner with my friends, Warrant Officer Jack Stark, USMC, Rtd. and his wife, Ruth, both of whom knew I had served in the Philippines, I was handed a copy of a pamphlet honoring the 50th anniversary of the Marines in World War II.[1] I returned to my home in Phoenix the following day. It was then that I began to look over the pamphlet. It recounted the story of the "Flying Column" in the Philippines and the liberation of the prisoners from Santo Tomas. It also described how the Marine Air Group 24, First Marine Air Wing, provided continuous close air support air cover with Marine SBD dive-bomber aircraft for the operation. Then I read: "Two radio jeeps and a radio truck with a total of three officers and four enlisted Marines were assigned to the mission."[2] *He was writing about the seven of us!* I was a technical sergeant in charge of the three other enlisted Marines.

I wanted to learn more, and I wanted to tell the story of my time in World War II. I began to do some research at the 1st Cavalry Division, the National Archives in College Park, Maryland, and the U.S. Marine Historical Center in Washington, D.C. Soon I realized the story was not complete without hearing from the internees themselves, and including their own accounts of what happened to them in those horrible years. I realized, though it is my story, more importantly it is their story too.

And so what follows is a significant part of World War II history told by one Marine who was part of the miraculous "Flying Column" of the U.S. Army 1st Cavalry Division. I, an enlisted Marine, and seven of the more than 3,700 internees who were rescued by this daring operation, tell the story.

Like all stories, it has many aspects to it, many sides and viewpoints. Recounted here is the story of the liberation of the internees at the Santo Tomas University Internment Camp as told by the internees themselves, who endured three and a half years of imprisonment under the Japanese. Leading up to the internees' stories is my story, that of a Marine, from the small town of Coalgate, Oklahoma, partly by circumstance and partly by choice, thrown into the war in the South Pacific. Toward the middle of this book our paths—those of the internees and me—meet, when we rode into camp with the 1st Cavalry and received their thanks and gratitude for their rescue.

Our paths were to meet again—this time in the writing of this book, which I offer as a tribute and a remembrance to those who fought, those who endured, those who died, and those who returned to their homes. Indeed, in the appendixes to this book are the more complete stories of two of our group from MAG-24—one who endured, Captain Francis R. B. (Frisco) Godolphin, USMCR, and one who died at the hands of our enemy, Captain Jack A. Titcomb, USMCR.

I have researched the historical background of the liberation, the decisions of great men, and the tactical decisions to ensure a wider understanding of the important role of the "Flying Column" and the Marine close air support to it and to provide context for the personal stories related here. We often forget in reading history books that history is something that has been lived by the participants. It is those lives and those voices I seek to recover here. When those of us in the military were fighting the war, we did not have a clear picture of what was happening. Decisions were made and orders were given that we carried out, without full knowledge of why they were made, and with no certainty of how they would turn out. But we were in good hands by experienced and well-trained leaders. If nothing else, you will see that was true in this campaign.

Here is the outline of the story you will read: General Douglas A. MacArthur, Commander-in-Chief of the Southwest Pacific Allied Forces, had ordered the 1st Cavalry to go to Manila, Luzon, in the Philippines and rescue the 3,700 men, women, and children, most of them American civilians, who had been interned at the Santo Tomas University Internment Camp in Manila for three and a half years. The 1st Cavalry's "Flying Column" accomplished this feat with a 100-mile dash down Central Luzon in only 66 hours, for the first time fully mechanized. I was one of the seven U.S. Marines attached to the 1st Cavalry with some 900 Army troopers. Our job was to direct from the front lines in our two jeeps and a radio truck the close air support provided by Marine Corps dive bomber airplanes.

The story related here tells of encounters with strong resistance by the Japanese. Some 230,000 Japanese troops had moved from Manila and Central Luzon to the eastern range of mountains of Luzon. The Japanese military believed they could resist our advances more effectively from the mountains. So we traveled in the lowlands as fast as we could, forcing our way down open highways and clear terrain, the way cleared by our strafing and bombing of the resisting Japanese troops. The speed of the column and the reconnaissance and air power supplied by our Marine planes made it possible to cross most bridges over deep rivers before they were destroyed. This operation was conceived and planned by a few of America's finest military leaders. February 3, 1945, was the date the Americans first reentered Manila since the Japanese take-over. That was the date of the liberation of the internees at Santo Tomas Internment Camp.

In Chapter 5 are the stories of the internees, told by seven who lived in the camp. I conducted personal interviews with the seven featured in this book from March 22, 2000, to November 13, 2000, as well as many contacts afterward. The stories they tell are of death by starvation, murder, and disease, of the horrible conditions under which they were required to live, as told by the internees themselves. For 462 of the internees, we arrived too late.[3] Many internees, mostly men, died because they had sacrificed their food to feed the children.

This book does not recount the whole Philippine Liberation by all of the Allied forces that participated. The horrible Bataan Death March alone would fill many volumes. There are many good books about this terrible tragedy. The American prisoners taken on Hell ships, most of whom died, is another story that should be told, few of whom are still alive. The many POW and internee camps in the Philippines are yet another story. Los Banos Internment camp, built to relieve the crowded camp at Santo Tomas; Bilibid Prison; several others in the Baguio area— each internee must have a different story of their own horrible internment. I tell only the part of the Liberation in which I participated.

In addition to wanting to tell my story and have the internees' stories heard, I am writing this book for another reason. Many other countries have fully supported their military and civilian citizens, POWs, and internees in protesting their inhumane treatment by the Japanese during World War II. Sad to say, the United States has not. Rather, in 1988 the U.S. Congress recognized only what the United States had inflicted on Japanese-Americans during their internment in the United States during World War II, allocating $20,000 in "reparations" to each, a total of $2 billion, yet allocating nothing to their German and Italian counterparts, who constituted nearly half of the internees in the camps.

The U.S. State Department has taken the position that all rights of the U.S. POWs and internees were waived by the U.S.–Japanese treaty of 1951. The internees have filed many lawsuits, but one by one they are being thrown out. An article in *Parade* magazine, for June 17, 2001, states:

The U.S. State Department and Justice Department intervened for the Japanese corporate defendants on the basis of the 1951 Peace Treaty, a clause which purports to waive all future restitution claims. But the treaty contains another clause, which the U.S. government to date has chosen to ignore, stating that all bets would be off if other nations got the Japanese to agree to more favorable terms than our treaty. Eleven nations, including the then Soviet Union, Vietnam and the Philippines—received such terms from the Japanese.

Tom Brokaw calls our generation, the generation of World War II, "the Greatest Generation," and he is right. America's citizen heroes and heroines who came of age during the Great Depression and the Second World War went on to build modern America. This generation was united not only by a common purpose but also by common values—duty, honor, economy, courage, service, love, family, country, and above all, responsibility. It was a generation that persevered through war and was trained in it. It was a generation that then went on to create interesting and useful lives and build the America we have today. When the United States entered World War II, the U.S. government turned to ordinary Americans and asked of them extraordinary service, sacrifice, and heroism.

Many Americans met those high expectations and then returned home to lead ordinary lives. When the war ended, more that 12 million men and women put their uniforms aside and returned to civilian life. They went back to work at their old jobs or started small businesses; they became big-city cops and firemen; they finished their degrees or enrolled in college for the first time. They became schoolteachers, insurance salesmen, craftsmen, and local politicians. Most never became known outside of their families or their communities. For many, the war years were an adventure to last a lifetime. They were proud of what they accomplished, but they rarely discussed their experiences, even with each other. They became once again ordinary people, the kind of men and women who always have been the foundation of the American way of life.[4]

Once we came back we just didn't talk about it. It is difficult now to explain why. Maybe it was because the war seemed like a bad dream—a nightmare—and that once we got back we just wanted to get on with our lives. When we thought about where we had been, what had happened, and what we had seen and lived through, it brought back bad memories, not good ones. There were some good times, especially in the friendships we formed. We made friends easily over there because we worked together and lived together. We were all the same there, fighting for a common purpose.

The bad memories came from the horror of what we saw and the losses we suffered. I lost a good friend over there. Several others I knew did not make it back. When you lose a member of your family, you lose a part of yourself. It's the same way when you lose a friend: something is gone from inside you that cannot be replaced. Maybe that is why we did not want to talk about it.

I remember lying in a foxhole dreaming of a little white house with a picket fence around it and little kids running around in the yard. Dreaming of the future is what helped get many of we younger ones through. My hope is that we did set an example for future generations. We also simply had a job to do, and, together, we did it. Never in the history of our country have so many pulled together to get a job done. Many heroes did not come back or came back and were never the same again. Finally, we are now starting to reflect and remember—and tell our stories. I hope it's not too late, and that more of us will come forward.

Many who expected to be drafted volunteered so that they could choose the branch of service they preferred. Others who volunteered to serve in the military would never have been drafted, including some who had family responsibilities but enlisted because they believed it was the right thing to do. Two such men became good friends of mine in the Pacific: Capt. John A. (Jack) Titcomb, USMCR, who was killed by a sniper's bullet in northern Luzon, the Philippines, on March 1, 1945 (see Appendix A) and Capt. Francis R. B. (Frisco) Godolphin, USMCR, with whom I worked in Luzon (see Appendix B). Many just like these two served their country well. We will always be indebted to them for their sacrifice.

We, as a country, owe it to them to know these stories. While people in the U.S. at the time were doing without gasoline and nylons, the internees had to do without food and medicine. Even today many of them cannot get over the horrible things they endured. It is shameful that we, as a nation, have not done more for them. We also owe a debt to our brave fellow American GIs who laid down their lives. There is no way we can repay them. But we can recognize them and we can thank them through their families.

We fought in the jungles of the South Pacific, trudging through the mud, in the heat, and enduring bad conditions. When we defeated the enemy, we won more jungle and more mud! But when we arrived at Santo Tomas Internment Camp, we were welcomed with open arms by fellow Americans thankful for what we had done. That was our reward— and what a wonderful reward it was.

My hope also is that the reader will get a sense of what that experience was like for those of us who lived it to be part of a worthy cause. It also describes how some died for it and how it felt for some of us to witness it. The book describes the day-to-day concerns of the soldier living through a history-making event. Through my eyes, those of a Marine involved in the liberation, and the eyes of the internees at Santo Tomas, readers will come to know a little more about who this "greatest generation" was and the challenges we all faced.

Finally, an important note about those we were fighting against and how we saw them. "Japs" is what we called them! And that is the word you'll see most often used in this book. But that was then, when they were our enemy. Today they are the Japanese, and we have great respect for them. But we didn't then. They were Japs to us. Bill Dunn explains it best: "When is a Japanese a 'Jap'? That's easy! It's when he's flying an enemy plane, occupying an enemy bunker, pacing the bridge of an enemy warship or merely trying to eliminate you from this earth."[5]

Acknowledgments

The heart of this book comes from the internees themselves, who were so gracious and so appreciative of my efforts: Gil Hair, Executive Director, The Center for Internee Rights, Inc., Miami Beach, Florida, and his mother, Jane; Rosemarie Elizabeth Hoyt Weber, whose father was taken from Santo Tomas to die on a Japanese Hell Ship, and her husband Ralph Weber; all seven of the internees whose gripping stories are in the book—Dorothy Khoury Howie, Miami Beach, Florida; Sascha Jean Weinzheimer Jansen, Vacaville, California; Edgar Mason Kneedler (deceased), Palm Springs, California; Mary Jane Brooks Morse, Vancouver, B.C., Canada; Caroline Jane Bailey Pratt, Davis, California; Madeline Ullom, Lt. Col. U.S. Regular Army Corps (deceased), Tucson, Arizona;

and Peter Robert Wygle, Ventura, California.

Other military and friends had a hand in this book as well: William Harry Boudreau, 1st Cavalry Division Historian, Plano, Texas; Steve Draper, Director of the 1st Cavalry Division Museum, Fort Hood, Texas; Bob Aquilina, Historian, U.S. Marine Corps Historical Center, Washington, D.C..; Gerald (Jerry) Daley, WWII Sgt. Division Hq. 7th Recon Squadron, Tulsa, Oklahoma; Donna Boutelle, Professor California State University, Long Beach, California; the Godolphin family, especially Jeanne Godolphin Smeeth, San Francisco, California; the Titcomb family, in particular Andrew Titcomb, his wife Joanna, and their son Jonathan, Perkinsville, Vermont. Special friends Jack Stark, Warrant Officer, USMC Rtd., and his wife Ruth, Dallas, Texas, and Bob Olson, Lt. Col. USAF Rtd., Amarillo, Texas, who helped find information I needed on the Internet.

Of course I am so grateful to Brigadier General Robert E. Galer for his foreword, added to the book after it was completed.

There would never have been a book without the help and guidance of my editor, Catherine Kreyche of Washington, D.C.

Finally, to my family, especially my three great grandsons, who suffered some neglect for the two years I was researching and writing this book. And to my daughters Jane and Peggy—Jane for helping me proofread the manuscript and Peggy for helping me research military records in the Washington, D.C., area.

To all, my heartfelt thanks for providing the help and advice that made this a much better book.

Prologue

Yesterday, December 7, 1941, a date that will live in infamy . . ." I heard those words over the radio when they were first uttered, and they still ring in my ears. It was the day after the Japanese attacked Pearl Harbor, and President Franklin D. Roosevelt was speaking before Congress, asking that war be declared on Japan.

The day before the president's speech, I was home with my mother. We first heard on the radio news that Sunday afternoon of the Japanese attack.

I was in a state of shock and disbelief. Why would any nation, especially such a small one, bomb the mighty United States? A day or two later the country learned more. At 7:55 a.m., on December 7, the Japanese attacked Pearl Harbor, Hawaii. American casualties that day, all of which were incurred in less than two hours, were 2,341 killed and 1,143 wounded. Eighteen ships were sunk or damaged. Among those sunk were the battleships USS *Arizona,* with 1,177 men lost, the USS *Oklahoma,* with 400 men lost, USS *California,* USS *West Virginia,* and USS *Utah,* with 50 men lost. *We were at war!*

The war started just after I had returned home from college. I was waiting to leave after the holidays for a special National Youth Administration school, part of one of President Roosevelt's New Deal programs, to be trained as an Army aircraft radio repairman. I followed through with my plans. In July 1942, I completed school and accepted a job as a U.S. Army radio technician at San Antonio Air Depot in San Antonio, Texas. Working on U.S. Army Air Corps planes, I had a draft-deferred job. Knowing this, I felt guilty, especially when I walked the streets of San Antonio with my buddies and saw that everyone our age was in uniform except us.

It was October 1, 1942. My friend Gordon Blue and I had a day off and were walking the streets of downtown San Antonio. We had read in the local paper that the U.S. Marine Corps was desperately looking for "good men" with radio training and experience. We had talked earlier about how "stupid" we felt not being a real part of the war. During our stroll we happened to walk past the Marine Recruiting Station. We looked at each other and walked in to find out what they had to offer two radio "experts." Little did I know that, for days later, I was sure that investigation led to the biggest mistake of my life. Only after the war was over did I realize that it was one of the best days—and that I had made one of the best decisions—of my life.

The recruiting sergeant wanted to know about our jobs at San Antonio Air Depot. As we told him, his eyes lit up. It was then that I realized that recruiting sergeants must work on a commission, not a salary. The officer in charge, a Marine Corps captain, then came out to meet us and ushered us down the hall into his office. He explained that we would go to boot camp (a satellite of hell, I later learned!), in San Diego, California. After that, we would be sent to Cherry Point, North Carolina, for Marine Corps Radio School, and from there to Corpus Christi, Texas, for radar school. We would be promoted to the rank of staff sergeant and go overseas with a Marine Air Wing. To go to a radar school and travel around the country and the world—all this was more than we expected. We agreed to continue forward.

We were given our physical examinations. Gordon passed his, and so did I—almost. I had heard that the Marine Corps did not accept men who wore glasses, so I took mine off. I was nearsighted, but I passed the first eye test without them. Then we were given the color test. Gordon was taken first into another room. He passed. I was next. The test required distinguishing colors. I was handed a book that had large circles made up of colored dots, four circles to a page. Within each of these large circles of dots, you were supposed to see a number in another color. The sergeant started my test. He turned to the first page of the book and said, "First circle, top left. What number do you see?" I saw no number. He went on, circle-by-circle, page-by-page. I was getting the drift, so I started guessing at the numbers. I got none of them right and failed the test miserably. I felt terrible. It looked like my friend was going to get in and I was not.

We were on the third floor of the building. The sergeant walked me over to the window. He said, "See that health food store across the

3

street?" They have fresh fruit juices and stuff like that. Go over there and ask for a large glass of fresh carrot juice. It will cost about 50 cents. Drink it all down and come back here in one hour!"

These were my first orders, and I wasn't even in the Marine Corps yet! Gordon and I walked over to the store. Gordon got a chocolate shake, and I got my carrot juice. There was no place to sit in the store, so we went back to the building where the recruiting station was and waited in the lobby for an hour.

Then we went up to the Marine Corps office. The sergeant was waiting for us. He asked me, "Did you drink the juice?"

"Yes," I replied.

He then took me back to the testing room and sat me down again in front of the book. He opened to the first page and asked, "On the top left circle, do you see the number?" He waited a few seconds.

Weakly I said, "No. I see some different colored dots."

Then he said more insistently, "Don't you see a number? What do you think it is?"

I said, "Three!" "Right!" he said.

"Now, the next circle. What is the number?"

"It looks like a 7."

"Right!" he said.

"That carrot juice works every time!" And so it went as we worked our way through the book. Sometimes it looked like two numbers, so I would just say what I thought it was. I passed the test.

He said, "You are now in the Marine Corps!" I will never know if I got those numbers right or not.

After signing all the papers in the Captain's office, we were told to be back six days later for the swearing in ceremony, ready to leave for San Diego. We had just a few days to leave our jobs and get everything in order. When we reported back, we were sworn in along with about twenty other recruits. The next day we left for San Diego.

After boot camp we were transferred to Cherry Point, and from there went to the Naval Air Technical Training Center, Ward Island, Corpus Christi, Texas. There we received classified training in the repair and maintenance of Navy and Marine Corps airborne radar and radio equipment. When we had completed the school we received orders to be shipped overseas and join an active Marine air unit in the South Pacific. After a short furlough we found ourselves back in San Diego. The city was teeming with servicemen perhaps not all of them well appreciated. It was reported that the parks had signs that read, "Dogs and Sailors, keep off the grass!"

Before the war had become imminent for the United States, there were fewer than 1 million men and women in all of the U.S. armed services. During the war more than 12 million were in the Army, Navy, Marine Corps, and Coast Guard. A large percentage of this increase came from men and women like us volunteering for service. In the newspapers, we were referred to as "citizen soldiers," but everyone, literally everyone, was severely affected by the war. Our country had been attacked and we had responded to the call. For myself, I could not have anticipated what lay ahead.

Chapter 1

Introduction to World War II in the South Pacific

Island Hopping

On September 20, 1943, we embarked from San Diego, California, on the USS *Mount Vernon*. The *Mount Vernon* was the largest maritime ship in the fleet. It had been a luxury ship until the U.S. Navy took it over during World War II.

We were told that approximately 6,000 troops were aboard. Our group stood on the loading dock for hours in full combat uniform, packs on backs, sea bags with us, and rifles over our shoulders, waiting to board. Finally, we were ordered to board the ship on the long, huge plank with many steps to the main deck. I was in the front of our group. As we walked into the ship, it looked like we were entering a large hotel lobby.

I saw hotel-type elevators and walked toward them. A Marine sergeant major standing there barked, "Down!" pointing to the ladder to the lower levels. We were escorted three or four levels down to our quarters. The bunks were five high. I grabbed a top bunk, having been told that, if you were below deck, the top bunk was the best place to avoid seasickness—to avoid suffering from the seasickness of the guy in the bunk above you!

As luck would have it, the bunk I chose was just below a large air-conditioning vent that I could open and close. That was very convenient, since it got very hot in that hold so far down in the guts of the ship.

While en route, I saw someone in the "lobby" whom I recognized as the British navy officer Lord Louis Mountbatten, commander of the Southeast Command. Lord Mountbatten was on his way to work with General MacArthur in Brisbane, Australia. In our combat fatigues, my fellow soldiers and I were in awe of the full-dress-uniformed Mountbatten. I saw him a couple times during the voyage.[6]

The first few days were the roughest, having to get used to the crowded environment. We were limited to where we could go. Besides our "quarters," we could walk the main deck and watch the water as we moved through it. And at night we could go to the aft of the ship and watch the churning, foaming water of the ship's propellers.

As on most large transport ships, the dining area had waist-high tables where you stood to eat—two meals a day, standard for troops being transported by the Navy. Many of the Marines became seasick, and many meals were lost and others not eaten. Some of us looked various shades of green. I was seasick for the first couple days but never lost a meal.

Since we were stuck sleeping in a hold with no air and could not see outside, we enjoyed climbing up to a deck to sit around during the day.

We were not in a convoy, so our ship zigzagged, which we could see from the deck. Like many Navy vessels, we changed direction every few miles so that we could travel more safely.

Some of the men found ways to entertain themselves. Every day, one of my staff sergeant friends would put on his swimming trunks, throw a towel over his shoulder, slip up the ladder to the elevators, and climb to the officers' deck. He would plop himself down in a lounge chair, and one of the ship's attendants would come by and serve him drinks and sandwiches—anything the "officer" wanted. When the deck got crowded, he would slip back and rejoin us. If he had been caught, he probably would have been thrown overboard. But he never was. In fact, he did this every day and began to get a good tan.

We stopped for a short time at Pearl Harbor for fuel and supplies and then got on our way. No one went ashore. In the distance, we could see the wreckage of a few of the ships from the attack on Pearl Harbor two years earlier.

On October 23, twenty-eight days after we had left San Diego, we arrived at Noumea, New Caledonia, a French protectorate. It appeared to be a fairly large city. We went ashore and were taken somewhere out of town to our "staging area." With tents out in an open field, it was obvious we were in temporary quarters, so we knew we would not be there very long.

We were given a weekend liberty to go into Noumea. There were countless tourist traps. And we had been warned about the "Pink House" in the heart of the city. This house of ill repute had GIs lined up around it for a block or so. We avoided that like the plague. The souvenirs did not appeal to me, but I did buy one dumb thing—an aluminum watchband

I was told was made from a Jap Zero fighter plane. It was made of a very shiny metal that lost its shine before we got back to camp. I had broken my leather band and needed a new one, but it turned out this thing was never close to a Jap Zero.

We stayed there only a few nights and then were taken in a small Navy vessel to Vila, Efate, in the New Hebrides Islands, where there was a more permanent camp. The tents were in a coconut grove, with no buildings in sight. Here we joined up with Headquarters Squadron, Marine Air Group 24 (MAG-24), 1st Marine Air Wing. Now there were 3,415 enlisted men and 458 officers, and our numbers would grow as we moved through the islands and to the Philippines.[7] We had some indoctrination about the group and what our responsibilities would be. We learned we would be going to the Russell Islands for a short stay and then make the landing at Bougainville. There we would establish a radio and radar repair group for all the airplanes in Marine Air Group 24 as well as others in the 1st Marine Air Wing. We didn't know any of the particulars at that time, but it was good to at least have some idea of what we would be doing and where we would be.

What I remember most about the island of Efate were the land crabs. These were like ocean crabs but were black and weird looking. They were everywhere because of the coconut trees. They could cut the husk off a coconut and get into the fruit of it with their claws. The crabs were sickening, the way they traveled sideways down through the trees. But that wasn't the worst of it. They would crawl into the tents and onto our camp cots during the night. We would feel something climbing in bed with us and throw it off with the blanket, flinging the crab across the dirt floor. We soon learned to bring a supply of bread from the mess tent after the evening meal and put the bread out in the middle of the tent so that these creatures would chew on it instead of us.

On November 14, we sailed from Efate on the USS *Tryon* for Banika, one of the Russell Islands in the Solomon chain of islands just north of Guadalcanal. At a camp there we spent a month getting ready for the landing on Bougainville. We learned to be ready to move out fast with all our gear and rehearsed getting ashore quickly. We also checked over radio repair equipment and planned how to get our repair facility set up as quickly as possible.

We received our first mail here since leaving the States. Mother had written me all the news. Since all incoming and outgoing mail was censored, especially our mail going home, we could say nothing in our letters home about where we were or what we were doing. So I wrote Mother and asked, "How is my good old friend Roy at the movie theatre?" She was aware I hardly knew Roy. He was much older than I and worked at the movie theater but certainly was not a "good old friend." But she also knew that his last name was "Russell." She then looked at a map and knew exactly where I was: the Russell Islands. She wrote back, "I know where you are!" Our families liked to know where we were so that when they read about the war in the newspaper and the place was not mentioned, they could interpret that as good news.

Guadalcanal, New Georgia, and some of the smaller islands in the northern chain of the Solomon Islands had been secured. The many long battles with heavy casualties on both sides there set the stage for future opposition to the Japanese in the Southwest Pacific. After much deliberation, General MacArthur decided to bypass the Japanese stronghold island of Rabaul and instead attempted to destroy it by taking a small perimeter of the island of Bougainville and establishing three airfields there from which to attack. So our next mission was Bougainville in the northern Solomon Islands.

Landing on Bougainville Island

On November 1, 1943, two regiments of the 3rd Marine Division, the 3rd and 9th Marines, and the 3rd Raider Battalion landed on the beach at Cape Torokina, in the north part of Empress Augusta Bay, on Bougainville Island, the largest island in the Solomons. The remainder of these Marines and the Army's 37th Division followed later. Over the next few days, these Marines moved inland to increase their position. Small enemy patrols were everywhere, but the main obstacle was the jungle and the muddy swampland.[8]

The plan was not to take the entire island, some 100 miles long, but just to establish a reinforced perimeter some 15 miles deep and 30 miles long. The landing force had seized the beachhead, destroyed or overcome the enemy, and won sufficient land area to build and support three airstrips. These airfields were being built specifically to destroy the enormous Jap facilities on the island of Rabaul and all the surrounding area where they had a foothold.

Air infantry support had been used sporadically and effectively during the Guadalcanal and New Georgia campaigns, but not in the planned, scientific manner that utilized the full possibilities of immediate, direct, and close-bombing support for the ground troops. An accepted version of Marine close air support reports it as: The direct support given by aircraft to front-line infantry units which are in combat with the enemy. This support is normally in the form of strafing, rocket firing, or the dropping of demolition, personnel or fire bombs on enemy troops and material, which are in immediate contact with the assault units. The purpose of Close Air Support is identical to the purpose of close support by any other weapon. It is to destroy enemy personnel, emplacements, or material, which may be holding up the advance of our infantry or causing casualties to our troops.[9]

Close air support provided by Marine airplanes was being planned for the Bougainville campaign. Some three months before D-Day on Bougainville, three officers (bomber pilots) and six enlisted Marines from the 1st Marine Air Wing were assigned to the 3rd Marine Division to study the capabilities and limitations of close air support. Captain Warren H. Goodman, USMCR in his "Role of Aviation in the Bougainville Operation," later reported the results of this study: It was decided that the capabilities of close air support as weapon "had not been utilized to the fullest possible extent." Planes that were requested had often bombed ground troops. The ground troops thus had little faith in air power. Further, white smoke, which had been used to mark targets, was used by the enemy to confuse the airplane crews. Because of this, friendly troops were being withdrawn from their positions to create a margin of safety for the bombers. That, in turn, allowed the enemy to advance and occupy the vacated ground.[10]

Close air support was made available to the Bougainville landing troops, but no request was received until November 9 when the 3rd Marine Division requested 18 TBFs (torpedo bomber aircraft) to assist in the capture of Piva Village. Colored smoke was used instead of white, and 12 TBFs from VMTB-143 and VMTB-233 dropped 100-pound bombs on the targets. The enemy retreated leaving 40 dead.[11]

A second call was made on November 13, resulting in strikes by 18 Navy TBFs from VC-38 and VC-40 the next day. One-hundred-pound bombs were dropped within 100 yards in front of the Marines. The Navy pilots were credited with 95 percent of them on target.[12]

The third request was at "Hellzapoppin Ridge," near the beachhead where 300 Japs were encountered, dug in, and presenting strong resistance. Three SBDs and three TBFs were called in from the recently completed Torokina airfield on December 13. One plane missed his target and the bomb landed 600 yards away on friendly troops, killing two men and wounding six. This was the only accident of that kind on Bougainville and was assumed to be responsible for the Army's rejection of the efficiency of close air support in an Army Field Manual report. Nevertheless, the Marines had additional successes in the use of air power before the successful taking of Bougainville.[13]

On December 15, control of the landing force passed from the 1st Marine Amphibious Corps to the Army's XIV Corps. The Army's Americal Division replaced the 3rd Marine Division. This Marine Corps campaign on Bougainville had cost the Marines 423 killed and 1,418 wounded. Enemy dead was estimated at 2,458, with 23 prisoners of war captured. However, it was estimated that there were thousands of Japanese troops on the island beyond the perimeter, which had four lines of defense. These Japs were completely cut off with no line of supply and no way to leave.

The U.S. Navy Seabees had come in early, first to build roads and finally the three airstrips. In fact, the 25th, 53rd, and 71st Naval Construction Battalions (the "Seabees") had landed on D-Day with the assault waves of the 3rd Marine Division. They began immediately to get ready to build roads, camp areas, and three airfields. They had completed the new Torokina airstrip near the landing beach, and it was operating in December. These were older guys, for the most part, and they did a remarkable job and were greatly admired by all the Marines, the Army, and everyone else. We used to say, "Don't hit a Seabee—he may be a Marine's dad!" The 3rd Marines erected a large sign on the main road inland, which the 53rd Seabee Battalion had built and had named "Marine Drive Hi-Way." The Marines' sign read:

SO WHEN WE REACH THE "ISLE OF JAPAN"
WITH OUR CAPS AT A JAUNTY TILT,
WE'LL ENTER THE CITY OF TOKYO
ON THE ROAD THE SEABEES BUILT.
THIRD MARINE DIVISION
2ND RAIDER REGIMENT

The 3rd Marine Division returned to their "home" on Guadalcanal after receiving a "Well done!" from Admiral Halsey. He sent them a message, which read, "You have literally succeeded in setting up and opening for business a shop in the Japs' front yard." The 3rd Marine Division left Bougainville for Guadalcanal on Christmas Day, 1943.[14]

MAG-24 left the Russell Islands for Bougainville on December 13, 1943, on LST-166. The LST was a type of troop transport where the entire front of the ship drops down on the beach so that equipment and men can debark from there. It carried about 600 troops, trucks, and other equipment on the main deck. This was the oiliest-smelling ship I had been on. You could not get away from the smell. There was no smoking allowed, and the lights were totally out at night.

I had met another staff sergeant and he and I both wanted a cigarette. So late one night we slipped from down in the hold, where we were located, to the main deck. One of us could light up a cigarette while the other watched.

The LST did not have a railing around the main deck—only a heavy cable between posts, which could be removed if need be. We wanted to go to the far aft of the ship where we were least likely to be seen. He went ahead of me, grabbing this cable with his right hand at normal step intervals, moving on up the deck. What we didn't know was that a section of this cable was missing where the gangplank was put out. When he grabbed the cable at that point, it was not there, and his momentum carried him overboard. I can still hear:

H – H – H – E – L – P – P –!

I ran for the quarterdeck to report a man overboard. There was a total blackout, even radio silence, so all they did was send a message in code to the LST behind us using the red light on top of the ship's main mast. I stuck around to make sure the other LST had received the message and spent that night down in the hold wondering if my friend had drowned. And I didn't find out for a day or two after we landed, when I ran into him on the beach at Bougainville. The LST behind us had fished him out of the ocean. Since we were in a war zone, this matter was dropped.

The voyage took only three days. We landed at Empress Augusta Bay,

Bougainville, British Solomon Islands on December 15, 1943, and were transported immediately to our MAG-24 Camp area, which was about ten miles inland from where we landed. We were not far from the end of the perimeter; in fact, we were about three miles from where the Army 37th Division had their defensive lines. Before we left the island, the Australians would relieve the 37th. Little did we realize when we arrived that we would be at that same location for a full year, supporting two airstrips and preparing for the Philippines campaign. We lived in square canvas tents. Each had a long octagon-shaped wooden tent pole in the center. On the outside, the tents were tied down with ropes to stakes in the ground. One tent accommodated five or sometimes six Marines. The tents were much like those in the television show *M*A*S*H*. "The Swamp" is where we lived for 12 months, except the tents we were in had open sides and dirt floors. If it rained or there were hurricanes—and there were several—we let the side flaps down. Sounds bad now, but it really wasn't all that bad. You can get used to anything.

Our tent stood under a huge eucalyptus tree, with its roots fanning out on top of the ground. Our camp had been thick jungle, but the Seabees had cleared it out for us. A Lister bag, a canvas bag kept full of water suitable for drinking, hung on this big tree. That tree was handy for us. We had hung a mirror on it and a little wooden shelf. In turn we would fill our steel helmets with water, set them on the shelf, and shave and clean up. A barrel on a large wooden A-frame served as our shower. It was filled daily. Sometimes, when there was a lull, we would drive a jeep down to the beach and jump in the water, sans clothes. That was our treat. We were warned of barracudas in the ocean waters, but I never saw any.

A Japanese prisoner was questioned by an intelligence officer and asked, "Who do you think are the best jungle fighters?" He answered without hesitation, "The Australians! The Americans don't fight in the jungle. They cut it down and build roads."

As for our restroom, you can imagine what they were. In the camp we had no need for lady's and men's rooms, but we had a "head," as it is called throughout the Navy and Marines. We had an "eight holer." A large, long trench was dug about six feet deep and covered with a wooden frame with eight round holes. All this was enclosed in a tent to protect us from the elements.

This "head" was kept sanitary by actually burning it out with gasoline once a day. The best time for this chore was, someone had concluded, while most of us were at breakfast. They would pour gasoline in the hole and set it on fire. While we were enjoying our fried Spam and powdered eggs, it would be burning out. We usually ate breakfast around 0600 (6:00 a.m.), and the head would not be open for business until about 0700, or until someone checked to make sure the fire was out.

One morning, whoever was responsible for this burning-out procedure was a little late. So the fire in the hole was started late. A line of guys began to form waiting for the head to be opened for use. In fact, our Chaplain was at the front of the line. Finally, the person assigned for the burning went in and said the fire was out and it was safe to enter. What he had not noticed was that the fire was still smoldering a little.

One of the guys who came in, sat down and lit a cigarette. Instead of blowing out the match, he threw the lit match in the hole. Whoom! It blew eight fellow Marines off their thrones. It was somewhat of a disaster (no pun intended). Every one of them had been burned and was taken to sick bay. It sounds kind of humorous now, but it certainly was not at the time. Everyone recovered, but new rules were instituted about burning out the head.

A bad hurricane hit our area one night, and one of the large eucalyptus trees blew over and fell right down a row of tents. It destroyed something like fourteen tents. One man was killed and several were injured. Clearing out the jungle had left the large trees exposed with not many roots in the ground, which is why they could blow over in a storm so easily. We learned this the hard way. After that, if the wind came up, we could be found in our foxholes.

In the Marines, we went by our last name. My buddies called me "Holland." We had been assigned to our tents alphabetically by our last name. In our tent were Sergeant Groome, Staff Sergeants Hansen, Hess, and Holland, and Corporal Acker. How did he get in there? He arrived late and we had an extra space, so they put him in with us. We had a great bunch.

The first thing we had to do was to construct a Quonset hut. It came in a kit, and the only wood was the thick plywood floor. The round-shaped rafters were metal, and when we nailed the metal roof on, we drove the nails into the "pinched" metal part of the rafters. We had the hardest time of it figuring this out. We set up our Radio and Radar Repair facility for service to the Marine aircraft for both the Piva North and Piva South airstrips. The Piva South strip was for the larger bomber aircraft of all types—B-24s, B-17s, R4Ds (DC-3s), and others—and the Piva North was for our Marine planes, the fighters (F6Fs, F4Us, etc.) and dive bombers (SBDs) and torpedo bombers (TBFs, TBMs, etc.).

In the first days after we landed at Empress Augusta Bay, we found a perfectly good travel trailer near the beach. It was a twenty-foot-long and had a lot of room. It was obvious it had been left there from before the landing. So we had it towed up to our camp area along with all our jeeps, trucks, and other equipment. With the help of the Seabees, we were able to convert this trailer into a final test lab. The trailer was parked on the backside of the Quonset hut, out of the way.

When one of our planes came in, we met the plane after it had taxied to a revetment, talked with the pilot, and found out if there were any radio or radar problems. Most often when a unit had failed, we would swap it out with one we had checked out and knew was in top shape. We had no time to tinker around trying to repair something in a plane. After we made the change, we would check the failed unit thoroughly.

When we received new radio and radar repairmen into our MAG-24 Communications Group, it was my job to take them to an aircraft and check them out on all the equipment on the plane. Like all of us, they had been trained to work on the equipment on the bench but knew very little about how it was installed and worked when in the plane. One thing we always checked them out on was the "relief tube." This was a cone-shaped device made out of rubber connected to a rubber tube, which ran to the bottom of the aircraft. It was there for the pilot's and gunner's "relief." We would take a new guy, have him sit in the backseat, and tell him this thing was an "emergency intercom." We would instruct him to put the device up close to his mouth. Then we would get into the cockpit to see if we could hear him over the "emergency intercom." Of course we couldn't, but we continued the ruse and would tell him to put the device closer to his mouth and shout louder. Four or five guys were usually watching this scene, cracking up.

Every aircraft had an IFF (Identification Friend or Foe) unit. It was a small black box about the size of two shoeboxes. Its purpose was to repeatedly identify the aircraft as "friendly," either a U.S. or an Allied plane. This unit, of course, was highly classified equipment that could not under any circumstances fall into the hands of the enemy. If one of our planes was shot down or had to make an emergency landing, the crew was trained to throw the bright red switch on the unit. This would trigger an explosive device, a small, long hand grenade that would destroy the guts of the unit but not damage anything outside the black box. When exploded, however, all of the sides of the box would bulge out.

On occasion, a pilot would accidentally pull the switch and blow up the unit. When this happened, the pilot usually wouldn't mention it when we met the plane after landing to see if anything was wrong. But later he would come into our shop carrying the bulging unit in his arms and say, "Can you fix this?" We would just take a new one to the plane, install it, and check it out. It was critical that this device work properly, or the plane could be shot down by friendly fire.

Christmas Day came in 1943 with little fanfare. We had been on Bougainville less than two weeks. There was an active volcano on Bougainville, Mount Bagana, and it shook us out of our cots Christmas Eve night. We were very near this mountain and thought a bomb had dropped from a Jap plane. We had to get used to it, since it rumbled and shook quite often.

We did have a church service on Christmas morning, at an open-air place with coconut logs where we would sit to watch movies after dark. We were promised two fresh eggs for breakfast, two cans of (hot) beer, and turkey for Christmas dinner. The "turkey" turned out to be turkey a-la-king, served on bread like stuff on a shingle. It probably came out of a can. And the fresh eggs were boiled. Some of the guys played poker all night for the beer. A couple of Jap snipers got through the lines, forcing us to dig in for a few hours. They always tried to provide something interesting for the holidays. That was Christmas, 1943.

A few months later, I had an opportunity to get a close look at the volcano—from the top. One of our Marine SBD Dive Bombers, like the ones later used to support the Flying Column in the Philippines, had just had a complete engine overhaul by our MAG-24 aircraft mechanics. While the pilot of this plane, a Marine lieutenant, and I were checking out the radio equipment, which had also been refurbished in our shop, he asked me if I would like to accompany him in the rear seat on the flight test. After every engine overhaul, the plane had to undergo a rigid test procedure, including the flight test. I said I would be glad to go and asked if it would be possible to fly over the volcano. So we took off and he headed directly for the volcano, circling around the top of it several times. Between the puffs of white smoke, I could look down and see a fiery red glow.

His flight-test plan included flying down around the islands of Guadalcanal and Munda and returning to Bougainville. This would be several hundred miles and would take several hours. We made it down to Guadalcanal o.k., but when we were approaching Munda, the engine started sputtering. He told me on the intercom that we were going to have to land at the Munda airstrip. There the mechanics looked the plane over and told us it would require a couple days to repair the engine. So we reported to the officer of the day, who had a message sent back to MAG-24 about our predicament. We were assigned an officer's cabin for the two nights we were there and spent most of our time in the officers' club. I stuck close by this lieutenant. We had a great time and returned to Bougainville two days later. When we landed, all the crew I worked with met the plane to harass me about taking a "vacation" in the middle of a war.

All this doesn't sound too bad, but there was a bad side. Little happened in the daytime, except that a plane might come in on one of the airstrips half blown up, the gutsy pilot making every effort to bring it home. Many times these planes would crash and burn on the strip. Almost daily, one or more planes would come in with the landing gear either shot out or not working. The pilots would attempt a "pancake" landing, gear up. Most of the time this would work, but sometimes the plane would flip over and catch fire. This seemed to be the biggest danger to the planes making it "home."

Almost every day we were subject to Jap sniper fire. With thousands of Japs left on the other side of the perimeter, some would occasionally get through the lines. This was a continuing fear for us. And almost every night there was an air raid. At one time there had been more than 1,000 Jap aircraft at Rabaul, and we were only 235 miles away. If the Japs could get a plane in the air, the pilot would always head for Bougainville, even knowing he would not return. So we were continually on guard and were quick to jump in our foxhole when we felt it necessary. Then there was Machine Gun Charlie. This was an old, dilapidated Jap bi-wing plane that would fly over almost every night. To drop a bomb on us, the pilot would have probably had to drop it out of the plane by hand, but just flying over would sound the air-raid alarm, and that is what the Japs wanted—to keep us on alert.

The Japanese are excellent gardeners, as everyone knows. They had no outside source of food on the other side of the perimeter or on Rabaul. So they would plant massive gardens. These were watched very carefully by our spotter planes, who flew over them several times a day to keep an eye on what they were doing. We had outfitted a TBF plane with a huge gasoline tank where the torpedo would normally rest. When our planes spotted the Japs out harvesting their gardens, we would spray the garden with gasoline from this plane and then drop an incendiary bomb on the garden to set it on fire.

By early March 1944, things began to get hectic. The Japs on the other side of the perimeter became desperate. One captured Jap soldier was quoted as saying, "You Marines are trying to push us off the island, and your Navy won't let us off." The 37th Army and American Divisions began making almost continuous contact with the enemy. It appeared the Japs were about to counterattack. On March 8, the 145th Infantry of the 37th Division was hit hard by Jap artillery. It took five days of very severe fighting to drive the determined Japanese back. However, the enemy kept coming and coming and it was a full nine days before there was a lull, on March 17. Then, on March 24, they launched another series of assaults. The Americal and 37th Division Army artillery fired the heaviest artillery support mission ever to be put down in the South Pacific. That broke the back of the Japs, and the fight was over on March 25. This ended the serious offensive of the two divisions and ensured that our two Marine airstrips were out of the Japs' artillery range.[15]

Our Piva North airstrip, very near our camp, was heavily damaged by Japanese artillery fire, but our faithful Seabees jumped right in on the problem and had it repaired in a very few days. This attack really changed our lifestyle on Bougainville for months to come. From then on, we were on the alert all the time.

In addition to all the other perils we had to endure on Bougainville for a solid year, we had a couple of serious health hazards—jungle rot and malaria. Jungle rot was a kind of skin disease, similar to poison ivy, but much worse. No one seemed to know how you got it. The medics treated it with a purple medication, which made it look even worse.

I probably contacted malaria when I stepped off the USS *Mount Vernon* in New Caledonia. To treat malaria, they gave us Atabrine, since no Quinine was available. The Atabrine worked, but it made our skin very yellow. Most of the time, when we went through the chow line for breakfast we would have to open our mouths wide, and they would throw in an Atabrine tablet. They made sure we swallowed it too. No pill—no breakfast.

Malaria came from all the mosquitoes that bred in the jungle swamps created by the frequent rainstorms. They tried to spray standing water after a storm, but it didn't help much. We went shirtless and wore cut-off pants almost every day as we worked on planes and wherever we were sent, but we all knew one strict rule: get caught after sundown without a long-sleeve shirt and full-length pants and you would get put on report. They would have surprise visits to our tents after dark to make sure we were obeying this rule.

One night, our Sergeant Major Jackson came through the camp with his corporal, taking names. He walked through our tent, and every one of us had only undershorts on. It was hot, but that did not matter to the Sergeant. He went around the tent, giving names to his corporal to write down. First was Groome, then Hess, and then Hansen. For some reason, young Acker was not there. I was also lying on my cot with only shorts on. But by the time he worked his way around to me, I had reached down, pulled my scratchy, wool marine blanket over me, rolled over, and pretended to be asleep. He did not take my name.

A couple months later, after the artillery shelling we went through, all of MAG-24 received a commendation. The way I found out about this was from a newspaper clipping with my picture my mother sent me from the *Daily Oklahoman,* an Oklahoma City newspaper. After that, there was a blanket increase in rank for everyone in our group, except the ones who had been on report. Presumably, the commendation was for enduring the shelling. I was promoted from staff sergeant to technical sergeant (Tech. Sgt.) on June 30, 1944. None of my buddies in our tent received the promotion because of the name-taking incident. They were not too happy.

As the year moved on, our efforts on Bougainville became fairly routine. Our three airstrips continued to support air strikes on Rabaul and other Jap holdout positions in the area. It was reported that we had destroyed as many as 700 Jap airplanes, which was the downfall of the Jap air power in the Pacific. Intelligence reports said that more than 98,000 Jap troops had been isolated on Rabaul and the rest of New Britain, about three-fourths Army and one-fourth Navy. As for us, we were becoming concerned about where we were to go from there.[16]

Very unexpectedly, most of the original enlisted men of Headquarters, MAG-24 received orders to return to the States. They had received sufficient points under the Marine Corps system to be rotated home. Among them were our MAG-24 communications chief, Master Sergeant Grebenstien, Technical Sergeant Rexer, and all the others who were in

Headquarters, MAG-24 when we joined them many months before on Efate. Because I was the ranking technical sergeant, I was made communications chief, replacing Master Sergeant Grebenstien. I was in charge of about fifty men and responsible for all the communications activities of the enlisted men for Headquarters, MAG-24—all because of a Marine Corps blanket.

After about six months on Bougainville, things began to calm down in terms of resistance by the Japanese on the other side of the island. We still had about a 30-mile perimeter of the 100-mile-long island, but the four lines of defense worked effectively. We did what we could to make our lives more bearable.

Our tent buddy, Sergeant Bill Groome, rebuilt a discarded airplane radio receiver and hooked a small speaker to it for use in our tent. By then, each of our tents had a 40-watt light powered by a large generator, but it was lights out at 2100 (9:00 p.m.). But on this little radio, which had the broadcast band, we could get several Australian stations and, of course, Tokyo Rose, who mentioned MAG-24 several times over the months. It was a huge relief to have a radio to break up the boredom of our routine and the long nights in the tent.

The guys in the next tent, who ranked us, asked if they could run a small wire from the radio with a speaker over to their tent. So we helped them fix this up. After several weeks, we noticed that our little radio had very little volume. You could hardly hear it. We began to look around and found that sixteen tents had hooked up to our radio. Some of them used telephone wire, which knocked down the volume for everyone to the point we couldn't hear much of anything. We disconnected these tents from the source and invited the men to come to our tent to listen to the radio.

Our enterprising MAG-24 operations officer, Lieutenant Colonel Keith B. McCutcheon, had collected all the information he could on the subject of close air support. He believed strongly in the capability of close air support for supporting ground combat troops. Through his untiring efforts and with the full backing of our 1st Marine Air Wing Commanding Officer, Major General Ralph J. Mitchell, the push continued to convince the Army on how we could support them in the next major target.[17]

We had two radio jeeps, which we had brought with us, but we only used them to remotely check out our MAG-24 planes. A fine radio transmitter and receiver had been installed in these two jeeps, but they were only for low frequencies, not VHF, which was used by most of our Allied planes. Sometime later, a complete Hallicrafters radio truck arrived with a gasoline-generator trailer and every kind of equipment capable of communicating anywhere in the world. We knew pretty well at this point that we would be using our jeeps and this radio truck somewhere in the near future.

Rumors persisted that we would be involved with the Army in the next major campaign, but it had not been decided whether this would be in the Philippines or Formosa. That decision had yet to be made. Then, in early August 1944, word reached us that Marine planes from MAG-24 and 32 would indeed be involved in the Luzon, Philippines, campaign. In September, Captain Francis R. B. Godolphin, USMCR and Captain Samuel E. McAloney, USMCR came from Hawaii to join the 1st Marine Air Wing on Bougainville to get ready for the Philippines. They had been attached to the 4th Marine Division and had participated in assault landings and campaigns of Roi Namur, Saipan, and Tinian as air liaison officers. Captain John A. (Jack) Titcomb, USMCR, our group communications officer, had been put in charge of the planning and operations of MAG-24's Ground Close Air Support for the Luzon campaign.[18]

We of MAG-24 began to prepare our men and equipment for the support we were to provide the Army on Luzon. We did not know when this would occur, where in Luzon we would be, or with whom we would be working. All the while we had to keep our MAG-24 planes flying off Bougainville.

Lieutenant Colonel McCutcheon, from his knowledge of close air support, organized forty different lectures on the subject. These were given to 500 pilots and gunner crews.[19] Colonel McCutcheon had directed training exercises in the Bougainville jungles with the Army's 37th Infantry Division and had supervised two months of extensive training in close air support tactic and communications procedures.[20]

While we were still servicing the planes on the two airstrips, Captains Godolphin and McAloney directed the refurbishment of the MAG-24 radio jeeps. To provide pilot-to-ground communications between the planes and the jeeps, we added to both jeeps the same VHF transceiver (SCR-542) that the planes had. This required a lot of ingenuity because we had so little to work with. A generator was installed on the jeep motor, floating an aircraft battery to provide power for the transceiver. There was little room in the jeep motor area to add anything. One of our technicians who had left the Massachusetts Institute of Technology Engineering school to join the Marines designed a special VHF antenna base to be mounted on the back top of the jeep, which could provide maximum reception both to and from the planes. After we got these two jeeps and the radio truck operational, we also participated in training exercises with the 37th Division. We were ready.

One of our tent buddies, Staff Sergeant Robert E. Hess, at this writing now residing in Sandpoint, Idaho, learned that they were closing the officers' club, which added support to the rumor we had been hearing that we were shipping out soon. In closing the club, each officer received an allotment of six bottles of booze if he wanted them. Hess also found that a sergeant friend of his, an aerial photographer, had received the six bottles from his pilot, who did not want them. Rudy (our nickname for Hess, borrowed from Rudolph Hess, one of Hitler's cohorts, at that time a German POW in London, England) came to me and asked if I would go in with him and get two bottles of Three Feathers bourbon from this sergeant friend for 20 bucks a bottle. We got them, hid them very well, and began to plan for a party when we got the official word we were leaving Bougainville.

A day or so later, Rudy was called to the Navy hospital for an examination. He had earlier been diagnosed that he would need to have his tonsils removed. Since we were leaving, they thought it should be done now, since no one knew how long it would be before he saw a hospital again. So they removed his tonsils and a couple days later discharged him to return to our tent.

When Rudy got back to the tent, he was in some pain and bleeding a little from the surgery. He could not eat anything, so he suggested opening one of the bottles of the bourbon. We mixed it with our supply of hot grapefruit juice and the concoction wasn't bad. However, it wasn't long before the other guys came in and wanted to try some. When they came from the tents next door, we opened the second bottle. The party was on.

We ended up getting hold of the other four bottles from Rudy's sergeant friend and he also joined the party. Even our Sergeant Major

Jackson (who had taken the names of those in our tent with no shirt on after dark) joined the party. After the party broke up, Rudy went to sleep on his cot but during the night began to bleed from the tonsil surgery. One of our tent buddies, who had been on duty, came in and saw blood dripping down Rudy's cot. He ran for a medic, not knowing what the problem was, and they took him to sickbay where he spent the night. He woke up the next morning, not knowing where he was or how he got there. After a couple days on soft food, he recuperated and was released. When we did get the official word we were leaving, we had already had our party.

On December 11, 1944, Headquarters Squadron, MAG-24 boarded the USS *John T. McMillan*, a cargo liberty ship which had been converted, sort of, to carry military troops.[21] With 2x4 lumber, the Bougainville Navy Seabees had gone aboard and built bunk racks below decks, four bunks high, for us to put our own folding camp cots on. A sergeant friend of mine and I put our cots on a hold (door) cover, which was a cube-type metal cover over the ladder (stairs) to the lower decks. It was a flat surface with barely enough room for two cots. We covered it with a piece of canvas. Most of our travel would be in the South China Sea, probably the roughest waters in the entire world.

The head (toilet) was on the main deck, made out of oil drums cut in half the long way and welded together. A wooden board with about ten holes in it was mounted on top of the barrels. Water rushed continuously from one end out the other and over the side of the ship into the sea. The shower was a piece of pipe with holes drilled in it and running cold water. It ran all the time with the salty ocean water. Whenever you used that shower, you came out sticky. When the ship stopped in the ocean for any reason, we were allowed to jump over the side, sans clothes, for a swim. We were given two cans of C-rations a day, our meal in a can, and then lined up for something to drink. Once in a while, we had a meal prepared on field ranges on the main deck.

We were on this ship for forty-two consecutive days, except for the nine days we were allowed to go ashore at Milne Bay, New Guinea, for Christmas 1944. We also made two stops at Hollandia, Dutch Guinea, before and after Milne Bay, but were not allowed to get off the ship. We debarked at Milne Bay, New Guinea, on December 22, 1944, and went ashore. A U.S. Army unit provided us with real barracks to sleep in. The Army guys treated us well. Some of us went to their supply tent, and they gave us any kind of clothing we wanted, like short-sleeve shirts, which we did not have, underwear, and so forth.

The next day after we got to Milne Bay, my boss Captain Titcomb told me we had left one of the two walkie-talkies on the ship. He told me to get someone to go to the ship and retrieve the other one. I said I would go myself. An Army guy drove me down to the dock and showed me the water taxi, which ferried people to the several ships docked in the harbor. I got on the little boat and was the only passenger. The driver asked me where I wanted to go. I pointed out our ship, and he took me there. I crawled up the rope ladder onto the deck. A Navy Chief met me and asked what I wanted. I asked him where our radio jeeps and the radio truck were. I didn't see them. *I was on the wrong ship!* It was about 5:00 p.m., and that had been the last run of the day for the water taxi. I had no way to get back to shore until morning. The chief was able to radio the Army to get the message to my captain I would not be back until the next day. The chief then gave me a private room and invited me to dinner in his mess. We had steak and all the trimmings. The next day, the water taxi took me to the right ship and waited for me to board the vessel and retrieve the radio. I thought I might be in trouble when I got back to shore, but I wasn't. The captain thought it was funny. No one else ever knew I spent a night on the "wrong" ship.

The Army provided us with three good meals a day every day at Milne Bay. Christmas Day 1944, we had a real military-style Christmas dinner. There was a party and dance that night at the Army base. There were five thousand troops, mostly Army, and six nurses to dance with. I stood on a barrel in the crowd and saw those nurses about a mile away. That's the closest I got. We were at Milne Bay a total of nine days. On New Year's Day 1945, we returned to USS *McMillan* and shipped out for the Philippines—our destination was Lingayen Gulf, Luzon, where we were to land twenty days later.

Chapter 2

The Philippines Campaign

Landing at Lingayen Gulf

Many people even today do not realize how close the Philippine Islands came to being bypassed by all U.S. troops until the end of the war. Fleet Admiral Chester Nimitz, Commander in Chief, Pacific Command had accepted a plan by Admiral E. J. King, and concurred in by the Joint Chiefs of Staff in Washington, D.C. This plan was to bypass the Philippines in favor of taking the Mariana Islands, then on to Formosa and finally Japan. General MacArthur, however, was determined to liberate the Philippines as soon as possible and rescue the Filipino people as well as thousands of American military prisoners of war and civilian internees on the way to Japan.

In July 1944, President Franklin D. Roosevelt traveled to Hawaii to meet with Admiral Chester Nimitz and General MacArthur to hear both sides of the controversy and make his decision later. General MacArthur was ordered by General George C. Marshall to the meeting but was not told that the President would be there. He took no staff officers with him and no plans or maps. MacArthur recounted, "Admiral Nimitz, with his fine sense of fair play, asked if I had been informed of the subject to be discussed, and if I had been asked to bring my important staff members. When I told him I had not, he seemed amazed and somewhat shocked."[22]

For several days, both Admiral Nimitz and General MacArthur presented their plans for the future strategy to be employed. No decision was made at the meeting and President Roosevelt returned to Washington. General MacArthur received a letter from President Roosevelt on August 9, 1944, sent while he was on his trip home, which said in part: "I am on the last leg of my return journey to Washington. It has been a most successful, though all too short, visit and the highlight of it was the three days that you and I saw each other in Honolulu. You have been doing a really magnificent job against what were great difficulties, given us by climate and by certain human animals. As soon as I get back I will push on that plan [MacArthur's plan for the Philippines] for I am convinced that it is logical and can be done."[23] The Joint Chiefs of Staff held on to the Formosa plan as long as they could, but President Roosevelt finally ordered the MacArthur plan, which was to attack the Philippines next.

It is hard to comprehend what might have happened had the Philippines been left hanging until the close of the war. As it turned out, some

20,000 Japanese troops killed and raped more than 100,000 Filipinos under orders of their commanding officer, Admiral Iwabuci, knowing there was no escape for them other than to be killed or by suicide. What would have happened to the 17 million Filipinos had all 230,000 Japanese troops been left on the Islands?

The American military invaded Luzon, the Philippines, on January 9, 1945. Four divisions of the U.S. Army landed against ineffective Japanese resistance. That same day General MacArthur arrived in the USS *Boise,* and went ashore on a landing craft. This ship served as his temporary headquarters. A special pier had been built so that the general could get off the landing boat without getting his feet wet. But he chose to wade ashore, just as he had at the Leyte landing, and just as his combat troops had done before him.[24]

At the time of the invasion, I was one of a thousand Marines aboard the USS *John T. McMillan,* which was circling around somewhere in the China Sea, waiting to go in. Our Marine Air Group-24 commanding officer, Colonel Lyle H. Meyer, 14 pilots, and 283 enlisted men arrived at San Fabian ahead of us on January 11. These Marines had immediately gone to work helping the Sixth Army Engineers unload and lay steel matting on the Lingayen Air Field, which was close to the gulf. In doing so, the Marines went a long way toward proving that they were eager to work with the Army ground troops and building trust between the two groups. On January 20, Lieutenant General Walter Krueger, Commanding General of the Sixth Army, wrote to Colonel Clayton C. Jerome, commanding officer of Marine Aviation Operations in the Philippines, lauding their efforts: "I desire to express my personal appreciation and official commendation of the 24th Marine Air Group for the outstanding manner in which it performed its part in that important mission. The rapid completion of this strip was mandatory. When a critical manpower shortage developed that jeopardized the construction program the 24th Marine Air Group responded magnificently in the emergency by providing excellent working parties to assist in unloading and laying of the landing mat. Although having no previous experience in work of this nature, the men performed their duties enthusiastically and efficiently. Their efforts represented a valuable contribution to the speedy completion of the Lingayen airstrip and reflect great credit upon the officers and men."[25]

The original plan was for our MAG-24 to share use of the air base with the Army Air Corps. However, even before Colonel Meyer's men began work on the airstrip it had been determined that there wasn't enough room for our Marine SBDs and their support personnel.

Colonel Clayton C. Jerome, Commanding Officer of the Marine Aviation Operations in the Philippines, began to look for a suitable place to build our airfield and establish our ground operations. After looking over several sites, he decided on a broad area between the towns of Dagupan and Mangalden. Almost everyone thought he was mad. He was planning to build an airstrip on a rice paddy. But his military experience in the Philippines in 1927 had taught him that a rice field, properly graded and packed, made a good, solid foundation for takeoffs and landings during the dry months. He figured three dry months were due, and three months was all he needed.

The 6,500-foot runway was soon completed, leaving sufficient room on both sides for camp facilities for all of the MAG-24 and MAG-32 flight and ground personnel. Colonel Jerome was designated commander of Air Base Mangalden, and commander of Marine Aircraft Groups, Dagupan. He named the new air base MAGSDAGUPAN, recognizing the name of the two Marine Air Groups and the base's location between Dagupan and Mangalden.[26]

We finally landed at San Fabian, Lingayen Gulf, Luzon, on January 21 and debarked from the *McMillan* early in the morning of January 22. After boarding Army trucks, we were taken to our airstrip, which was in the final stages of construction. On leaving the ship we were given six cans of C-rations. It was made clear to us that this was all the food we would get for the next three days. My six cans lasted about a day and a half. But the local Filipinos supplemented our diet, showering us with bananas, raw eggs, and some unrecognizable food delicacies. Except for Christmas at Milne, we had lived on C-rations for thirty-four days aboard the ship. Not only sick of the food, we were also sick of being trapped on that tub, which we naively referred to as "the Prison Ship." (At the time, we had no idea how truly horrific conditions on a Japanese prison ship were.) The *McMillan* had been completely ill equipped to carry troops: it had no hot food, no facilities, no quarters. The first night we slept on the ground was an absolute joy. We spread out and at last could breathe good clean air.

Soon we were assigned to a tent near the airstrip. The tent had camp cot space for six of us, the same arrangement as on Bougainville. In fact, I was back with most of my old buddies again.

The afternoon of the third day off the ship one of my buddies and I began to get hungry. Captain Titcomb had told us to "get lost" because heavy equipment was working in our area finishing revetments, the spaces where the planes were parked. So Sergeant Bill Groome and I, in search of food, walked out onto the main highway and hitched a ride in an Army truck to Dagupan, the small village about ten miles away.

The driver dropped us off, and we walked the main street just gawk-ing. There were lots of stores, most of them closed, but some of them open for business. Jewelry stores and the like, they were just the kind of places that would catch the eye of a GI. We hadn't seen a town since we visited Noumea, New Caledonia, more than a year before. We finally spotted a restaurant with what looked to be Chinese writing outside, so we went in. When we sat down at a table, an old Filipino lady who looked like sixteen miles of bad road walked over and quickly said, "We got fish heads and rice!" I had been thinking "hamburger," so this took some mental readjustment on my part. We both nodded our heads for her to bring the food out.

In front of each of us she placed a whole fish. At first I tried not to look at the fish's burnt-out eye sockets, but I got over my initial squea-mishness. It turned out to be one of the better meals I've had in my life—at least one of the most appreciated.

While I was eating I thought about money—I had none. I asked my friend. He didn't have any money either. We never "drew" any money because we had no need for it and nowhere to spend it.[27] Then I remem-bered the dollar bill I had folded in the back of my billfold. Before we left San Diego, a bunch of us had a "shipping out" party at a restaurant that had eight bars. We all signed a dollar bill for each of us, promising to have them with us when we returned home. When we finished the meal, the old waitress came up and said, "Seventy-five cents." That was the total for both of us. I laid the dollar bill down on the table, and we walked out. We caught a ride again on an Army truck and got back to camp. Fortu-nately, no one had missed us.

Preparations for the Manila Campaign

When we arrived at Lingayen, our leader, Captain Titcomb, made it clear to us that our first objective was to set up, in a tent near the new airstrip, a radio maintenance and repair shop similar to what we had at Bougainville. Marine planes would be coming in soon, and we needed to be ready for them.

I now wore two hats. As communications chief for MAG-24, I was responsible for the radio shack where we repaired all MAG-24 Marine aircraft radio and radar equipment. I was also supervising preparation of the two radio jeeps and a Hallicrafters radio truck, which were to assist the Army in close air support. We did not know where we would be providing this support, but the intense focus on preparations indicated that we would soon be seeing action.

The radio truck and the two jeeps were parked near the radio shack where we were getting the shop organized. We rarely had to be told what to do, because of our training and experience on Bougainville. We had a similar setup in a Quonset hut there, and we all knew we had to provide the same maintenance service as we had for the planes based there. Everyone "turned to," and we had the place up and running in a few days.

Next Captain Titcomb told Staff Sergeant Byers and me to get the truck and jeeps ready to roll. He told us we were on standby to join the 1st Cavalry Division and head south. This confirmed our suspicions that we were heading for Manila. Titcomb had talked with Captain Godolphin and found out that he and Byers would be in the truck, which pulled behind it a large gasoline-powered generator for the radio equipment in the truck. I would be with Godolphin in one of the jeeps. In the other jeep would be Captain McAloney and PFC Armstrong. So we fired up the three vehicles and checked them out. Then we inventoried all the spare parts to make sure we could repair the radios if they broke down and packed extra radio units to use in case the equipment failed.

Our equipment and spare parts were loaded into a small trailer that would be pulled behind one of the jeeps. For the next couple of days, Byers, Armstrong, and I continued getting the truck and the two jeeps ready. We made a final check of the radio equipment communications between the two jeeps and the truck and checked them out with the planes on the ground. We saw Titcomb and Godolphin daily. They would stop by to see how things were going. One of them always came up with something else they thought we might need when we hit the road, be it spare parts, extra equipment, or personal items.

All the while, there were air raids at night. We could hear anti-aircraft off in the distance but saw no Jap planes. Then, on January 30, close to midnight the night before we left, Jap planes came in and strafed. We scrambled for our foxholes. Fortunately, none of the planes on the airfield were damaged.

Marine Aviation Close Air Support

As soon as the light bulldozers had turned the rice paddy into an airfield, the dive-bomber squadrons began flying up from the Northern Solomon Islands via Owi, Peleliu, and Leyte. The first planes arrived on January 25: forty-six SBDs from VMSB-133 and VMSB-241. Meanwhile, ground echelons had been arriving since the day we landed at Lingayen. By January 31, MAGSDAGUPAN had seven squadrons with 168 SBDs, 472 officers, and 3,047 men. Headquarters of the 308th Bomb Wing (Army) had designated Colonel Jerome commander of the base. The airfield became home to almost as many Army planes. Major Sherman Smith was named "strip commander."

The 1st Marine Air Wing had learned on September 20, 1944, at Bougainville that seven of its SBD dive-bomber squadrons would be used for the Luzon campaign, which was to follow the campaign in Leyte. Two units were involved: MAG-24 and MAG-32. Their squadrons and their colorful nicknames were:

MAG-24	MAG-32
VMSB133 – "Flying Eggbeaters"	VMSB142 – "Wild Horses"
VMSB236 – "Black Panthers"	VMSB243 – "Flying Goldbricks"
VMSB241 – "Sons of Satan"	VMSB244 – "Bombing Banshees"
VMSB341 – "Torrid Turtles"[28]	

The dive-bombers of the two Marine aircraft groups on Luzon performed creditably during the early phase of the invasion. Use of the Douglas Dauntless dive-bombers by the Marines was unique in at least one respect: The Marine squadrons were the only units still flying that type of aircraft. The Army had stopped using them as early as 1942, and during the summer of 1944 the Navy had turned to more heavily armed and faster aircraft. The SBD dive-bombers had performed valiantly for the Marines from Midway to Bougainville, due to the accuracy obtained with the aircraft in pinpointing targets. However, the airplane was rapidly becoming obsolete. Its combat radius was only 450 miles, and the planes had seen a lot of use. The planes that replaced the SBDs had larger fuel tanks and could travel farther. The Luzon campaign was to be these dive-bombers' swan song: the planes were scheduled for retirement at the end of the Philippines campaign. But Marine aviators and their outmoded aircraft had one more chance to show what they could do.[29]

Following their long indoctrination in close support at Bougainville, the Marine pilots expected to start immediately bombing a path for the advancing infantry. Such was not the case. Neither the Army Air Force nor the ground troops were ready to have strikes directed on targets by jeeps on the front line. They considered this too dangerous for their troops. The first few days' missions by Marine planes were set out at MAGSDAGUPAN the evening before the attack.

The first air strikes began on January 27 with raids on San Fernando and Clark Field Air Center. These had to be cleared by an assigned Army Support Air Party, all the way up to Sixth Army and through the 308th Bombardment Wing. Lieutenant General Walter Krueger and his Sixth Army were two-thirds of the way down from Lingayen south to Manila before any close support was requested. Heavy Marine air strikes continued from planes based at the MAGSDAGUPAN airstrip. During the last five days of January, five Marine SBD dive-bomber squadrons flew 255 sorties and dropped 104 tons of bombs.[30]

On January 27, the 1st Cavalry Division had landed at Lingayen and immediately moved to an assembly area at Guimba, 35 miles inland. Finally, Captain Godolphin briefed us about our mission. We were told to get our personal gear ready and check out the two jeeps and radio truck for the last time. We would be joining up with the 1st Cavalry Division to go to Manila.

What we didn't realize at the time was that the 1st Cavalry Division would become the "Flying Column," which had come about as a result of General MacArthur's order to rescue the prisoners at Santo Tomas.

We did know that we were to provide the Army with close air support. Our assignment grew out of Marine Lieutenant Colonel Keith B. McCutcheon's doctrine of close air support, developed in the Solomon Islands. For the first time, Marine air liaison parties would operate on the front lines. Any ALP team, like Godolphin and I, working in conjunction with the ground force commander, could call for air support when opposition was encountered, guide the aircraft to their targets, observe the effects of bombing or strafing, quickly correct any pilot errors, and redirect the bombers to their targets. The dive-bomber squadrons of MAG-24 and MAG-32 saw this as the long-awaited chance to prove their value to the ground forces.

McCutcheon, in recounting the story of the close air support, said that the 308th Bombardment Wing did not want to authorize the 1st Cavalry Division to levy requests on us directly.[31] Since the division could not tell a day ahead exactly when the targets would be identified and what they would be, we suggested that they submit a request for nine aircraft to be on station overhead from dawn to dusk. Captain Godolphin was the one who made these arrangements. Godolphin, who had similar experiences previously on the Marshall and Mariana Islands and had taught close air support classes on Bougainville, went over to the 1st Cavalry Division headquarters in Guimba to work out the details of our participation. There Godolphin ran into a Lieutenant Colonel R. F. Goheen. Goheen, who had been a student of Godolphin's at Princeton University, took Godolphin around and introduced him to some of the officers, including Brigadier General Hugh Hoffman. The personal connection helped to establish the lines of communication.[32] The division would request the aircraft from the 308th Bomber Wing. The 308th would flag us. We would take it from there.

Before we left, we again tested each of the vehicles' radio equipment by communicating with an SBD airplane parked on the ground. Equipment included VHF airplane transceivers like those on the SBD aircraft, microphones, earphones, speakers, and batteries. When we asked Captain Godolphin what radio code we were going to use, he said: "Well, we need something that we won't forget. How about 'K-ration'?" We surely would not forget that! Godolphin designated our jeep "K-Ration 1" and Captain McAloney and PFC Armstrong's "K-Ration 2." Captain Titcomb and Staff Sergeants Byers and Miller in the radio truck were "K-Ration 3." Captain Godolphin told us he had given this some thought. "K-Ration" represented our "Supper, Breakfast, and Dinner, or SBD [planes]."[33]

Our two jeeps and truck finally left MAGSDAGUPAN on January 31 at 1730 with two armed escort jeeps, one in front and one in back. Guimba was 40 miles away, but we arrived there about 1900. The Army there was expecting us. When one of the 1st Cavalry guys saw us coming, he shouted, "Here comes our relief!" With that we knew what we were in for—7 Marines with about 800 Army soldiers. Despite the kidding, they couldn't have treated us better. They knew we were there to protect their flank. Captain Titcomb had written earlier in his daily diary, "They're a great bunch, this First Cavalry Division. They have spirit and pride and drive just like the Marines!" I agree.

The Rescue of POWs at Cabanatuan

On January 30, the day before the Flying Column started out, the U.S. Army Rangers rescued the American military prisoners of war at Cabanatuan.[34] Bataan survivors from the Army, and a few Navy, and Marines were being held sixty miles north of Manila. The Army Rangers had arrived in Cabanatuan about 24 hours before us.

American Bataan survivors were incarcerated at Cabanatuan when the Rangers arrived. Many of the others had been taken just a short time earlier to Bilibid Prison in Manila, after the Japs were sure the Americans were coming. They knew where we were and knew also that these would be the first POWs to be rescued. The Rangers fought through twenty-five miles of Jap lines and broke down the gate to Cabanatuan Prison just before dark on January 30.

They could hear the prisoners shouting, "The Yanks are here! Assemble at the main gate." Many of them were not able to get to the main gate because they were in terrible physical condition and needed help just to move.

The Rangers helped to their feet those prisoners who could walk. Others had to be carried out. At first the prisoners were suspicious when the Rangers arrived.

"Buddy, we're Yanks," the Rangers said. "We're Americans! Up quick and get over to that gate! Here's a pistol. Here's a knife. You're a soldier again!"

When they realized what was happening, one of them said, "They are Americans! They're here! God, they've come! Christ, are we glad to see you."[35]

The Japs had sent 2,000 troops to stop the rescue. But out of the trees and bushes came Filipino guerrillas, who repelled the attack. Later, when the Rangers were congratulated on another job well done, they would say, "Don't forget the Filipinos. We broke through the Jap lines but they got us into the camp."[36]

There were 513 rescued from the camp: Army, Navy, and Marines, a few British and Dutch, and one Norwegian. Of these, 486 had been on the Bataan Death March. The Rangers and Filipino guerrillas suffered 30 casualties, 27 dead and 3 wounded. But they had killed about 500 Japanese and knocked out 12 Jap tanks.[37]

Our three serials of the 1st Cavalry Division rolled out shortly after midnight on February 1. The serials surged down three different back roads that came together at the town of Cabanatuan, still controlled by some 8,000 Jap troops moving slowly northward and who were waiting for us. This presence of Jap resistance in the same area had earlier delayed the Rangers twenty-four hours from going into the compound to rescue the POWs. However, the delay allowed our 1st Cavalry Medical Squadron of men and ambulances to arrive after the rescue and help treat the sick and wounded Cabanatuan prison POWs and transport them back to temporary hospitals for medical treatment.[38]

Chapter 3

The Flying Column

On to Manila—100 Miles in 66 Hours

When General MacArthur arrived at 1st Cavalry Division headquarters at Guimba on January 31, he gave startling orders to the 1st Cavalry Division's Commander, Major General Verne D. Mudge: "Go to Manila! Go around the Japs, bounce off the Japs, save your men, but get to Manila! Free the internees at Santo Tomas! Take Malacanan Palace (the presidential palace) and the Legislative Building!"

MacArthur had just ordered one of the gutsiest actions by any military organization in American history. General MacArthur stated, "I have the utmost confidence in the 1st Cavalry Division being the first into Manila." He ordered the 100-mile dash through enemy territory heavily infested with Japs with what was called the "Flying Column." He and General Mudge were well aware that the Army 37th Division was only 25 miles away from the capital city, heading down northern Luzon, but these soldiers were on foot. The 1st Cavalry was totally motorized and could move faster.

At the same time, the need to move quickly meant that there would be no time for the usual approach to reconnaissance, protecting flanks, or consolidating positions. When resistance was encountered the Army troops were to charge right through it. Speed was the most important consideration. Large, lengthy battles with the enemy were to be avoided. Surprise and pushing through with as many men, tanks, and artillery as possible was necessary to prevent the annihilation of all the 3,700 internees at Santo Tomas. The concern was that the Japanese would kill the internees if they knew the Americans were coming. And even if they did not kill them many more American prisoners would die from disease and starvation.

Over the years there has been much speculation that General MacArthur had received reliable information that the Japanese were intending to murder all the prisoners of Santo Tomas once they knew their recapture was approaching. Thus, the 1st Cavalry was to release the internees at Santo Tomas in the same way that the Rangers had recaptured the POWs at Cabanatuan—by surprise attack. Most believe the plan was conceived only a few hours before MacArthur gave the order.

Even if a traditional approach to reconnaisance and protection of the flanks was not feasible, some form of support was still critical to the plan. That is where our work lay. Our Marine planes in the daylight hours were to provide it in a form the men of the 1st Cavalry had never before

48

seen. The order was given to MAGSDAGUPAN: provide an air alert (on station) of nine planes from dawn to dusk over the 1st Cavalry Division. The SBDs were ordered to guard the division's flank of the division as it sped to Manila.

When General Mudge briefed his men on the details of the operation, he outlined the entire concept and issued verbal instructions. At the end of his presentation he asked, "Are there any questions?" There were none. He had made absolutely clear what was to happen.

The 308th Bombardment Wing had already ordered the Marine Aircraft Groups, Dagupan, to provide an air alert—nine SBD planes would fly from dawn to dusk over the 1st Cavalry Division. This plan included ALPs, air-trained teams in direct contact with forward ground commanders who could call in instant action with their airborne weapons. The air alert system was ideal for supporting fast-moving troops and in a sense replaced the 1st Cavalry's artillery, which could not be moved or set up as quickly.

At the same time the Flying Column of the 1st Cavalry Division was ordered to go to Manila, the 37th Infantry Division, partner of the close-support dive-bombermen in the experiment at Bougainville, was ordered to make a similar dash on the right (west) flank. The XI Corps troops of the Eighth Army landed southwest of Manila to drive from the other direction.

The following Marine ALP assignments had been made officially: "With General Chase and the 1st Brigade was the radio jeep with Captain McAloney, driven by radio operator PFC P. E. Armstrong. With General Hugh Hoffman and the 2nd Brigade was Captain Godolphin and his driver-radio man, Technical Sergeant R. B. Holland. In the radio truck, traveling with General Mudge and division headquarters were Captain Titcomb, Staff Sergeant A. A. Byers, and Staff Sergeant P. J. Miller."[39]

General Mudge had organized the 1st Cavalry Division Flying Column into three brigades, or serials, as follows:

First Brigade (1st Serial)

BG William C. Chase, Commanding Officer of the Flying Column and Brigade Commander, 1st Serial

Lt. Col. William E. Lobit, Commanding Officer

From the 5th Cavalry: the 2nd Squadron; Reconnaissance Platoon; Anti-Tank Platoon; Battery "A," 82nd Field Artillery Battalion; Company "A" 44th Tank Battalion; 3rd Platoon, Troop "A," 8th Engineers; and the 1st Platoon, Troop "A," 1st Medical Squadron

Second Brigade (2nd Serial)

BG Hugh Hoffman, Brigade Commander

Lt. Col. Haskett L. Conner, Jr., Commanding Officer

From the 8th Cavalry: the 2nd Squadron; Reconnaissance Platoon; Anti-Tank Platoon; the Maintenance Section; and one section of 50 caliber machine guns; Company "B," 44th Tank Battalion; Battery "B," 61st Field Artillery Battalion; 1st Platoon, Troop "C," 8th Engineers; and the 1st Platoon, Troop "B," 1st Medical Squadron.

Third Brigade (3rd Serial)

MG Verne D. Mudge, Commanding General, 1st Cavalry Division and Brigade Commander

Lt. Col. Tom Ross, Commanding Officer

The 302nd Reconnaissance Troop and the remainder of the 44th Tank Battalion.[40]

After all units had joined up, the strength of the Flying Column was:

1st Cavalry Division—estimated 800 troops

44th Tank Battalion—43 tanks each with a crew of four, 172 men

Marine Air Groups 24 and 32, 9 SBD dive-bombers over the Flying Column from daylight to dark, out of an available 168 SBDs—9 pilots and 9 gunners, or 36 men, per SBD group

Marine ALP close air support teams in two jeeps and one radio truck—7 men

U.S. Navy bomb-disposal expert—1 man

Total: 1,016 men—(Army, Navy, and Marine Corps)

General MacArthur had received intelligence that more that 230,000 Jap troops had retreated from the Manila and Central Luzon area to the north and to the east. Knowing the Philippines as he did, the general anticipated that Japanese general Tomoyuki Yamashita would move his troops into the rugged mountains to the east, flanking the central plains. That meant Jap resistance would probably be on our left flank in the Flying Column as we headed south. He was later proven correct, and our Marine planes were responsible for protecting that flank. Yamashita was aware that the American invasion forces were too strong to be stopped on the central flatlands. He reasoned that it would be harder to defeat his forces in the mountains, so he scattered them over a long area of the eastern mountains.

In addition to the 230,000 troops, 18,000 Japanese troops were reported in the area of Manila, the majority of them Japanese sailors from sunken ships in Manila Bay. A U.S. Army official document, "After Action Report, XIV Corps, M-1 Operations," declassified by the National Archives and Records Administration on July 20, 1999, reported: "The enemy strength in greater Manila was estimated (approximately February 1, 1945) to be 18,000. Of this number three fourths were supposed to be navy personnel, and one fourth army. From various sources and from the nature of his resistance at the entrance of the city, it was deduced that within the city itself (1) there were few if any organized combat units, (2) the enemy defense would be of a passive nature, (3) enemy communications were crippled, (4) most enemy weapons had been recovered from destroyed aircraft and sunken ships, and (5) there was no enemy reserve or mobile combat force. As it was later proven, the enemy expected the American forces to approach from the South. Thus as the two divisions moved into the city from the North, Rear Admiral Mitsuji Iwafuchi, the overall defense commander, found his organized positions facing the wrong way, his poorly equipped troops about half the strength of the American forces, his command deprived of communications, and his forces without hope of assistance from air or naval units. However, the stubborn resistance of the garrison did credit to his truculence as a fighter, and the ruthless destruction of property was a reflection of the tenacity of his efforts."[41]

The three serials moved out of Guimba simultaneously on three separate and primitive roads at one minute past midnight on February 1. The dash to Manila had begun. The nine-plane air cover would be overhead from sunup to after sundown; the planes would circle continuously up and down the valleys, searching every road and trail for signs of enemy movement. When roadblocks were spotted they were reported and, with permission quickly secured from General Chase, bombed.

General Chase had not been thoroughly briefed on how this protection of his flank by our Marine planes was going to work. When we arrived, he asked what equipment we had. When told we had a radio jeep ready to forward his orders to our Marine pilots overhead, he ordered Captain McAloney and PFC Armstrong, "Just stay behind me in your jeep."

Because the cavalrymen were in a hurry, they sought to avoid prolonged engagements with the enemy. The Marine flyers were there to recommend alternate routes whenever they seemed desirable. Since the Japanese were in the mountains to the east, there was always the danger that they would attack the slender three-pronged column.

That night we moved carefully, under a complete blackout, crossing rivers and rice paddies. Colonel Lobit's 5th Cavalry crossed the Pampanga River, capturing the Valdefuente Bridge just as Jap demolition squads were about to blow it up. General Mudge himself had moved up with them and led his troops through Jap mortar fire onto the bridge. He helped throw the explosive charges that had been attached to the bridge into the river. In the meantime, Colonel Conners of the 8th Cavalry crossed the Pampanga River at another point to the southeast and seized a stretch of Highway 5. A force of Jap troops in a barrio (a small town) were caught between these two squadrons. A Jap truck loaded with dynamite was hit by a bazooka (1st Cavalry weapon). It exploded leaving a large hole in the road, but the hole was later filled and we were able to cross over it.[42] Heavy fighting followed for most of the night. The 12th and the 7th Cavalry then moved up and completed response to this resistance. The Flying Column was again in a position to move ahead.

We quickly learned that Jap troops were in the area when we entered a barrio and no Filipinos were there to greet us, even during the night. Before we reached Cabanatuan, General Mudge had given orders to Lieutenant Colonel Tom Ross and his 44th Tank Battalion Sherman tanks to reconnoiter the town of Gapan. After they crossed the Santa Rosa River, another fierce battle with a large Jap force ensued. However, we captured the main portion of Highway 5 leading into the town of Gapan. Unfortunately, Lieutenant Colonel Ross, Commanding Officer of the 3rd Brigade, lost his life during this attack.[43] He and Captain Charles Kudrle, also of the 44th, were ambushed by a Jap heavy machine gun. Captain Kudrle was severely wounded but managed to crawl under a hut and into a foxhole. Lieutenant Colonel Ross went to his death firing his Browning Automatic Rifle in his defense.

It did not take our Marine planes long to provide valuable reconnaissance and air cover, and the 1st Cavalry Division's air support coordinator did everything he could to help our ALP unit carry out every mission he ordered. General Chase's radio jeep stayed close to him at all times. In fact, he had decided it was better for him to ride in the jeep with McAloney and Armstrong much of the time as they traveled down the road. The Marine SBD dive-bombers stood guard on the exposed left flank of the column and searched the area 30 miles in front and 20 miles behind the column, except when they were carrying out an attack. The planes scouted enemy concentrations, as well as a bridge the column had intended to cross but the Japs had bombed out. This reconnaissance made it possible to reroute the column. The 1st Cavalry Division later gave a generous tribute to the Marine support: "Much of the success of the entire movement is credited to the superb air cover, flank protection, and reconnaissance provided by the Marine Air Groups 24 and 32. The 1st Cavalry's drive down through Central Luzon was the longest such operation ever made in the Southwest Pacific Area using only air cover for flank protection."[44]

Most of the time we operated in an "air alert" situation, which meant that when our planes were in the area we could give them direct orders for strikes as we received them. However, all strikes had to be coordinated with the 1st Cavalry's air coordinator because our two jeeps and the radio truck were receiving requests for air support for the entire Flying Column. Occasionally, in a "ground alert" situation the request would be transmitted by the radio truck to the planes on the ground at MAGSDA-GUPAN. This could happen during the night when there were reports of large concentrations of Japanese troops whose locations were provided by reliable Filipino sources. In most cases, however, the planes were to report to the nearest radio jeep and request further orders.

In an air alert we would carry out bombing or strafing requests as in the following example:

"K-Ration-1 to Black Panther. Come in."

"Black Panther to K-Ration-1. Go ahead."

"K-Ration-1 to Black Panther. We have a target approximately 1,000 yards ahead of our position. Watch for our William Peter [white phosphorous].[45] Over."

"Black Panther to K-Ration-1. Go ahead."

"K-Ration-1 to Black Panther. It's on the way. Over."

"Black Panther to K-Ration-1. We have it. Stand by."

"Black Panther to K-Ration-1. We got it. Over."

"K-Ration-1 to Black Panther. Good. Hit 1,500 yards south of the William Peter. Over."

"Black Panther to K-Ration-1. Roger. We will hit 1,500 yards south of William Peter. Over."

We always asked them to repeat their orders. After the SBDs made their runs, whether dropping two 250-pound bombs or one 500-pound or one 1,000-pound bomb or strafing Jap troops, our 1st Cavalry observers would report on the results:

"K-Ration-1 to Black Panther. You got it. Right on target. Thanks."

"Black Panther to K-Ration-1. Roger. Over and out."[46]

That is the way it worked—and it worked well.

By daylight on February 2, the route through Cabanatuan was open to traffic for the whole Flying Column. Early that day, right after we were beginning to move steadily, we heard on my jeep's radio speaker: "All A-24s, THIS IS K-RATION-1. CALL OFF YOUR STRIKES AND RETURN TO BASE. REPEAT—ALL A24s RETURN TO BASE!" The A-24 was the Army version of the SBD, which they had stopped using months before. I was shocked. K-Ration 1? I was K-Ration 1! I said to a 1st Cav guy sitting with me in the jeep, "That's us!"

"Who the hell was that?" he asked. I thought a moment. I knew who it was. It was a Jap on our VHF frequency. We had been warned that this might happen. I picked up my microphone and said, "Get off the air, you Jap son-of-a-bitch! Pilots, pay no attention to that Jap! DO NOT RETURN TO BASE! If you hear that Jap again, ask him to say "HONOLULU"! We knew the Japanese had difficulty saying English words with the letter "L" in them. That shut him up, and I didn't hear from him again.

Several instances were reported of the Japs breaking into our radio communications, but for the most part, these efforts failed. A report of one that worked involved nine of our SBD's assigned to a target in Balete Pass, in northern Luzon. The planes could not reach their target because of bad weather in the area, so they were diverted to a target in the Baguio area. Baguio was the summer capital of the Philippines, and this area is where General Yamashita, Commander of all Japanese forces, had set up his head-quarters. The SBD pilots, after a strafing run on this new target, received a radio message stating "you are bombing and strafing friendly troops!" The flight leader directed the nine planes to return to the base at MAGSDAGU-PAN only to find out that the message had not been sent by any of us.

A second such incident involved a strike that was directed by a radio message to return to base with their bombs. Again, they learned when they returned that we had sent no such message. However, I heard about no more incidents after my radio encounter with the Jap.[47]

As we began to move down Highway 5, we saw overturned Jap trucks and other vehicles shot up and destroyed. Quite often the column came upon places where it was necessary to bypass demolished bridges by fording the streams. The troopers took these obstacles in stride and the column continued to roll. When the spearhead of the column reached the town of Baliuag, there were signs of Jap patrols and other signs of recent Jap occupancy. The cavalrymen quickly placed the town under American control, established outposts there, and later pushed on.[48]

The stretch from Gapan to Baliuag, about 25 miles, was touch-and-go all the way. Once in a while we would get up to 30 miles per hour, and would think we were going to get there quickly. But that never lasted long. We would always run into an obstacle, like a strong Jap position, which forced the 1st Cavalry to dismount and fight their way through.

All along the road, happy Filipinos cheered us on. They would shout, "Mabuhay, mabuhay, veectory, veectory," and give us flowers, chickens, eggs, and bananas. I never did figure out what to do with a live chicken or a raw egg, but I knew it was given from their hearts. Frankly, we loved all this attention and it made what we were doing a little more worthwhile.

Later that day, the 2nd Squadron, 8th Cavalry ran into a full Japanese battalion near Santa Maria. Quickly, Godolphin was called by General Hoffman to request a strike, but our planes were advised of the proximity of our troops. Instead, they made several low-level runs, not firing a shot, and the Japs scattered in all directions. This made it possible for the squadron to rush in and clean out those who were left.

The speed of MAGSDAGUPAN communications was well illustrated when Colonel Walter E. Finnegan of the 7th Cavalry Regiment dashed up to Godolphin's jeep with a report that a Japanese plane was in the area. Captain Godolphin pointed to the lone enemy plane still burning on Marikina strip 2,000 yards away. Staff Sergeant Byers in the radio truck had already relayed the information from the captain's jeep to two P-51s, vectored them to the plane, and watched them shoot it down.[49]

As this was happening, the 5th Cavalry, driving south, called in SBDs from both MAG-24 and MAG-32. They were diverted from their prearranged assignment to bomb and strafe the town of San Isdro, just ahead of General Chase's troops. The soldier who noted that all bombs hit the target reported, "Target left in shambles."

South of Baliuag all the bridges were out across the Angat River, which we had to cross. Where the bridges were destroyed, the water was too deep for the tanks, trucks, and jeeps to get through. The 2nd Squadron, 8th Cavalry and the 2nd Squadron, 5th Cavalry crossed east of Pla-ridel and found deep holes where they crossed. But they began filling in the holes using bulldozers so that we would be able to ford the river.

At Baliuag, General Mudge and the two brigade commanders, General Chase and General Hoffman, set up their separate command posts for the night. General Chase was in a Filipino house. Local Filipinos told him that General Yamashita, the Japanese commander, had stopped at the same house several days earlier during his withdrawal to the north. At midnight after this very busy day, February 2, the head of the Flying Column was only 15 miles from Manila.

The local Filipinos at Baliuag were very perceptive. They knew we were coming down Highway 5, and they also knew that when we got to the river we would be stopped indefinitely. So, sometime before we got there, they prepared a luau (similar to that of the Hawaiians) for us. They had dug a long, deep hole in the ground. They built a fire in the bottom of the hole, and when the coals were red-hot, they covered them with banana leaves. Then they placed a side of beef on top of the banana-covered coals and covered the meat also with leaves. They cooked it for several hours, perhaps even overnight.

All we could see around the area were trees and small grass huts. Since the Filipinos were all around we knew we did not have to worry about any Japs, so I asked someone to watch my jeep radio and come get me if they heard it. I walked over to the hole as they removed the meat. The ladies served full plates of the meat the men had cooked, along with bread and several kinds of vegetables. It was wonderful.

I was sitting on the grass by myself when two young girls, probably teenagers, came over with their plates of food and asked if they could join me. They both spoke exceptionally good English. They asked, "Where do you come from?" and questions like that. We talked until we had finished our meal. That was a treat for me.

My water canteen was empty and I asked the girls if there was a place to fill it. They walked me a short distance in the direction of the town and off the path through some trees. There stood a large tank on a tower, with clear spring water running continuously out of a pipe. I asked, "Is this where everyone around here has to get their water?" They said it was and explained that it was for all of the community. I asked, "Where do you bathe?" The younger of the two said, "Right here. Late at night, one of us watches while the other bathes." The other one said, "Yes, we will be bathing here tonight about two hours after dark." H-m-m-m. I quickly figured that would be about 9:00 p.m.

We went back to where everyone was still eating and, even though I was not too hungry, I ate another plateful. Later, I noticed my canteen was just about empty again and I thought that I would go back and fill it with that good, spring water. Maybe around 9:00 p.m.

The next day the column rolled on until the forward troops hit the "Hot Corner." This was near the town of Novaliches at an intersection near the Ipo Dam, which the Japs had decided to defend at all costs. Colonel Conner's "E" Troop went there to deal with the problem and heavy fighting followed. The 2nd Squadron, 8th Cavalry moved on to cross the nearby Novaliches Bridge. Our Marine planes had been sent to check the bridge out and reported that it appeared intact. Soon it was discovered the Stone Arched bridge over the Tuliahan River was heavily set with demolition bombs and the fuses had already been lit. Lieutenant J. G. James P. Sutton, a Navy bomb-disposal expert, who was with us to respond to just this situation, ran onto the bridge with Jap bullets sing-ing all around him and cut the burning fuses. After the Japs were cleared away from the bridge area it became passable.[50]

We didn't know it at that time, but Lieutenant Sutton, in the little time he had, cut the fuses but failed to remove the explosives. They remained on the bridge, and after the forward echelon of the column crossed, the Japs returned, lit the fuses again, and completed the demolition, making it extremely difficult for the much-needed reinforcements to follow.

The forward echelon of the Flying Column, which had crossed the bridge before it was blown up, was able to push on and secure Tuliahan at about 1800 hours. It then reached Grace Park, an airfield about a mile north of Manila that had been destroyed. They crossed the Manila city limits at 1835. *The United States Army had returned to Manila.*[51]

From this point, Colonel Conner and his 8th Cavalry and Colonel Lobit and his 5th Cavalry pushed ahead toward Santo Tomas Univer-sity where the American civilian prisoners of war were interned. Colonel Conner ran across two former Filipino scouts in the American Army. He was skeptical of their volunteering to show his troops the best way to Santo Tomas, but after checking them out thoroughly decided to do so. It was a real break. During the trip through the city, Troop F of the 8th Cav-alry broke off to go to Malacanan Palace, one of the objectives ordered by General MacArthur. They quickly surprised the Jap forces on the palace grounds and drove them out. Shortly afterward the Japs attempted to re-enter the palace grounds and 40 Japs were killed. Five Jap staff cars were found outside the walls of the palace the next morning, indicating that some high-ranking officers had been there.

As the forward column moved down Quezon Boulevard, all the 1st

Cavalry vehicles assembled into a close column. Unnoticed in the darkness for a short time, four Jap trucks moved along the rear of the column, keeping their distance. Suddenly the jeep in the rear of the column noticed the enemy truck and opened up with .50-caliber machine gun fire. This started a battle between the moving forces. Two 1st Cavalrymen were killed and several were wounded. The Jap trucks along with their troops were demolished.

Release of Santo Tomas Internees

When the Philippines was a protectorate of the United States, Santo Tomas University in Manila was the oldest institution of learning under the American flag. It was established in 1611 by Dominican fathers and was devoted to the blessings of Christian religion and education. Santo Tomas University was the largest facility of its kind in Manila. Its 48-acre campus was enclosed in high concrete walls, except for the front, which had high iron bars. In 1942, the Dominican priests had no choice but to release Santo Tomas to the Japanese.

The university was a day school, which meant there were no student dormitories, only large buildings with classrooms. Therefore, there were no suitable facilities to house the at-times more than 4,000 prison internees, many of whom had been there for over three and one-half years. The ingenuity of the internees made life at the camp somewhat endurable, but there was little they could do about the lack of food, which was the primary cause of illnesses and resulted in many deaths. Never in U.S. history has there been anything to compare with this inhumane confinement of American civilians.

This is surely one of the most miraculous days of World War II. Many versions of this day, which saw the release of 3,700 internees at Santo Tomas, have been told over the years. While the stories differ, depending on who saw what, some facts have been established, and the excitement of that day has been recorded in many places.

On Saturday, February 3, 1945, it was nearly time for the evening roll call at the Santo Tomas Internment Camp in Manila. Among the 3,700 emaciated and tattered men, women, and children who had been prisoners of the Japanese there during the three long years since the fall of Manila, hopes and spirits were high. American aircraft had been seen and identified by the internees several times during the past few days. Of course, the planes were newer models than anybody in the camp had seen before, but there was no mistaking the American markings. And if American planes were coming in close, maybe the Japanese were planning to give up Manila as they had been forced to give up Leyte. The change in the attitudes of the Japanese prison staff had been noticeable. Discipline was relaxed. The internees knew something was happening, and that things were looking better for them all the time.

At 1645 (4:45 p.m.), as the internees went to their quarters for the roll call, nine Marine SBD dive-bombers, among those on station every day supporting the Flying Column, buzzed the prison compound so low that it seemed certain they would take the roof off of the guard tower.[52] The Japanese guards saved face by ignoring the planes, but every one of the internees who could do so ran to the windows to get a glimpse of the Yank aircraft. The prisoners noticed something their keepers missed. From one plane a pilot dropped something that landed in the northeast courtyard of the Main Building. One of the Main Building residents quickly retrieved the object, which was found to be a pair of pilot goggles—with a note attached. The note said, "Roll out the barrel. Santa Claus is coming Sunday or Monday."[53]

The words of the message spread like wildfire among the internees in the Main Building. Their fellow internees who lived in the shanties in the quadrangle and in the other buildings wondered why there was so much excitement. They were still wondering when the shooting began later in the evening outside the compound. The inhabitants of the Main Building were afraid that the guerrillas had gone off half-cocked, creating a disturbance that would delay the arrival of Santa Claus or make it impossible for "him" to get there at all. The Jap guards shot at inquisitive heads peering out the prison windows.

As darkness fell, amid the noise of rifle shots, cheering Filipinos shouting "Mabuhay!" could be heard. The roar of internal combustion motors and the clank of metal was audible through the prison windows. One internee said, "They're our tanks. They're American tanks." Another said, "How do you know they're American tanks? You never saw American tanks! They are probably Jap tanks retreating." There was no answer to that. Then the shanty-dwellers began to file into the Main Building. Lieutenant Abiko, the Japanese supervisor of prisoners, had issued the order, "Tell all the shanty-dwellers to get into the Main Building within twenty minutes. The Americans are in town." The shanty dwellers then began to file into the Main Building.

The internees listened anxiously as the firing drew nearer. Stealthy glances from the windows revealed little, but throughout the building starved and wrinkled faces broke into smiles and grins. Internees so recently bowed by their long imprisonment now walked on air, hoping, yet fearing to hope, that Santa Claus was really arriving.

They watched the Jap guards go to their posts. They saw two Jap trucks carrying seven Jap soldiers roll hastily out of the front gate as the tumult neared the rear of the compound. In the growing darkness the rattling treads of the tanks became the jingling bells of Santa Claus' sleigh. Or were they Japanese tanks? Then the tanks turned left and stopped in front of the main gate. Indistinct voices floated up to the internees leaning out of the windows, bent on missing nothing. A flare was sent up. Its light showed the time on the Main Building's clock. It was 8:50 p.m. Everything was quiet.

A voice came out of the darkness: "Where the hell is the front gate?" The Americans had arrived for sure. A tank named "Battlin' Basic," of the 44th Tank Battalion, crashed through the gate.[54] Santa Claus in the form of the 1st Cavalry Division had come to liberate the 3,700 internees of Santo Tomas.

Colonel Conner was in his jeep right behind the tank Battlin' Basic. Bill Dunn, the CBS correspondent who had been with General MacArthur, was in the jeep with Conner. Behind Conner in another jeep was *Life* magazine photographer Carl Mydans, who had been an internee at Santo Tomas himself. He was one of 160 internees repatriated on the ship *Gripsholm* after being imprisoned a year and a half, and he had many close friends in Santo Tomas. Carl did a very dangerous thing. He jumped out of his jeep, stepped through the hole in the wall left by the tank, and hollered, "Hello, anyone!" This is Carl Mydans. Are there any Americans in there?" He heard nothing. He shouted again and again and finally went back to Bill Dunn and said, "Bill, I'm afraid to go in there, afraid of what we're going to find. *I don't think there's anyone still alive.*"

That, of course, was everyone's fear. There had been rumors that the Japs would kill all the internees before we got there.

About that time a Jap came out of nowhere and threw a grenade over the wall where Conner and his men were planning the best way to enter. A piece of shrapnel hit Colonel Conner in his calf. It was not a serious injury but could very well have been.[55]

Shortly after that the lights began to come on and screams of joy could be heard echoing all over the Santo Tomas campus. "Battlin' Basic" had moved into the campus followed by two other tanks and the forward echelon of the 1st Cavalry. The internees began to run up, throwing their arms around these strange-looking big men who they knew were the American soldiers who had come to save them.[56]

As dawn broke the next day, February 4, the Flying Column was strung out for more than fifty miles, from Santo Tomas University to the town of Novaliches. The plan was for General MacArthur to join up with General Mudge and then go into Manila and Santo Tomas. However, at 0830 the 2nd Squadron of the 5th Cavalry had discovered that the bridge over the Tuliahan River had been destroyed and the Japs had established a roadblock on the south bank of the river. Movement was abruptly halted.

The 1st Squadron, forward-most in the column, was ordered to send two troops ahead, one to secure the south bank of the Tuliahan River and the other to assist engineers in constructing a bypass. "B" Troop disposed of the small Jap holding force and reported that the crossing was secured. "A" Troop, the division engineers, estimated that it would be the next morning before crossing the river would be possible. All the while there was growing concern as to how much longer the small force at

Santo Tomas University could hold off the reported number of Japanese in Manila.

I was with a group halted for several hours at the Tuliahan River at the same bridge Lieutenant Sutton had performed his heroics. We knew that General MacArthur was somewhere in the area. At around 1000 (10:00 a.m.) he arrived. I was sitting in my jeep when I looked over and saw him with General Mudge and other officers a few feet away. They were in a huddle, apparently discussing the bridge situation.

Unexpectedly, General MacArthur came up to me as I sat in my radio jeep. I was busy talking to the pilots of our Marine planes overhead who were reporting on conditions on the other side of the blown-out bridge. I had a "Tommy gun" (a Thompson submachine gun) lying on my lap. I normally kept my own carbine with me wherever I was, but Staff Sergeant Byers had to go somewhere and swapped with me so that he would not have to carry the heavier Tommy gun. The general listened as I talked with the Marine planes. He could hear both sides of the conversation.

He asked me something about the planes—I forget what. At the time, I hoped he would leave because I was busy and my responsibilities were uppermost in my mind. At the time, we were very anxious. We knew Japs were all around us, but we didn't know how many. We felt like sitting ducks because we could not move forward or backward. We had to be attentive to these pilots, answering their questions and copying down their reports. The general finally said something like, "Keep up the good work," and turned and walked away.

As he left, I saw Captain Titcomb, my boss, walk toward the general and salute him sharply. General MacArthur just turned and looked the other way. That was the general. I didn't like what he did, and it bothered me because I had a lot of respect for Captain Titcomb and I could see this hurt him. I thought about this incident even more later, after a sniper's bullet killed Captain Titcomb. That time with General MacArthur was the last time I would ever see Titcomb. Looking back I know that if the general had responded to every salute, he would be saluting all day. I understand that now but didn't at the time.

The 5th Cavalry's account of the destruction of the bridge over the Tuliahan River near the town of Novaliches states that there was a feeling among the men of the 5th Cavalry that they had let General MacArthur down, since MacArthur wanted to show up on the campus of Santo Tomas.[57] Nothing could be further from the truth. It was just unfortunate that Lieutenant Sutton, under heavy Jap fire, only had time to cut the fuses and get out of there, leaving the explosives behind. All the Japs had to do was come back after our advance troops had left and blow up the bridge. No one was to blame. It was just something that happened in the heat of battle. Also, I remember hearing machine gun fire in the trees nearby. They had to get General MacArthur out of there under those circumstances.

Meanwhile, back at Santo Tomas, on the first morning of freedom for the internees, February 4, the situation was still hectic. The badly needed supply of food for the internees was more than 100 miles away. General Chase's 1st Cavalry troops on the campus were sharing their K-Rations with the internees, particularly the children. Santo Tomas University was surrounded by a dying city. Fires burned everywhere and explosions from demolitions could be heard as the enemy systematically razed buildings and bridges. Thousands of homeless citizens moved near the camp, seeking food, shelter, and escape from the inevitable battle. Inside the grounds of the internment camp more than 3,700 liberated internees looked to the American forces for food and protection. The 37th Division was approaching the city from the north, but was still too far away to give assistance at Santo Tomas, and the 11th Airborne Division, which had landed on Luzon four days before, on January 31, was still far to the south. Not only rations but ammunition had run low. The numerous firefights with Jap resistance on the way to the city had nearly exhausted the supply. If the Japs had made a determined counterattack against Santo Tomas, it is doubtful the cavalrymen could have withstood it.

Hostage Situation

The predicament was further complicated by 65 Japanese troops who had holed up in the Education Building on campus. There they held hostage 276 of the internees, mostly men and boys, under the threat of death demanding safe-conduct to the Manila city limits. For the first few hours after the cavalrymen entered the university grounds, there was a continual exchange of rifle fire between the Jap holdouts in the Education Building and the troops outside. The Americans ceased fire when they learned that hostages were being held. The Japanese fire then also slacked off. General Chase's mission was to effect the safe liberation of all internees, and he was deeply concerned over the welfare of those still in the hands of the Japs. He appointed Colonel Charles E. Brady, executive officer of the 1st Cavalry Brigade, to negotiate with Lieutenant Colonel Hayashi, commander of the beleaguered Japs, for the release of the prisoners.

At first intermediaries were used, but on the night of February 4,

Colonel Brady himself, accompanied only by an interpreter, internee Ernest Stanley, entered the Education Building. After fifteen minutes, Colonel Hayashi appeared with six armed guards and set forth his terms for the release of the hostages. He demanded that his men be freed with all their automatic weapons, grenades, and individual arms. Lengthy talks followed. It was finally agreed that if the internees were left unharmed, Colonel Hayashi and his men, carrying only individual arms (one weapon to a man), would be escorted through the front lines and released.

Before daylight on February 5, Colonel Brady and men from "E" Troop, 5th Cavalry met the Japanese force at the entrance of the Education Building and escorted the group to a point approximately one mile from Santo Tomas. There the Japs were released. Colonel Brady's action saved the lives of the 276 internees, and won him the Silver Star.

From the eyes of one of the internees is this account: On Monday (February 5, 1945) I stood with others and watched as sixty-five Japanese men who had been in charge of our camp were escorted out five blocks to their troops and given their freedom. This was their reward for not harming the internees. Soon after that, at 10:00 a.m., with American troops firmly in charge of Santo Tomas Internment Camp, our hearts leaped for joy as the American flag was raised high above us on the main building. We waved, wept, and sang "God Bless America." We sang "The Star Spangled Banner" with more patriotic fervor, joy, and appreciation than ever before. Our voices, full of tears, mingled with those of the soldiers. The day of freedom began for us as the rising sun went down over STIC, and the stars came out—forever.[58]

As stated, only two men conducted the negotiations for the release of the hostages. The internees had an intense hatred for three people: first and foremost, Japanese lieutenant Abiko. Second was a longtime resident in the Philippines named Tobo, who was in charge of the "package line." In the early days of the camp, internees were allowed to pick up packages at the front gate brought to them by their friends or servants still on the outside. Tobo would demand his part of whatever was in each package: food, clothes, and so forth. Third was Ernest Stanley, the interpreter for Colonel Brady in the hostage situation. Stanley was a British civilian who had arrived in Manila just a few weeks before Pearl Harbor. Stanley spoke fluent Japanese, and soon after he came to the camp, he allied himself with the Japanese hierarchy. He became the Japanese interpreter for the camp and was allowed to live away from the internees in the Japanese commandature. He seldom spoke to any of the internees, except when translating for the camp's internee Executive Committee.

When the 1st Cavalry soldiers arrived shortly after 9:00 p.m. on February 3, one of the American officers shouted, "Where is Mr. Stanley?" The internees immediately thought, "Now he will get his." Stanley appeared and the officer handed him an Army steel helmet and a carbine rifle and said, "Mr. Stanley, how glad we are to see you." It turned out that Stanley had been planted in Manila and was operating as an intelligence agent for the United States, sending information outside the camp through Tobo. Tobo, a Nisei-American, had been planted in Manila as a hairdresser sixteen years before and acted as a link between Stanley and the guerrillas. It is likely that information from Stanley, passed through Tobo, had reached General MacArthur, which led to the urgency of establishing the Flying Column to release the internees of Santo Tomas.

In Carl Mydans' photograph of Colonel Brady marching the Japanese out to the edge of Manila after the negotiated release of the intern-ees held hostage, Mr. Stanley is wearing a white shirt and has a big smile on his face (see photograph section). For 36 hours, he acted as translator for Colonel Brady during negotiations with Japanese Colonel Hayashi. We can now appreciate why he is smiling in this picture—a three-and-a half-year job well done.[59]

Early on February 5, we arrived at Grace Park on the north edge of Manila. We had been told that we were going to set up a temporary command post there. There was scattered activity in every direction, and with all the requests for air reconnaissance, we were spread thin. Captain McAloney and PFC Armstrong were still on the campus of Santo Tomas and could cover the area west and north of Manila. We would take the rest, behind us and to the east and south. As far as we knew, the 11th Airborne was still coming up from the south. So we looked for a suitable place to settle in for a day or two. The Grace Park Air Field had been totally destroyed. Ironically, our planes had bombed this airfield before and after the landing at Lingayen. And what we didn't destroy, the Japs demolished before their retreat.

Not long after we settled in, Captain Godolphin received a call on the radio from Captain McAloney at Santo Tomas, saying that General Chase would like to meet with Godolphin and McAloney. He wanted to discuss further assignments for air cover by the Marine planes. He asked that we go over to the university. I drove Captain Godolphin the 10 miles or so to the university, escorted by two jeeploads of 1st Cavalry troops. We arrived there sometime after noon.

When we arrived on the campus, we immediately drove to where our other Marine radio jeep was, on the right, inside the main gate and across from the Main Building. Godolphin and McAloney went off to see General Chase, and I had a great visit with Corporal Armstrong, a fine-looking lad of about 19, who served as the other jeep driver and radioman. He filled me in on the hostage situation, which had just been resolved a few hours before. These 65 Japs who had held the internees hostage for a day and a half were marched right in front of almost all the 1st Cavalry GIs who were there. Armstrong and others told me how difficult it was to just stand there, with a rifle in their hands, and let these "bastards" just walk out. Of course, each of the Japs was carrying a weapon too. What is remarkable about this event is that if one shot had been fired, just one by either side, there would have been a wholesale massacre of everyone around. I have often thought about that.

Later while on campus talking about this incident to several people, I was told that we precipitated the long delay in completing the negotiated settlement so that word would be sent to the guerrillas, who were waiting for the Japs when they were released at the Manila city limits. This was one of many rumors I was never able to verify.

Although I had to stay in sight of Armstrong and his jeep in case Godolphin returned and wanted to get out of there, I wandered around the Santo Tomas campus by myself and got lots of hugs from many internees, especially when they saw I was a Marine. They hadn't seen many Marines.[60] In strolling around the campus I met several of the internees. Like the other GIs, I was appalled at their physical condition. The men were pale and undernourished; the women looked a little better; the children, for the most part, appeared to be in good condition. It was obvious that whatever food was available had mostly gone to the children.

After several hours I got a signal from Armstrong and dashed over to my jeep. Captain Godolphin was ready to return to Grace Park, so we left. As it turns out, it was just before the Japs began shelling Santo Tomas. On the way, Godolphin told me some things about his meeting with General Chase, that the general agreed we were to set up our headquarters and work out of Grace Park since it was centrally located.

Japanese Shelling of Santo Tomas

One of the many tragedies of the Pacific War is the shelling of the campus of Santo Tomas, which began late on February 5 and continued, unrelenting, through February 7. Seventeen internees were killed and many others were wounded.[61] These poor emaciated souls, most of whom had spent the entire three and a half years in this God-forsaken place, suffered unspeakable inhumanities, and then, after their release, were deliberately killed by this shelling. To add to this tragedy, shortly after their release on February 3, the victims had been reported alive and well to their relatives in the United States and throughout the world and were soon to return home.

Surviving internees have found it difficult to talk about the tragedy, and accounts of it are too sparse. One exception is Eva Anna Nixon, who wrote in her memoirs about what she saw at the time: "On Wednesday, February 7, the whole camp was stunned by the holocaust of real war. Little did we dream that morning as we watched the shells fall out in front of the main building that many of us would die that day. I picked up a piece of a Japanese shell, still hot, which fell at my feet as I talked with Dr. Walter B. Foley that morning. Could I know I would never talk with him again? I stood in the lunch line with the intelligent lawyer, Mr.

McFie, and we had discussed the future of the Philippines and China. A few hours later he was dying with his brains blown out. When I last saw Mildred Harper get into bed and heard her laughter ring through the blackout, I didn't know that shell fragments would put a stop forever to her merry laughter. And when Gladys Archer stopped me in the hall, I had no idea that in minutes her head would be severed from her body. And there was beautiful Veda—but they gave her blood plasma and she will live, even though her eye and ear are gone.

"We had awakened that morning to happy news. The Army food supplies were arriving. The menu for supper went up: Corned beef hash, green beans, fruit cocktail. We went back again and again to the back hall where the menu was posted just to re-assure ourselves. We were so happy that we became careless about the falling shell, the snipers, and the shrapnel. When a shell fragment hit the window of our room, a woman said, 'Look, our window has a shrapnel wound,' and we all laughed.

"While we sat in the hall exchanging stories that afternoon, there was a buzz over our heads, a loud crash, and then cement, glass, and dirt came tumbling down around us. We ducked our heads and huddled close together. As soon as the dust settled, we looked out the window into the patio where water was pouring from the roof tanks through a shell hole and cracked and crumbled stones.

"Evelyn dashed down the stairs. 'Did you hear that! It buzzed right over our heads up there, and you should have seen us hit the floor! No siesta for me!'

"'I don't have any shrapnel to take home, and I'm going to see if I can find some,' said a woman next to me. 'There ought to be some around after that blast.'

"But she didn't have time to find her shrapnel. There was another loud explosion just back of us. The corner of the building above our head crumpled. Someone screamed.

"Another loud explosion, more cement and glass, more confusion and noise! An American soldier came by and said, 'Stay away from windows and doors. Get back against the wall and stay down low. Don't go back into your rooms.' He stood straight and spoke as calmly as if he were telling us where to stand in line for registration, though at that very moment he was risking his life to save ours.

"We huddled against the wall and silently clung to each other. Another blast shook the building, and everything became hazy and dark. We covered our faces and braced ourselves as the building tumbled about us. The shell hit directly back of us and wind gushed out the door near us. A nurse, the color drained from her face, ran down the hall followed by two soldiers carrying a stretcher bearing two children dripping blood.

"We huddled together like hunted animals, realizing that the next moment might bring death. I was too stunned to pray, but as I sat waiting in that haunting silence, knowing my face was as ashen as those around me, and knowing we all shared a common hope for life, the words of a grand old hymn sang themselves through my mind like this:

> Our God, our Help in ages past,
> Our Hope for years to come,
> Be Thou our Guide while life shall last,
> And our eternal Home!

"I never hear that hymn without remembering the exploding shells, the falling cement and glass, the strained, white silence of those hours—and the eternal faithfulness of God.

"After a few hours the shelling stopped. We thought it was over. So we started moving around again to survey the damage. Then suddenly there was another blast, a direct hit on the corner room of the main building. Down through the crowded halls again came the casualties, blood-streaked, frightened people, running, with stretchers and mangled bodies. More explosions! The whole side of the building seemed to be caving in. We moved with the mob back around to the safest northeast corner of the building as shells which sounded like eggs frying in hot grease whizzed over our heads.

"We took refuge on the sidewalk, which was to be our bed, dining room, and living room for the next week. We were a large company—men, women, children, and soldiers—huddled together for safety up against the wall of the building. As the night exploded by, we heard stories of death and destruction.

"Early one morning while we slept on the sidewalk, it rained. The day grew chilly, but we huddled close to the wall and to each other to keep warm. When at last the rain stopped and the sun came out, we were thankful for warmth. That picture was printed in the papers across the United States, through which my family came to know that I was still alive. That was the day also that Clarence Townsend of Salem, Ohio, Friends Church came into the camp and hunted me up and started bringing me up-to-date local news from home. That was the day the first load of bread rolled into camp and the cheers went up. "Bread, bread, bread!" It was the first bread he had seen for three years.

"Standing in line to get food for our group that day, I discussed with those in front and back the joys and tragedies we shared. The person back of me was already marked for death by tuberculosis. But there in the line that day he philosophized, 'I was sure glad to see that bread. You know, we're not out of danger yet, but I'd rather be shot than starve to death.'

"The young French woman in front turned around and burst into tears. 'Who wants to die at all? I don't want to die of starvation, nor do I want to die in the shelling. We've come through all this. I love life. I've learned to appreciate it more now. Why do I have to die? O God, I don't want to die!'

"We were silent as she fought to get control of emotions. We stood with bowed head, partly because we respected her in the depth of her tender feelings, and partly because we knew she had expressed the desire of every soldier on the battlefield, and every single one of us.

"At last our starvation days were over, and after a few days the firing toward us ceased. We were delivered from the things we feared, though for weeks we continued to live in the midst of the tragedy and horror of war. The exploding guns, dive bombers, observation planes, wounded soldiers in ambulances, wreckage of huge stone buildings, or of dead bodies under stacks of rubble and debris, increasing numbers of fresh graves and white crosses—all these things underlined the meaning of war and the cost of liberation.

"In those war-filled months before we finally left Manila for the U.S.A. on April 10, 1945, we had time to ponder the meaning of life. As I remembered the days of hunger, I thought more deeply about the truth expressed in Luke 4:4, when Christ said, 'Man shall not live by bread alone.' And as I walked, broken-hearted, in the field of white crosses, just having learned that I had a brother shared in this price, I prayed for God to show me what was meant by the words of Jesus who said, 'I have come that they might have life, and that they might have it more abundantly' (John 10:10).

"Easter, our last holiday spent in camp, held deeper meaning for me than any other. I felt that I, too, had experienced something akin to resurrection. I knew then that life could never be the same again. I knew that in the years left to me I would always carry a sense of responsibility for all those who in their youth had been cut off from life for freedom's sake. And may I never forget another who in His early years also died for me—but rose again—to set all my suffering, anxiety, and death in the eternal perspective of His loving purpose."[62]

On February 7, General MacArthur made his triumphal entry into Manila. He was met at the city limits by a group of officers and men including Lieutenant General O. W. Griswold, Major General Mudge, Brigadier General Chase, and personnel from the Flying Column who had made the dash into the Japanese stronghold. General MacArthur's first words praised the historic feat accomplished by the 1st Cavalry Division. General Chase was then informed that he had been recommended for promotion to major general and had been placed in command of the 38th Infantry Division, which was fighting on the Bataan Peninsula. Showered by the plaudits of the grateful Filipinos, General MacArthur rode through the city. Despite the sniping and artillery fire going on in every quarter, MacArthur visited the Malacanan Palace and the front-line troops who were engaged in a firefight with the enemy along the Pasig River.

The 5th Cavalry was relieved from the Santo Tomas University on

February 7 by the 37th Infantry Division, which had fought its way into Manila on February 4. By that evening the 1st Cavalry Division had killed 1,587 Japs and had captured 51 prisoners-of-war. Their own losses during the Luzon Campaign up to that time were 36 killed in action, 141 wounded in action, and 4 missing in action.

Novaliches Watershed

While we were at Santo Tomas, we learned that the "G" Troop of the 2nd Squadron, 7th Cavalry under the command of Captain Erick D. Berquist had advanced to Novaliches Dam. They made a surprise attack and captured this important facility, which provided Manila's entire water supply. The dam had been thoroughly mined, but the decisive action of Captain Berquist and his men resulted in the annihilation of the Japanese demolition unit before they could detonate the high explosives. The following day, February 6, the 7th Cavalry Regimental Headquarters and the 2nd Squadron, less "G" Troop, moved in and secured the Novaliches watershed and the Balera Filters, a water filtration plant, in the nick of time. When the filter plant was taken that evening at 1900, it was found that the Japs had wired it completely for demolition and were scheduled to set off the explosives at 1930. The next day more than a ton of explosives were removed.

The 1st Squadron, 7th Cavalry provided protection for the line of communication in the vicinity of Santa Marie–Novaliches when it joined the remainder of the regiment in repulsing Japanese attempts to infiltrate and blow up Manila's water facilities. Some Filipino guerrillas had verified that the Japs had also intended to poison the water. Tons of poisons were later found. Captain Godolphin and I were ordered to take our jeep, break off from the column, and join up with the 1st Cavalry's Seventh Regiment to provide air cover for these troops. We were to forget the plans made with General Chase when we were at Santo Tomas and get up there with the 7th Cavalry as quickly as we could.

We left Grace Park early the morning of February 7. When we arrived at the Novaliches Watershed, the Seventh Regiment, 1st Cavalry had set up a command post near the filtration building. It appeared the building itself might provide some protection from enemy fire. I always had to have my radio jeep near the command post, so I parked the jeep close by the command post tent and near a tree.

We were briefed on the situation and prepared ourselves for what we expected would be a pretty rough time. It was fairly quiet until suppertime. We dug our foxholes and prepared for the night. While I was at Milne Bay, New Guinea, for Christmas in 1944, the Army gave us anything we wanted in the way of clothes and supplies. Someone had talked me into taking a camouflaged hammock. It was green, had a plastic waterproof roof, mosquito netting all around, and a zipper to get in and out. I had never seen one of these before, nor have I since. The hammock folded up and fit in a little bag, which I had thrown in my sea bag. I had never thought to use it before, but because of all the water around and little pools of what appeared to be overflow from the plant, the mosquitoes were thick. I had been diagnosed with malaria on Bougainville, and I was concerned to protect myself. I moved my jeep up so I could tie one end of the hammock to the tree nearby and the other to the jeep. Just about directly underneath the hammock, I dug a foxhole with my handy-dandy folding shovel. I was all set up—or so I thought.

This was my first night at the Novaliches Watershed.[63] The 1st Cav cooks set up a table with gallon cans of fruit cocktail, blackberries, and other fruit to go with our K-ration evening meal. I put the blackberries in my mess kit and got something to drink. The chaplain, Thomas E. McKnight of the Seventh Regiment, was standing behind me in the chow line and we began to talk. He asked if he could join me for the meal and followed me over to my jeep. I explained that I had to stick close by the radio. Relaxing on the green grass, we finished the meal and continued to talk for what seemed to be hours. He was encouraging to me and thankful for the presence of our air support. It was getting late, so he excused himself, shook my hand, and left. We had a great visit—one that was very comforting to me.

About midnight, the Japs attacked us with machine guns, mortars, and finally rockets. That was my first experience with rocket missile artillery. These rockets screamed, and it was a frightful noise.[64] When this mortar attack started during the night, I came out of that mosquito netting without using the zipper, tearing it up completely. I fell into my foxhole where I belonged. I grabbed my helmet off the grass, but I had left the small folding shovel in the foxhole. I hit it when I fell in and cut my left hand below the thumb. I could not see in the dark, but after things quieted down a bit, I felt blood running down my arm. In the light of the artillery, I saw it was bleeding pretty badly, so I pulled off my undershirt and wrapped it around the hand. We had always been told that no one could be hit below the level of the ground except by a direct hit from above, and I was certainly not going to raise my head above that hole.

I spent that entire night in my foxhole as I am quite sure everyone else did too. I remember welcoming daylight. I unwrapped the undershirt from my hand and it started to bleed again. I found a handkerchief to wrap around it and went looking for the medical aid tent. It was pretty close by. I walked into the tent. It was crowded with injured people. I fixed my eyes on a guy who had lost his leg; the medics were trying to stop the bleeding. One of them came up and said, "What the hell do you want?" I said I had cut my hand and needed a bandage. He pointed over to a table with medical supplies and said, "help yourself." I did not see any bandages, so I grabbed some gauze and tape and got out of there as fast as I could. I went back to my jeep and wrapped it up. It was nothing big. Apparently I had just hit a blood vessel.

After that, I went looking for a cup of coffee. While in line I was told by one of the 1st Cav guys that the chaplain had been killed during attack the night before. I left the line without coffee and went over to my jeep where he and I had eaten our dinner and said a prayer. Yes, I cried too, for the conversation I had with him only the night before had meant so much to me. At the time, I didn't even know his name. He must have detected I was concerned about the whole situation. I kept thinking that if a chaplain could be killed, so could I. This was truly a reality check for me.

The 1st Cavalry Division's account states: "The record of the 7th Cavalry in carrying out this mission is replete with shining examples of gallantry and self-sacrifice. Among the 7th Cavalry personnel to receive the Silver Star decorations for heroism during the Novaliches-Balera action were: Chaplain Thomas E. McKnight of Stockton, Calif., who left his foxhole during the mortar attack to answer the call of a wounded man and was killed while administering to him."[65]

Things got crazy that day. Captain Godolphin had determined where in the jungle this enemy fire was coming from, so our Marine planes were kept busy. The 1st Cav would drop two colored incendiary bombs and direct SBD planes to strafe between them. We could hear the Japs scream when the planes' machine gun fire hit them. Someone told me there were literally hundreds of Jap soldiers out there. You couldn't see them, but you sure could hear them. Unofficial reports were that more than 600 Japs had been killed.

During this battle, the Jap troops charged our position in a last attempt to regain control of the waterworks. I was standing near my jeep when I heard heavy machine gun and rifle fire. We were on a little knoll where the waterworks was located, so I grabbed my carbine from my jeep and walked over to see what was going on. When I looked down in the little valley, I immediately hit the deck. I was ready. Just a minute later, I felt someone kick my shoes. I looked up and it was the 1st Cavalry Division colonel. He said to me, "What the hell do you think you are doing? Get back over to that jeep. We're going to need those planes in a few minutes!" I wasted no time getting back to my jeep seat and it wasn't long before we called the strike by our nine Marine planes.

Later in the day, I was walking around, taking a break, and a guy I believe was from the United Press came up to talk with me about the previous night. I had spilled blackberry juice all over the front of myself from the dinner the night before. He looked at my wrapped-up hand and saw the stain and asked, "Did you get hit last night?" I replied, "No." He said, "What's that all over your jacket?" I said, "blackberry juice." Without saying another word, he turned and walked away. No story there.

The next night I decided to change my sleeping spot. I thought it would be safer to move into the filtration building. Most water filtration plant buildings, particularly back then, had very high ceilings. Spaced around the walls were French windows about the size of a sheet of paper. In the middle of the area water was spraying up into the air. Novaliches was the primary water supply for Manila, and the water was running all the time. However, the pumps that sprayed the water above the pools were shut off after dark, presumably so we could hear.

I found a spot near the windows and laid out my blanket for the night. Again the enemy artillery started. The building caught several hits and these small glass windows began to break. Soon I had small pieces of glass all over me. I was lucky I was not cut. I ran out of the building to my jeep and crawled under it. It was too far away to my first foxhole to make a run for it, and I had covered it up anyway. When the artillery quieted down, I found my little shovel and dug in like I should have in the first place.

There was a tall lookout tower beside the filtration building that looked like a lighthouse. I saw a lot of activity around this tower and asked about it. I was told that someone had reported seeing a small light in this tower the night before. It was described as maybe some fool Jap lighting a match or something to give a signal. So a big gun on wheels was brought up on orders from the commanding officer of that operation. The gun was fired and the top of the tower was blown to bits. There wasn't anything left large enough to tell if a Jap had been up there or not.

Godolphin and I were ordered to stay and work around the Novaliches Watershed area. Since the enemy had made two attempts to recapture the area, it was likely they would try again. In the meantime, Filipino guerrilla scouts had determined that 20,000 enemy troops were scattered along the Mariquina River, near the towns of Antipolo, Montalban, and Ipo, an area not too far from us. Strikes targeting this area had been going on from February 6 through the 10th with larger numbers of SBDs from MAGSDAGUPAN. The largest strike force Captain Godolphin and I directed included 81 SBD planes. A Filipino guerrilla lieutenant, a former civil engineer, scouted the area and made maps of the Jap positions. After Captain Godolphin carefully studied this information, he called in the dive-bombers. Major Manchester, a Marine SBD pilot, coordinated this strike, and his planes were circling as we radioed the information to them. Captain Godolphin had worked out each target in great detail. One by one, each target was hit. The last was about two or three hundred yards from our forward 1st Cavalry troops. As was planned, the first wave of nine planes came in and dropped their bombs. They were duds. This was sometimes done to test the accuracy of hitting a target in difficult areas. Captain Godolphin, with a big grin on his face, later said, "You should have seen the looks of discouragement on the faces of our infantrymen!" Nine other planes followed, dropping their 1,000-pound bombs and destroying all the targets.

The activity in the watershed area became so heavy that the 1st Cavalry air coordinator was holding up approval for strikes. This frustrated Captain Godolphin because the enemy was moving their troops, and by the time the approval came through the radio, the targets were gone. This was true for a Jap portable rocket-launcher that was tearing us up at night. Our spotters would locate it at night and by the time approval came through, it was gone. This happened for two days, so Captain Godolphin took the problem directly to General Mudge. When he explained the problem, General Mudge told him, "When planes report on station, you tell them what you want them to hit. Never mind what they have been briefed for. I will take full responsibility."

The next morning when the SBDs reported on station, the captain directed them to a clump of brush at one end of the Jap-held Marakina airstrip. That was where the rocket-launcher had last been reported. One pilot dropped his bomb on the target and reported seeing the twisted wreckage of the rocket-launcher after his bomb hit it.

This new way of coordinating strikes greatly improved their timeliness, frequency, and accuracy. However, in many situations, detailed briefing of the pilots was necessary before they took off from MAGSDAGUPAN on a strike.

Several days later Captain Godolphin and I were ordered to return to our former command post at Grace Park in Manila. All the 1st Cavalry commanders in the area were going to get together and plan future operations. After we got back there that morning, I was taking a breather by the jeep and a Filipino walked up with a bloodied prisoner. At first I thought he was a Jap soldier but it could have been a Filipino collaborator. I didn't know and I didn't ask. The prisoner was too messed up to tell. His pants were practically torn off, and part of the calf of one leg was gone. The Filipino was carrying a carbine just like mine. He asked me for some ammunition for his carbine. I knew what he wanted it for, so I pointed him to a 1st Cavalry officer across the way and told him to take his prisoner to him, which he did. I didn't see what happened after that.

Sometime in the early afternoon, while sitting in my jeep at Grace Park, I received a call from the radio truck. It was Staff Sergeant Byers. I had no idea where the radio truck was at that time. Before I had a chance to ask, he said, "Bob, I have two pieces of good news for you."

"What?" I asked.

"First, you have made Master Sergeant! Second, you're going home!"

"Going home?" I asked.

"Yes, your relief is here." He continued, "They called from the base and said to tell you that you have the points to go home and a whole bunch of Marines from MAG-24 are leaving."

I was stunned but managed to ask, "When?"

"Here's what you are to do. In the morning, you are to drive out east on Highway 5 to the intersection of Highway 51. You know where that is?"

"Yes, but I will make sure," I replied.

"It's only about 5 miles from where you are. Get someone to direct you where the planes have been landing. Talk with Godolphin; he has been advised today about your leaving. You are to be there at 0700 in the morning. A TBF plane will land on Highway 5 and when it stops, drive your jeep up to the plane. A Tech Sergeant (I didn't get his name—and I couldn't have cared less) will get off the plane. He is taking your place. You get your stuff and get on the plane. The pilot will take you back to MAGSDAGUPAN. That's it."

"Is this some kind of joke?" I asked.

"No, it's not. Have you got it straight?"

"Yes, I will be there," I said. I couldn't believe it.

Needless to say, I was there well before 0700 the next day. The plane landed, I shook the hand of my replacement, and I got on the plane just as I was told. We landed at our air base, and a Marine lieutenant met the plane and took me to MAG-24 headquarters. He sat me down and told me that the relief for 600 Marines of the First Marine Air Wing had arrived a day or two before. All 600 were being sent home. I remembered the same thing had happened on Bougainville when the original MAG-

24 personnel had accumulated their points and gone home to the states and I was made communications chief to replace the previous chief.

We were to fly to Manus Island, where we would catch a ship for the U.S. He told me that after I went home, I would probably receive orders to go to Marine Air Station, Cherry Point, North Carolina, for training in new techniques in close air support. He explained that the SBD dive-bombers would be replaced by the newer SB2C-4 "Helldiver" dive-bomber, manufactured by Curtis-Wright. We had seen one or two of these on Bougainville. I would be trained in the States on the newer SB2C radio and radar equipment in the plane and would be attached to a new close air support outfit. All I really heard was, "You are going home." I didn't even ask if I would be coming back to the Pacific.

We knew nothing then about the atom bomb and how it would bring this horrible war to a close. I probably would have been sent back to the Pacific after my training, most likely for the Formosa campaign, which would have had to have taken place before we could land on Japan. President Truman's decision to drop the atom bomb may very well have saved my life.[66]

I spent only one night at MAGSDAGUPAN. All us Marines leaving from MAG-24 were shuttled on R4D airplanes to Manus Island.[67] We were put in a tent and only spent one night there also. The next morning we boarded the USS *Dupage* and shipped out, arriving in San Francisco March 10, 1945.

Chapter 4

The Philippine Islands Liberation

Completion of Luzon Campaign

For the remainder of February and during early March, the SBDs gave close air support to the 6th, 25th, 37th, 38th, 40th, and 43rd Infantry Divisions, as well as the 1st Cavalry Division and the 11th Airborne Division. The Marine aviators and ground ALPs were accepted once the quality of their air support was recognized, and the Marines continued to perfect air-to-ground coordination of air strikes.[68]

The Marine aviators of MAG-24 and MAG-32 continued their excellent record in providing close support to the 1st Cavalry Division during the liberation of Manila. While fighting for the capital of the Philippines throughout February and into March, Marine pilots were called to provide close air support for Filipino guerrilla bands that were fighting the Japanese.

Two U.S. Army officers, Major Russell W. Volckmann and Captain Donald D. Blackburn, had escaped from the Japanese during the early days of the war. They made their way to Northern Luzon and organized in the mountains and jungles bands of guerrillas from among those Filipino forces that had been cut off from any line of supplies and the rest of Luzon. There were about eight thousand of these guerrillas; only about two thousand of them were well armed.[69]

After the Luzon landings, the Sixth Army organized these guerrillas as the United States Armed Forces of the Philippines, Northern Luzon. By mid-February, the Sixth Army was aware of the close air support the Marines aviation had been providing on Luzon. The 308th Bombardment Wing decided to attach Marines to Colonel Volckmann's guerrillas to direct close air support missions. On February 20, four officers from MAG-24 and MAG-32 met with Colonel Volckmann to devise a plan for providing close air support to the guerrillas. After the meeting, three officers, three enlisted men, a radio jeep, and a radio truck were transported to northwestern Luzon about fifty miles behind enemy lines to begin their work. The first mission was to eliminate the Japanese who were dug in on a ridge just east of the port of San Fernando, which was also held by the enemy.[70]

During the night Marine ALP radiomen dragged their radio jeep to the top of the ridge and hid it about fifty yards from the front line. The truck remained behind so it could communicate between the jeep and MAGSDAGUPAN. Twelve Army planes made the first strike, guided by the ALP. The planes dropped 100-pound fragmentation bombs by parachute. They went off on contact across the 1,000-yard ridge. This allowed the guerrillas to move in and take the ridge. After the plane left, the Japanese began to inflict casualties on the guerrillas. The radio truck then called in another strike, this time by Marine plane, which dropped 500-pound bombs and strafed the Japanese positions.

In numerous other instances Marine ALPs were similarly successful in guiding air strikes. In one case, the air strikes killed 137 out of 150 Japanese troops. The guerrillas reported that of the remaining 13, they killed 7 and were looking for the other 6.[71]

On March 1, Captain Jack Titcomb, one of the Marine officers serving as a member of the ALP with the guerrillas whom I had been with at Bougainville, was killed by a sniper's bullet "while asking for more planes for a strike, microphone in hand" (see Appendix A).

The air base at MAGSDAGUPAN, the base for the Marine planes, had escaped enemy attack throughout February, but on March 2 the Japanese struck the base. At 0200 a Japanese twin-engine bomber, known as a Betty, flew by at a high altitude. The aircraft gunners in the area opened fire on the plane. Then two additional Bettys came over the camp at an altitude of 300 feet or less and dropped nearly 300 anti-personnel bombs. The result of this air attack was 4 dead and 78 wounded. One SBD was lost, the result of a direct hit. Several others planes were damaged. The attack did not, however, succeed in interrupting air strikes.[72]

Between March 5 and 31, 186 missions were flown in support of guerrillas on Northern Luzon. As guerrilla operations spread to the other islands, the Marines provided additional ALPs and close air support. In each instance, the results were the same. The Japanese were either killed or withdrew.

Marine Air Support Commendations

By the end of the Luzon campaign on April 14, 1945, MAG-24 and MAG-32 Marine planes had flown 8,842 combat missions, dropped 19,167 bombs, and fired more than one-and-a-half million rounds of ammunition. The ground crews at MAGSDAGUPAN kept an average of 81 percent of the planes in combat readiness, and individual aircraft flew an average of nine hours a day. Letters of appreciation, military commendations, and words of thanks began to come in. The Secretary of the Navy issued the following Commendation to MAG-24:

The Secretary of the Navy takes pleasure in commending the MARINE AIRCRAFT GROUP TWENTY-FOUR for service as follows:

For exceptional meritorious service in support of the United States Sixth Army in Lingayen Gulf and Manila, Philippine Islands Area, from January 23 to April 10, 1945. After landing at Lingayen with the assault forces on D-day, Marine Aircraft Group Twenty-Four operated continuously against Japanese forces, flying a series of more than 8,000 daring and brilliantly executed sorties despite relentless air and ground force opposition. Dauntless and determined, these units penetrated numerous hostile defenses ahead of our advancing troops and, destroying vital ammunition and fuel dumps, bridges, gun bastions and troop concentrations, effectively reduced the enemy's power to resist and contributed materially to the sweeping victory of our ground forces in the area. The heroic achievements of Marine Aircraft Group Twenty-Four reflect the skill, personal valor and steadfast devotion to duty of the courageous officers and men, and are in keeping with the highest traditions of the United States Naval Service.[73]

Brigadier General William C. Chase remarked that he had never seen such able, close, and accurate air support as the Marine fliers were giving him. This was ample praise from someone who was at first skeptical about the effectiveness of such Marine air cover, and the men who had fearlessly led the Flying Column into the heart of Manila.[74]

Major General Verne D. Mudge, commanding the 1st Cavalry Division, made the following statement:

On our drive to Manila, I depended solely on the Marines to protect my left flank against possible Japanese counter attack. The job that they turned in speaks for itself. I can say without reservation that the Marine dive-bombers are one of the most flexible outfits that I have seen in this war. They will try anything once, and from my experience with them, I have found out that anything they try usually pans out in their favor. The Marine dive-bombers of the First Wing have kept the enemy on the run. They have kept him under ground and have enabled troops to move up with fewer casualties and with greater speed. I cannot say enough in praise of these men of the dive bombers and I am commending them through proper channels for the job they have done in giving my men close ground support in this operation.[75]

From the 1st Cavalry Division history:

Much of the success of the entire movement is credited to the superb air cover, flank protection, and reconnaissance provided by the Marine Air Groups 24 and 32. The 1st Cavalry's audacious drive down through Central

Luzon was the longest such operation ever made in the Southwest Pacific Area using only air cover for flank protection.[76]

Major General Edwin D. Patrick, commanding officer, Sixth Infantry, in a letter of commendation:

The close air support given this Division by the 308th Bombardment Wing and Marine Air Groups (24 and 32), Dagupan, in the operations conducted in the Marakina Watershed area has been outstanding. The advance of our troops over difficult mountainous terrain against a well-armed determined enemy is being made possible in no small part by these air strikes.

Particularly noteworthy have been the skillfully coordinated and accurate air strikes of the SBDs of the MAGD base at Mangalden field (MAGS-DAGUPAN). In one strike made on 28 February against Mt. Mataba, these Marine pilots dive-bombed a pinpointed target located between two friendly forces with accuracy comparable to that obtained by field artillery. The courage, patience, and willingness displayed by these men deserve high praise.[77]

Lieutenant General Walter Krueger, commanding the Sixth Army, in a letter dated May 16, 1945:

In the crucial stages of the Luzon Campaign . . . this support was of such high order that I personally take great pleasure in expressing to every officer and enlisted man . . . my appreciation and official commendation for their splendid work.

Commanders have repeatedly expressed their admiration for the pinpoint precision, the willingness and enthusiastic desire of pilots to fly missions from dawn to dusk and the extremely close liaison with the ground forces which characterized the operation of the Marine fighter groups. By constant visits of commanders and pilots to front line units in order to observe targets and to gain an understanding of the ground soldier's problems, by the care which squadron commanders and pilots took to ensure the maximum hits, and by the continuous, devoted work of ground crews in maintaining an unusually high average of operational crews, the 24th and 32nd Marine Air Groups exemplified outstanding leadership, initiative, aggressiveness and high courage in keeping with the fine traditions of the Marine Corps.[78]

Before the Marines left the Philippines, General Krueger added the following farewell message:

The war record of the First Marine Aircraft Wing [included MAG 24 and 32] is emblazoned with one success after another, from the bitter days of Guadalcanal, where they won the President Unit Citation, to Luzon, where the record speaks for itself and from praises uttered by men of the Sixth Army who have done the land fighting.[79]

From Major General O. W. Griswold, Commanding, XIV Army Corps:

The excellent close support furnished by Marine dive-bombers in the advance of ground troops east of Manila in the Wawa-Antipolo sector be-

tween February 1 and March 15 was a major contribution to the success of operations in that area. The coordination and skill displayed by those pilots with the resultant effectiveness of their strikes was a continuation of the fine work accomplished on Bougainville. It has been my experience, gained from association with that operation and the present one, that Marine dive-bomb pilots can always be depended on to render outstanding support to the ground troops.[80]

The accolades came in the form of more than thirty letters of commendation and appreciation from every Army command level. Whether initiated by F4U Corsairs or SBD dive-bombers, the Marine doctrine of close air support had been validated. Acknowledgment of this came in a final evaluation by Lieutenant General Robert L. Eichelberger, Commander, Eighth Army, who wrote:

The Marine Liaison Officers were always in front lines with the infantry commanders, and they were familiar with the forward positions, as was the infantry. By Radio they guided in the planes, and often the target of the strike was no more than three hundred yards ahead of the huddled doughboys. Nothing comforts a soldier, ankle-deep in mud, faced by a roadblock or fortified strongholds, as much as the sight of bombs wreaking havoc on stubborn enemy positions. It puts heart into them.[81]

Another letter from Lieutenant General Eichelberger:

I have heard a great number of reports from Major General Franklin C. Sibert of the Tenth Corps and other unit commanders on results of

Marine-type dive-bombing in the Philippine theater. The value of close support for ground troops as provided by these Marine fliers cannot be measured in words and there is not enough that can be said for their aerial barrages that have cut a path for the infantry. From all quarters, commanders down to the men with the bayonets, I have heard nothing but high tribute. Great going and keep blasting.[82]

From the official Marine Corps history of World War II came this observation:

A radical departure from orthodox methods was the adoption of direct communications between pilots and ground-based air liaison parties. The performance of Marine aviation on Luzon Island and in the Southern Philippines was to become an outstanding chapter in a long history of excellent achievement, combining raw courage with skill and flexibility. The activities of Marine air in the Philippines constituted one of few opportunities that Marine Air Groups had to show their skill in close air support.[83]

These are merely representative of the many commendations and letters of appreciation. A great number of personal citations and honors were presented as well to those who participated in this campaign.

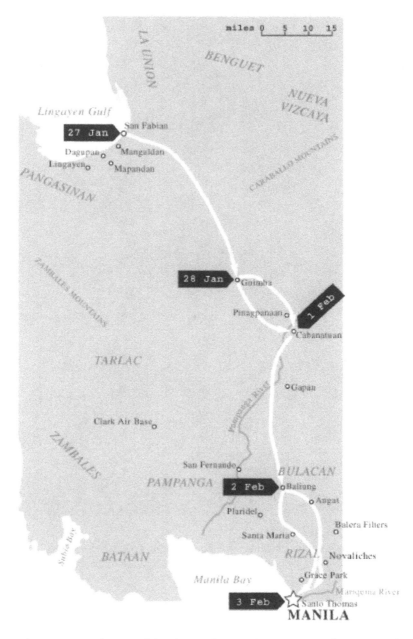

Map of Luzon, 100-mile route of the Flying Column, U.S. Army 1ˢᵗ Cavalry Division, from landing at Lingayen Gulf, January 27, 1945, to recapture of Santo Tomas Internment Camp, February 3, 1945. (Drawn by Walter Smith IV)

fig. 1

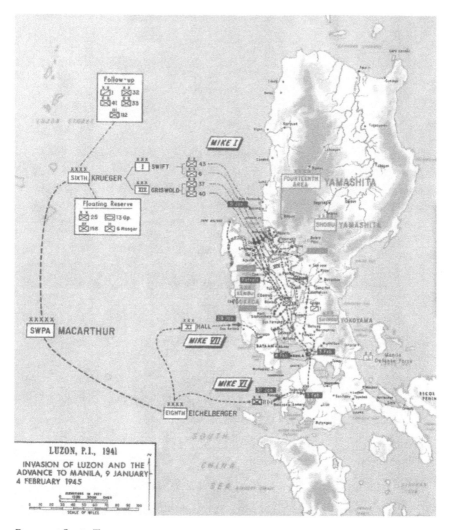

Rescue at Santo Tomas

A flying column from the 1st Cavalry Division liberated 4,000 internees at the University of Santo Tomas in Manila on the evening of 3 February. The battle for Manila followed and continued until 3 March. The 1st Cavalry, 11th Airborne, and 37th Infantry Divisions cleared the city.

fig. 2

Two emaciated Santo Tomas Internees, Lee Rogers (left) and John C. Todd, typical examples of the condition of men internees at time of rescue. In three years in the camp, Rogers' weight dropped from 145 to 90 pounds and Todd's from 178 to 102. (Life, March 5, 1945). (A Carl Mydans photo, permission from Time-Life/Getty Images)

fig. 3

Hostages—Santo Tomas internees being held in Education Building by Japanese soldiers, hiding behind windows on ground floor (Life, March 5, 1945). Internee Curtis Basil Brooks, Alexandria, Virginia, has identified himself as young boy in the third window from the left (in black clothes) and his twin brother, Bernard W. Brooks, Jr., in the fifth window from the left (also in black). (Carl Mydans photo, permission from Time-Life/Getty Images)

Internee shanties in the courtyard of Santo Tomas University where they lived most of the last year and a half of their internment. (U.S. Army Signal Corps photograph)

fig. 4

March through Manila—5 February 1945. Colonel Charles E. Brady and his 1st Cavalry troops escort Japanese Colonel Hayashi and his Jap soldiers to the outskirts of Manila in order to gain release of 221 Santo Tomas internees held as hostages. Colonel Brady on far left and internee Earnest Stanley, Japanese translator (in white shirt), reported to be a U.S. agent (Life, March 5, 1945). (Carl Mydans photo, permission from Time-Life/Getty Images)

Internee shanties on the grounds of Santo Tomas University away from the main campus buildings area. The wall around the Campus is seen in the background. (U.S. Army Signal Corps photograph)

fig. 5

Santo Tomas Internees cry and wave as they see the American flag for the first time in 37 months (Life, March 5, 1945). Captain Sam Wilson, U.S. Navy, who had escaped the Japanese and led the guerrillas in Mindanao during the war, brought this first American flag into Santo Tomas. The young boy in the striped shirt (bottom left corner) is internee Peter Wygle wearing a shirt that was knitted by his mother using one of the sets of more than 1,000 knitting needles made by his father. (Carl Mydans photo, permission from Time-Life/ Getty Images)

fig. 6

The basement of the beautiful Bay View Hotel, Manila, owned by Edgar Kneedler and his father, totally destroyed — burned out by the Japanese as they retreated USMC, Marine Corps League, p. 42, Spring 2002.

Internee Dorothy Howie with husband Jamiel, and daughter, Dianne — December 24, 1942. ("Dianne was one year old".)

fig. 7

Internee Sascha Jean Weinzheimer in 1943.

Internee Caroline Bailey Pratt, holding stuffed animals she had as child in Santo Tomas Internment Camp. Her family ate out of the beanbag (above) in December, 1944 before they were rescued in February, 1945. (Davis Enterprise, Davis California 1995)

fig. 8

Map of Luzon showing Peter Wygle's dad's walk from Baguio to Manila. (Peter Wygle, Surviving a Japanese P.O.W. Camp, *p. 28)*

Internees Peter Wygle and family — Sally, Mother, Dad, and Peter on the tower of Santo Tomas Internment Camp, February, 1945 (Wygle, Peter, p. 163)

fig. 9

Internee Mary Jane [Brooks] Morse and her mother Pacita Brooks in Manila sometime in 1942 during the Japanese occupation and prior to internment in Santo Tomas.

Madeline Ullom with friend Luke Legg receives Peter Wygle's knitting needles delivered to her by author on October 21, 2000

fig. 10

*(Left) "Many Fine Tributes Paid Capt. John Abbot Titcomb,"
newspaper article dated July 20, 1945 (reprinted from* The
Franklin Journal, *Farmington, Maine, July 20 1945)*

*(Below) Titcomb Field, Malaban, Mindanao, the Philippines
named in honor of Capt. John A. Titcomb. Chapin, USMCR,
And a Few Marines,* Department of Defense Photo 117638.

*Captain Francis R. B. Godolphin, USMCR, and Major Barr, USMC, who just bombed sus-
pected Jap positions from the air are down at the front within an hour to learn from the 7th
Cavalry Regiment about the accuracy of their bombing (Between Manila and Antipolo.)
(U.S. Army photograph)*

fig. 11

Chapter 5

Santo Tomas Internment Camp: The Internees' Own Stories

The stories that follow are the internees' own stories. There are similarities in these stories, along with each internee's own unique perspectives on life in the camp, as unique as the lives and ages of these Americans who survived the harsh conditions. Here are stories of ingenuity, of the importance of family connections, and of how the camp became a community unto itself. These stories reflect the strong memories of people who have lived through unforgettable trauma. The details in them have mainly to do with survival in increasingly harsh circumstances.

There are some interesting things to note and speculate on. Many of the stories told by those who were children in the camps do not attribute what happened in the camp to be caused by anyone in particular. This is echoed in some of the stories told by the adults as well. "They" is a word you see often.

Although there is repetition in the stories, the value in the different accounts is that they are told from both similar—and different—perspectives. With each story one learns more details about life in the camp; the early confusing days when the Japanese took over; the stories of families separated and then living together in the camp; the formation and functioning of the internee committees which "governed" the camp; the readjustments that had to be made as the camp grew in size and population; the changes the internees experienced when camp rule was switched from the Japanese diplomatic corps to the Japanese military; and the increasingly harsh existence, especially the losing battle against hunger and disease.

There are stories of ingenuity and gentle heroism, as with Mr. Wygle, the handyman who made thousands of knitting needles out of bamboo and repaired shoes. There are the efforts to hold onto something of the world they left behind at the camp gate—the duck obtained by Jamiel Howie for his family's Christmas dinner and the women of the camp who met monthly to put on makeup trying to remember what life was like before Santo Tomas—and what they hoped it would be like afterward. There are the talent and hobby shows that the Wygles, father and son, talk about. There are the stories told through the eyes and ears of children about the trials and the adventures of being in the camp.

And in the end there is the story that all of the internees will never forget: that of the Liberation and the last frantic days when American planes flew overhead and the 1st Cavalry entered the camp. Like a postscript, each story told by these internees talks of the long trip home to the United States and what became of them after the war.

All of these stories are separate and to be honored as the recollections of each individual interviewed. Together, these stories reveal what life was like for those who inhabited the camp, some of whom survived it and some of whom did not.

Edgar Mason Kneedler

Edgar Kneedler managed the Bayview Hotel at the time the Japanese occupied Manila. He entered Santo Tomas a few months after the camp was established. His story offers many observations of the Japanese during the occupation. What follows is based on the author's interview, which took place in Kneedler's home in Palm Springs, California, on August 23, 2000, and on a draft of his autobiography, which he had just completed. He provided me with the pages from his life's story that detailed his Manila and Santo Tomas prison experiences to supplement the interview.

My father was born in Collinsville, Illinois, just nine miles from St. Louis, Missouri. He studied medicine at Alexian Brothers Hospital, which later became the medical part of St. Louis University. When the Spanish-American War broke out in Cuba, the U.S. Army was looking for young doctors. They made my father a major in the U.S. Army Medical Corps and sent him to Havana. Later he was sent to the Philippines. He liked Manila and decided to set up his private medical practice there.

My mother, who was born in Brookfield, Missouri, had two sisters who had married men who worked in Manila. They wrote my mother asking her to visit them there. When she did she met the young, eligible

Dr. Kneedler. They were later married. I was born in Manila on May 5, 1914, and had two older brothers, Harold and Don.

When my father decided to retire from medicine, he developed property he had bought in and around Manila. That resulted in the Bayview Hotel, the Leonard Wood Hotel, the Paralta Apartments, the Ambassador Apartments, the Dewey Apartments, the Kneedler Building, and three private homes, including a beautiful summer home in Baguio.

I went away to the University of California, Berkeley, for college. My father wanted me to return to the Philippines after I graduated and get involved in the hotel business. I convinced him that I should have some hotel training, so I went to the number-one hotel school in the United States, Cornell University. On my way back to the Philippines, I stopped for a time in California and went again with a girl I had gone with at the University of California at Berkeley. Her name was Dorothy Douglas, and we married in 1939 and sailed to the Philippines on the ship *President Coolidge*.

I started as assistant manager of the Bayview Hotel and later became manager. Later, our first child, Ann, was born.

About 9:00 a.m. on December 7, 1941, the first bombs hit two small naval ships docked at the mouth of the Pasig River in Manila Bay. Some were also dropped in Luneta Park, near the Bayview, that same morning. The bombings became a daily occurrence, with the Japanese striking at Cavite Naval Base, Bataan, Clark Field, and all other installations their intelligence had marked for destruction.

My brother Don was convinced we should get our families out of Manila. He arranged the necessary military passes, and with two cars, chauffeurs, and servants they headed for Baguio. I stayed behind to run the Bayview Hotel and the other properties of our company.

If a building could be regarded as bombproof, the Bayview was the closest thing to it, and many of our friends knew this. The hotel was a steel-frame building with solid concrete floors overlaid with tile. We began getting calls asking if we had any room. People were afraid that they would be isolated in the outskirts or that their private homes would be easily destroyed by bombs. We offered every available space, and families who knew each other began doubling up. Soon the hotel was occupied at three times its capacity. We had sandbagged the entire lobby and even brought all the extra mattresses down from the storage and linen rooms for people in the neighborhood to sleep on. Everyone wanted to congregate, and the bar was the busiest corner in the place.

I don't remember having more than a couple of hours' sleep during the whole period of siege, from December 8 to New Year's Day, when the Japanese entered the city. Don returned from Baguio as soon as the family was settled.

About December 20, Dorothy called me from Baguio. She said she heard that the Japanese had landed at Lingayen Gulf, adjacent to the mountains in which Baguio was situated, and that they were heading for the Manila North Road, which would cut Baguio off from any access to Manila. I ran to tell Don. "Let's go up and get them right now," was his immediate reply. He got a U.S. Army sticker somewhere and stuck it on the windshield of the car, and we were on our way. It was about five o'clock in the afternoon.

The road to Baguio is flat until you reach the base of the mountains, when you start up the famous Benguet Trail, or the "Zig Zag," as it was called. In a few kilometers you climb a precipitous two-way road nearly 7,000 feet to reach the town. The U.S. Army sticker that Don had placed on the windshield got us through all the roadblocks set up by the Philippine Army. Don was driving like the "headless horseman," so the trip that was normally a comfortable five-hour drive we made in three hours. We stayed the night, and early in the morning packed children, wives, mother, and servants (three of whom were seated in each other's laps) into two cars. I was driving one car, and Don was driving the other. Dorothy's information was correct: as we passed the bottom of the Zig Zag where a road turned off to Dagupan, Filipinos told us that the Japanese were about ten kilometers away.

About an hour along the lowlands highway, Ann, who was seated in the front seat in the lap of Paz, her amah, looked out the window and called out in her one-and-a-half-year-old voice, "Eh-pane, eh-pane!" Sure enough, two Japanese fighter planes were flying to the right of us at low altitude. They shot on ahead for some distance and suddenly took a quick turn back down the highway, heading right for us. I was driving the first car. I jammed on the brakes and ordered everyone out. We scrambled to adjacent ditches and trees. Don followed suit. The two planes must have topped the cars by about fifty feet, machine guns poised and ready. We stayed where we were until we saw them disappear. We were convinced that if Ann hadn't seen them when she did, giving us time to stop and get out of the cars and show that we were civilians with women and children, they would have riddled both cars and killed us all.

The rest of the way to Manila was less harrowing. We heard, and barely saw, some of our B-24s overhead, but no more Japanese planes threatened us. The dear old Bayview looked pretty good when we rolled up in front of it.

The Japanese thought that selecting New Year's as the day to enter the city would represent the dawn of a new era in which they would "liberate" the Filipinos from the yoke of "Imperialist America." They may not have realized that they gave everyone in Manila a last big New Year's Eve fling—at least for a few years.

When the Japanese arrived in the city, it was in a strange-looking caravan. The marchers were accompanied by an almost ludicrous phalanx of bicycle riders. Cars and motorcycles were also part of the parade. Most of us sat in stunned silence trying to anticipate what to do next.

Housing was a prime concern of the Japanese, and an early contingent of officers soon arrived at the Bayview. Great God, I thought, how do you receive a group of the enemy arriving at your door when your whole experience in such matters has been to be cordial?! I certainly wasn't about to say, "Happy New Year!" They had interpreters, of course, and as they approached the desk they asked for the manager. I identified myself and a strange conference began. The officer who did most of the speaking was a Lieutenant Kano. I was soon to learn he was the son of Viscount Kano, head of the Yokama Specie Bank in London. He spoke perfect English with a British accent, since he was brought up and educated in London. It was one of the few brief moments of relief I felt in this trying moment, but since he was with the Department of Propaganda I had to be cautious in my remarks and my replies to his questions. They wanted all the information possible about the hotel: How many people were in it? Were they in their rooms? Where was the liquor supply?

The next step was to let the guests know that they must remain in their rooms. Several teams of officers would be inspecting the rooms, and they would no doubt ask the guests a number of questions. The remaining staff of room boys who hadn't bolted in fear delivered this message.

Excluding the penthouse, the Bayview had nine floors. The four teams started the tedious routine on the top floor, dividing the rooms between them for the interrogation. Dorothy, Ann, and amah Paz were on the seventh floor in a bay-front room. I went up to prepare them for the intrusion.

After about an hour's wait, our contingent of inspectors arrived at the room. There were four men—three officers and a civilian interpreter. The man who appeared to be the highest-ranking officer asked the questions through the interpreter. He was a plump, pleasant-looking man with a surprisingly courteous manner, whom Ann took to right away. She made a beeline for him with her arms raised, and he picked her up. She evidently won his heart. He turned to the interpreter and told him to ask us if there was a place we could send all the pregnant women and those with children two years or younger. I told him, "Yes." We had several houses that would serve the purpose. I lost no time rounding up those I knew who qualified—Irene Barnett, Mary Kneedler, and three other friends—and setting them up at our Dakota Street house.

Then came the decision by the Japanese to empty the Bayview of guests and billet them in various buildings throughout Manila until the site for a more permanent internment was selected. Buses were commandeered, and the exodus began. I watched the forlorn expressions on our friends' faces as they passed through the hotel entrance and piled into the buses. We tried to persuade the Japanese to let Mom and Pop stay in the hotel, but they said, "Only the manager." Mom was smart enough to go to the kitchen and fill two pillowcases full of rolls and buns to take along. Three days later I found out that they were congregated with about two hundred others into Villamor Hall, the Music Building of the University of the Philippines, put under guard, and left to fend for themselves. There were no beds or bedding, one toilet for everyone, and no provisions. Mom turned out to be the Angel of Succor, dispensing bread to all and sundry. They were there for three days.

It was then decided to turn Santo Tomas University into an internment camp. It had three large principal buildings with a few smaller annexes. The acreage covered several city blocks.

The Japanese ordered a sawali wall to be built around it. Sawali can best be described as a strong reed that has been stripped and woven into a mat. The wall was mace with two layers of sawali with wood framing between them.

At the time, I was still being held in the Bayview. I was told that I would be held there until they found a Japanese manager to take over. The situation at the Bayview was chaotic. Divisions of the army were being brought to the hotel to be housed. One division would take over one floor. If that division chose the fifth floor and another division considered superior in classification moved in, that division would make the earlier occupants move down to the fourth or third. Higher rank, higher floor. This game of musical chairs went on all the time.

Most of these men had never seen toilets before. I was called on repeatedly to show them how to use the john, particularly how to flush it. The push-button locks in the center of the doorknobs also threw them completely. They were always locking themselves in or out of the rooms, and you could hear "Manijah!" screamed from all parts of the building at any hour since the Bayview had an open court in the center right up to the roof.

The occupants were also continually asking me where the liquor supply was. My explanation that there wasn't any did not suffice, and I had to take officers up to the storeroom where we used to keep it to prove that. On several occasions I had to back away from an angered Jap who might have taken a swing at me if he hadn't controlled himself at the last minute. The higher ranks were always slapping the lower ranks, and this habit was passed down to the lowliest soldier in the army. Smacking someone across the face was their form of discipline.

We had a cheery collection of little Filipino shoeshine boys at the Bayview entrance who returned after seeing all the boots they might get to polish. Quickly they caught on to the low Japanese bow and would line up about seven abreast and bow when the officers arrived. The impressed officers did not know that as the boys bowed they mumbled under their breaths in Tagalog, "Anak ng puta" ("Son of a whore") or "Putang ina mo" ("Your mother is a whore").

The generation of Filipinos under American occupation all spoke English, since it was made the language for all schools and texts. When I was allowed out for a stroll in the neighborhood, I often heard this bunch of wonderful little kids trailing me and quietly chanting over and over in their choirboy voices, "Mr. Kneedler, don't you worry."

After the first week the Japanese presented Mr. Shigematsu to me as the new Bayview manager. He had been the flunky for a small flophouse in Sibul Springs near Manila. By now several more of our room boys had returned, including our tall number-one boy, Esteban. The day he returned, Esteban whispered to me, "We will stay here as long as you are here, Mr. Edgar." My reply was, "Esteban, don't make any such decision now. These characters may be here for a few years, and you and the other boys are going to need work."

One of the first things Shigematsu decided to do was to clear the lobby of the sandbags, so he ordered all the soldiers stationed around the hotel to drag them out and dump them in Manila Bay. This took a whole day, and the tile floor of the lobby became streaked with mud. He had it all cleaned up, and the next day came to me to see if we had any floor wax. Esteban was standing nearby, and his face lit up with a mischievous smile that only he and I understood.

When the Bayview was first completed we used to wax the lobby floor, but so many people slipped that Pop abandoned the idea, and we just scrubbed and rinsed it with big electric brush machines. Esteban gleefully assured me that we had a lot of cans of Johnson's Floor Wax in the linen room, and he couldn't wait to round up some of the other boys to do the job. I did say to Shigematsu in a sly way that I didn't think it was a good idea, but that was all he needed to insist on it. He was feeling his oats as the new "big boss" of the Bayview.

Filipinos have a unique method of polishing floors. To clean the dirt, they take two halves of a coconut husk, stand on them, and skate over the floor. The next step is skating on a square of folded burlap soaked with wax. I thought I noticed that Esteban was being a little generous with the wax!

Shigematsu was beaming with pride. He had started the floor waxing the morning the officers had left the hotel for their newly acquired offices. The job was finished by noon when the cars of the returning conquerors were lining up in front of the hotel. The Japanese walk is unique, and when you see it in high boots, especially on a short man, it is unequaled. Sure enough, the first one in fell backwards and hit the back of his head on the floor. The soldiers at his side trying to catch him went down with him. Following this, officers skidded and flopped, and in a matter of minutes there was a dog pile in the middle of the lobby. Esteban and the other room boys showed remarkable restraint in their expressions. They knew what was coming and made sure they were in the lobby to watch the show. Shigematsu began running around like a mouse in a maze helping officers to their feet, low bows being bandied all about like reeds blowing in a strong wind. The officers eventually made it to the elevators. One stroke that Esteban thought up himself was to wax the yacal stairway to the second floor where the dining room was situated. Yacal is a beautiful Philippine hardwood. About a half-hour after all the officers had returned I heard a fearful clatter in the lobby. Two officers came sailing down the stairs on their backs in tandem, with their shaved heads hitting every step, swords clattering a bongo beat. They shot right out into the middle of the lobby, supine as dreamers gazing at the sky from a meadow. That's when I vanished along with the gratified room boys who made an orderly retreat to have the first good laugh of the month in seclusion.

I had submitted several requests to visit my parents in the camp, and finally one day was granted permission. Accompanied by a soldier, I arrived at Santo Tomas in a caretela, a cage-like, two-wheeled, horse-drawn conveyance that was the principal means of travel for the Filipinos. The sight in Santo Tomas of thousands of Americans, British, Canadians, and others milling around the grounds in confusion was unnerving. I exchanged greetings and interrogations with friends, and finally someone told me in which building and classroom I might find Pop, since men and women were separated in these improvised dormitories.

I found Pop in his dorm seated on a wooden box, talking with one of his cronies about the dismal state of affairs. After we embraced, he wanted to know all about the properties and what was going on outside. Before I left, Lieutenant Kano had told me that our small (sixty rooms and suites) Leonard Wood Hotel had been converted into a "residence" for imported Japanese prostitutes who were there for the comfort of the officers. I reluctantly revealed the truth about his Leonard Wood. Thank God for Pop's earthy sense of humor. Even at a time like this, he simply looked into space and said, "Well, I guess we can burn 'er down after the war and salvage all the old screws."

Later I located Mom and a lot of our friends. We all tried to bolster our sagging spirits by some feeble attempt at encouragement, but I'm afraid the calamity of the situation was too evident to sound convincing. The time allotted for my visit was short. I returned to the Bayview determined to join the others in Santo Tomas.

A day or so later, a tall pleasant-looking Japanese officer named Captain Murao was presented to me as the new military head of the Bayview. I was to discuss with him all matters pertaining to the operation of the hotel, through an interpreter, and he would relay the orders to Shigematsu, considerably humbled after the floor-waxing incident. One couldn't meet a finer man in any race than Murao. In one of the frequent three-way conferences, he confessed that he and many other officers of the Japanese Army belonged to the Samurai families and were not in favor of this war. I hoped that Murao made it safely through to the armistice.

The strain of all this was too much, and I came down with a severe case of bronchitis. So the Japanese would leave me alone, I told them I was tubercular, and it worked like a charm. They had a great fear of TB since it was one of the health scourges of Japan. I later discovered that TB was written on my military pass in bright red calligraphy, and it served to give me considerable mobility in releases from internment and permission to stay outside the camp for extended periods.

Before leaving the hotel I did one of the more stupid and risky things I could have done. The *Life* magazine photographer Carl Mydans had to leave all his cameras and photographic gear behind and asked me to hide it. I contacted the mother Superior of the Hospital Español de Santiago in Antipolo, several kilometers outside Manila. She was my father's former surgical nurse when he was the head physician of St. Paul's Hospital in the Walled City. She agreed to store the equipment at the hospital, and one night the hotel room boys and I loaded it into a caretela and covered it with a tarpaulin, and the cochero and I headed for Antipolo.

We had to pass through three checkpoints and were interrogated at each. By some miracle no one looked on the floor of the caretela. That I was heading for a hospital with a medical pass kept them from getting too close.

Dorothy and the other mothers with young children had moved to the Assumption Convent, which the Japanese left unmolested. I managed to visit my family before I went into the camp. They appeared to be safer and much more comfortable than they would have been in the crowded corral of Santo Tomas. Some internees felt that all patriotic Americans should join their fellow citizens in the camp and not stay outside in hospitals or foreign homes or institutions. I saw nothing patriotic about it.

The day before I left for Santo Tomas, I was told that a "veddy hi offisah" would occupy the penthouse and that we must get it in order. That officer turned out to be an unnamed general. As a parting gesture to their upper brass, I placed a large bronze incense-burner of Pop's on a small table by the head of the bed. It had an open grill cover, and I had filled it with some rotting onions I found in the storeroom. "Sweet dreams, general," was my contemptuous salutation as I took the last view I ever had of our penthouse.

A brilliant Filipino employee of the Philippine Mint contributed one bright ray of humor in these gloomy days. The Japanese were to print their own version of the Philippine peso and take the original one out of circulation. This whimsical genius had the familiar cartoon of the head and smiling face of Mickey Mouse watermarked on the first issue of the Japanese peso. Up to the end of the war, everyone distinguished between the two currencies as so many "real pesos" or so many "Mickey Mouse pesos."

A lanky, rawboned American woman from Nebraska named Gladys Savary ran the French Restaurant and Boarding House across from the Bayview entrance on Calle Isaac Peral. She had married a Frenchman and was qualified to be a French citizen through her husband. As a third-party national the Japanese did not intern her. Gladys lived in a compound of three houses that she controlled in Pasay, the township that bordered Manila. The compound was walled in, which gave a sense, though perhaps ephemeral, of security. Gladys persuaded me to let Dorothy, Ann, and the servants move into the compound. She felt they would be safer under the French flag. She always met intruding Japanese with her brassy French and succeeded in producing an orderly retreat from her door. I agreed, helped them move, and then departed for the camp.

Americans are fiends for organization. At the Santo Tomas we had committees within committees for the purpose of organizing further committees to delegate work. An elected central committee of three men was accountable to the Japanese commandant, who was the titular head of the internment camp. Then there were committees on health, labor, family relations, food, gardening, sanitation, entertainment, petty crime, and more—and subcommittees within subcommittees. My first assignment was gardening, a pretty hopeless pursuit. The land on which the university stood was all refilled. If you dug down about two feet you ran into tin cans and refuse from earlier deposits. About the only thing that thrived was talinum, a leaf similar to the Italian arugola.

The next job I got was scrubbing the tropical slime off the walls and floors of the shower rooms and toilets in the Main Building. We had a crew of four men for the job. The one advantage to this assignment was that we could set the hour to close the facility down for cleaning and take care of our own needs instead of having to stand in a long line waiting our turn either for the john or a shower.

I also took turns on the food line serving the meager stews and rice and tea that were the regular fare. I remember once getting to the bottom of the huge copper pot that we put the tea in and serving one of the outstretched cups with tea and a lizard. The man looked at it with considerable composure and commented, "Well, at least it's meat." He tossed it out, of course, but it illustrated how unperturbed many of the internees had become to the conditions under which we now had to live.

In the earliest days of the camp, Filipinos were permitted in to set up markets where we could buy produce, mostly fruits and vegetables, with smuggled-in pesos or on credit, which in those first months of internment they were perfectly happy to extend.

Colonies of nipa huts had sprung up around the three buildings to relieve the crowding. Filipino carpenters were permitted in to build these for us. Nipa is similar to thatch and is used for the roofing. The rest consists of large bamboo poles for the frame of the shanty and strips of split bamboo for the floors. Sawali, which was used to construct the camp wall, was used for the walls of the hut. All joists and flooring were tied, since you can't drive a nail very successfully into bamboo. The nipa huts were originally used as cooking shacks and for daytime gatherings of families and friends. Soon the men were permitted to sleep there, and much later wives and families joined them if the size of the particular hut permitted.

These subdivisions sprang up like mushrooms, and we had names for them: Garden Court, Shantytown, Froggy Bottom. I bought a hut in Garden Court for 400 pesos ($200) from an internee who wanted to stay in the Main Building. It was a simple one-room affair with a small area for cooking and sleeping and room for a couple of chairs and a table.

Commandants were changed often. We figured that the Japanese must have had a collection of older colonels they didn't know what to do with whom they made commandants of the camp. One character we referred to as "the shell-shocked colonel" was named to the post. The colonel had a habit of conducting a tour of the camp for visiting Japanese officers. One day when I was seated at one of the huge bench-table combinations we used for our meals behind the Main Building, the colonel appeared with about eight Japanese officers. The ladies of the camp were also seated on the benches, paring and digging worm holes out of the sparse collection of vegetables sent in for our stews. About ten feet from me was Mrs. Saunders, a black woman and wife of a deceased colonel of the Ninth Cavalry, a black unit which was sent to the Philippines during the period of the so-called Insurrection. I'm six feet tall, and Mrs. Saunders towered over me. She must have been at least six-foot-four. She was a handsome, well-proportioned woman with aquiline features and beautiful dark skin. She used to run a popular boarding house in Manila and was a superb cook. Many from the American community showed up at her place on Saturdays for her cakes and cupcakes, which she sold to the public.

Apparently the colonel had never seen anyone like her. He stopped his group and cautiously approached Mrs. Saunders, who, seated, was taller than he was. "You Canadian?" he queried. I saw her bristle slightly, but she continued to pare and paid no attention to the question. Again the colonel asked, "You Canadian?" In a show of indignation she abruptly turned her back and refused to answer. The colonel resigned himself to no progress in the conversation and said in Japanese, "She's Canadian." That was all that was needed to set the match to the tinder. Mrs. Saunders slammed down the knife and rose up in all her imperious height and turned on the group, the fire of divine rage blazing from her eyes. "No, I'm not a Canadian," she flashed back. "I'm an American Negress; I was born in Texas, and I'm proud of it. And while you're here tellin' me things, I've got a few things I want to tell you. Now come along with me!"

Well, Mrs. Saunders took them on her own tour of the camp. You could hear her stentorian voice for yards, spiced with all the four-letter words I'd ever learned plus a few I had never heard before. I had to report for my job washing pots in the kitchen. I hadn't been there quite an hour when I heard Mrs. Saunders' trumpet-tongued sounds approaching the kitchen. In she charged with her meek entourage of frightened followers close behind. "Now, I want you to taste this pig food you've been feedin' us," she roared.

"It's nothin' but crap and corruption!" The "pig food" she was referring to was moldy cornmeal that we cooked for hours trying to remove the moldy taste; it didn't help one bit. I handed her a ladle, and she shoved a mouthful of this stuff into the mouths of all nine attending Japanese. I stood in stunned amazement as they sozzled the slop around in their mouths looking for an avenue of escape.

Then our lady of wrath announced, "Now I want you to see where you've got us older women housed—just like a bunch of gypsies. No place to put anything. The beds about eight inches apart and hard as nails." Her voice faded down the hall with her "captives" trailing after her in meek submission. I was sure they would drag her off to Fort Santiago, the gestapo prison in Manila, but apparently the group was happy to be released and wanted to forget the whole episode. When I saw Mrs. Saunders the next day I greeted her with, "Mrs. Saunders, that was marvelous! You said everything all of us have wanted to say for months and then some!" A peal of delicious laughter spouted from her. "Call me a Canadian!" she remonstrated.

After a year and a half in the camp a repatriation ship was arranged. About 150 persons over sixty years of age were selected to depart on the *Asama Maru* for Goa. The ship *Gripsholm* met them at Goa and transported them to the United States. Fortunately, Mom and Pop were among those chosen. They had mixed emotions about leaving us, but we insisted. It was too good an opportunity to get out of this mess.

Two physical symptoms developed from the lack of protein in the diet: one, the disease known as beriberi, which starts with swelling in the ankles that works up the body; the other a need to urinate every hour, or every half-hour in extreme cases. The name for the john in Japanese is "benjo." We had built several open latrines around the camp, and we would have to pass a stationed Japanese guard to get to them. In order to explain our mission we would have to pause, bow slightly, and say "benjo." The constant stream of internees trotting by made the guards irritable and suspicious as to our motives, especially in the middle of the night or in the early morning hours. They often shouted impatiently, "Benjo, benjo, alla time benjo," and on occasion they turned back the poor soul responding to the urgency. We circumvented the need for making repeated trips by keeping a large can in our quarters with an improvised handle and cover to serve as a thunder mug, to be carried to the latrine when nearing capacity. The guards began to suspect the contents of these receptacles, and on one occasion one of them demanded I open the can. I tried to persuade him otherwise, but that made him even more suspicious. With an "OK, buddy, you asked for it" coursing through my mind, I let him inspect my little treasure chest and soon proceeded on my journey, leaving him with no further doubt as to the contents.

I was able to use my pass to be released for a couple of weeks for a "medical examination" and visited Dorothy and Ann at the Savary compound. Dorothy pleaded that we should have another child. She was sure we would be here for several years under these conditions and argued that if we waited until after the war the age difference between the children would be too wide. It is the kind of emotional feminine logic that a practical man often submits to, as did I. This was the first year of occupation, and Dorothy was convinced that she was safe at Savary's and had accumulated enough canned powdered milk and other supplies to sit out the war. She did become pregnant, and Douglass was born nine months later, on May 13, 1943, in the Hospital Español de Santiago, delivered by Dr. Moretta, my father's former Spanish medical partner.

I was back in camp after this visit and, with perhaps one exception of visiting the hospital when Douglass was due, even holding Dorothy's hand during the delivery, I was unable to leave camp again because of tightened security.

The last year of internment was the most trying. The military had expelled the Diplomatic Corps, which had been running the camp. As I had feared, the military took over directly, with no intermediary buffers and a new commandant, Kodama.

The camp was divided into units, with monitors appointed over each section who had to regularly report the activities of the internees. The men of the camp were required to line up at various posts to be inspected and counted every morning. Two Japanese officers did the inspecting, and we had to bow low from the waist as they passed. A strict census was being kept, especially of the men. We optimistically concluded that all this was a sign that General MacArthur's "I shall return" dictum was coming to pass. We did have a clandestine radio in camp, listened to by a select few, but as is often the case with relayed messages, the facts were hardly recognizable by the time they had made the rounds. The general message, however, was that the Americans were coming back and that we would be rescued.

The Japanese did discover the radio, and as a result Grinnel and Dougleby, both formerly of General Electric of Manila and principal officers of our Internee Central Committee, were executed. All of us became acutely aware of the seriousness of our position and abandoned any hope for leniency, which may have existed in previous years. All communication with the outside was cut off, and the markets the Filipinos had been able to maintain were removed. We had to rely on the meager fare of the food line, so moldy rice and cornmeal was all that we could look forward to.

Beriberi was evident in varying degrees of advancement in every internee. Some who had managed to save a few canned goods, which were almost never opened unless they looked like they were going to explode, or had kept their cans of powdered milk for the final lap were able to supplement their diet with a small portion of protein. Those unfortunates who had nothing but line food watched the swelling tissues of beriberi advance upward from the ankle to the vital organs, resulting in death in most cases. No medical cure was available to arrest it. All that was needed was protein, which was in scarce supply. All of us looked like scarecrows. I stopped weighing myself after I lost the first thirty pounds, since it only served to alarm me further.

In November 1944 we first saw a squadron of Navy Grumman planes that surprised the Japanese by attacking the fleet of moored merchant ships in Manila Bay. Rumor was that they sank about two hundred. These blessed "angels" risked flying over the camp and dipping their wings to the leaping and shouting assembly of internees who defied the Japanese order to seek shelter during any such raid.

The next day the command went out that every internee who had a nipa shanty was to line up for buckets that were to be kept in the huts full of water in case of fire. We were also told that three Japanese officers would inspect every hut to make sure we were complying with the order. On the first day of inspection we sat dutifully awaiting the inspection team. When they arrived at my hut, the three officers inspected the bucket, which I had placed prominently in view, and seemed to be arguing. They left in a flurry of dissent. The next day the order came out that the buckets were not correct because they didn't have the red "F" painted on them as our fire buckets do. We were told to line up again for a little can of Red Devil paint and a brush and to paint an "F" on each bucket. We were advised that we would be inspected again the next day. Some of us, myself included, had set the bucket down without thinking to position the "F" in the line of sight. The same three officers entered, looked, and the same squabble of Japanese expletives started; then the officers departed.

The next day the order came out that because some of us had hidden the "F," we had to line up again for the can of red paint and the brush and paint an "F" on all four cardinal points of the compass on the buckets. This was not psychological torture the Japanese dreamed up for us, but a serious matter of decorum and correctness. You can imagine the commentary issuing from the internees over this. I strolled up the path to one of the other shanties where one of the British ladies was putting the finishing touches on her masterpiece. "There now," she exclaimed. "If the blighters aren't satisfied with this, I'll spell out the whole nasty word!"

After the Navy raid, anticipation of approaching liberation was on everyone's mind. The Japanese were edgy, increasingly strict, and, increasingly preoccupied. We barely noticed the passing of 1944 to 1945, except to have more hope that this surely was the year we would witness the return of MacArthur and the American troops.

Toward the end of January it was evident that the Japanese knew that they would be driven out of the Philippines, and the razing of Manila began. Sailors from the Japanese Merchant Marine who had been billeted all over Manila after the sinking of their ships joined what remained of the retreating army to bring about a holocaust of horror and destruction, later overshadowed by the devastation of Nagasaki and Hiroshima by atomic bombs. No one—Filipinos, Spaniards, or anyone from any other country left in Manila—was spared the slaughter and ravage that took place. Gasoline drums were placed in principal buildings, one of them being the Bayview Hotel, and fired on with artillery, causing total demolition. I was told that most of our Spanish friends, men, women, and children who congregated in the Casino Español when they were forced out of the buildings by fire, were machine-gunned in the streets. By strange good fortune, Santo Tomas was on Manila's outskirts. We could watch and hear the bombing and explosions from the upper windows of our buildings. "That looks like the Escolta (the principal shopping area) going up," one would cry. "Those are the Legislative Buildings!" "That must be the post office," and so on, as the terror and mayhem progressed. We heard on good authority that the Japanese were heading for the camp to stage the final butchery of what was left to represent the United States in Manila.

Thank God MacArthur heard it, too, and on the evening of February 3rd the First Cavalry (may God keep them all) broke through the lines in huge tanks, and, despite some dirty Filipino Quislings who directed them into Japanese artillery fire instead of the camp, they crashed through the sawali walls. I need not describe the exultation and rejoicing of the internees as the tanks' searchlights scanned the camp in their advance on the Main Building. We were so used to being shriveled up from starvation that these boys in their fatigues and helmets looked like they had come from another planet.

I was unable to contain my emotions, which were running the gamut from exultation to tears, and I simply had to rush back to my nipa hut and try to steady the flood surging through me. In a few minutes I heard my name being called out. An internee brought Carl Mydans, who was crying out, "Where the hell is Ed Kneedler?" After embraces and exclamations, the first coherent sentence I could voice was, "Carl, I saved all your camera equipment!" "My God," he replied. "I collected insurance on all that long ago and have brand-new equipment!" We then joined the celebrating, which lasted all night, but the dawn brought the realization that the carnage was to continue.

The camp became the front for two weeks. What Japanese forces remained were shelling us with artillery, and two of the principal buildings were hit several times, killing and wounding a number of internees. The Japanese in the camp holed up in one of the buildings, the Education Building, with many hostages but finally surrendered after a day of crossfire and extensive injury to both sides.

When relative quiet returned to the city, Carl Mydans asked me if I would accompany him and several American officers from Santo Tomas into Manila proper, since, having been born in the city and lived there for so many years, I would be the ideal guide. I agreed to go.

I had received news from Dorothy that she and the children were all right and, much to my astonishment and delight, that my cousin Ronald Naess was among the paratroopers who rescued that section of the city. Carl agreed that we should go to Pasay to get them.

The bridges crossing the Pasig River from the commercial center to the residential and principal hotel area had been destroyed. Our army had constructed steel pontoon bridges higher up the river, so we had to approach the heart of the residential and hotel district from Pandakan, another suburb to the north.

I felt like a babe lost in the woods. I couldn't find a single building or familiar landmark. Even the street signs had disappeared. I could only tell them to keep on driving. Finally we arrived at a broad avenue that looked like the Badlands of South Dakota in miniature. I suggested we turn right here. Within a block or two I suddenly recognized the steps and half of a statue, which were all that was left of Villamor Hall, the Music Building of the University of the Philippines. Behind Villamor Hall had once stood several of the principal buildings of the university, now a pile of rubble. "I know where we are!" I exclaimed, and was able to direct the expedition from that point. My mouth and eyes were wide open, and only gasps and expletives were coming out.

We turned left on Isaac Peral, the street on which the Episcopal Cathedral, the Peralta Apartments, and the Bayview Hotel were situated. I couldn't find the cathedral. The Peralta was gutted and shattered in places but still standing. The Bayview was a mass of twisted steel and rubble up to about the sixth floor, and the rest of the floors were gutted and pockmarked with artillery and shrapnel holes. As we continued up Dewey Boulevard, our eyes were met with destruction that no one could have imagined or written into a novel. We arrived at the Savary compound and found that the families were protected by the same contingent of GIs who had rescued them. Dorothy and the children looked better than most of us from the camp, having been fed better. The reunion was a highly emotional one. Since dangers still lurked everywhere, we decided to bring them all into the camp.

We were still being fired on in the camp, and artillery shells were whistling back and forth overhead to strike at the troops on either side of us. The soldiers didn't understand how we internees could walk about so nonchalantly, doing our chores. I suppose we were too ignorant or too tired to worry about the dangers.

After the attacks let up, plans for repatriation began. Transport ships arrived in Manila Bay, and, little by little, people were assigned to them and shipped back home. Don, my brother, and his family were eager to leave soon after they saw to their personal properties and those of the company. I stayed on a year before returning to the United States.

After he returned to the United States, Edgar Kneedler went on to become a screen actors' agent and a concert pianist. He passed away in his home in Palm Springs, California, on January 27, 2001.

Dorothy Khoury Howie

Dorothy Khoury Howie was a young wife and mother in the camp, who had a child while her family was in Santo Tomas. Her story provides unforgettable, vivid vignettes of camp life, before internment, during the emotional liberation of the internees, and through voyage back to the United States. This is her story:

I was born in Worcester, Massachusetts, on January 6, 1920, the youngest of nine children. My parents were Dr. and Mrs. Kamil Khoury. My mother's first name was Amelia. My father was an internist whose office was in Boston, Massachusetts. In 1925 my family moved to Brooklyn, New York. There I attended school at Bayridge High School and met my husband-to-be, Jamiel Howie, through a family friend. We were married on May 21, 1940.

Jamiel (Jimmy) was in the clothing manufacturing business. We moved to Manila in January 1941 where he started his own factory manufacturing embroidered baby wear. His company was Howie Infant Wear Corporation in Manila. We lived in the Bay district and liked Manila very much.

The Japanese started bombing Manila on December 8, 1941, and the bombing continued for a long time. Our daughter, Dianne, was born on Christmas Eve, 1941, at Hospital Español de Santiago in Manila while air raids continued all day long.

Jamiel registered for Santo Tomas on January 6, 1942, just a few days after our daughter had been born.[84] I remained in the hospital with Dianne under house arrest for two months, as an "enemy alien." Later, we moved to a rented house in New Manila until the baby was one year old.

Before Jamiel registered for Santo Tomas, we had been told that there was an option to claim to be from the country where your ancestors were from, even if you were an American citizen. For example, you wouldn't have to go into the camp if you were Lebanese or Syrian. Although we had that option, Jimmy said, "No, I want to be where the Americans are. If they are repatriated or liberated, that's where I want to be." So we did not take that option.

Mr. Sam's family took the option and said they were Syrian.[85] However, he was never repatriated. Instead he was killed with Duggleby and two others from the camp.[86] He had been imprisoned in Santiago, a town in northern Luzon, for six weeks for giving money for promissory notes.

You weren't allowed to do that. When he was caught a second time, he was killed with this group.

When I was taken into camp with Dianne in June 1943, I was six months pregnant with our second daughter, Beverly.[87] We lived in the Annex, where the women and children stayed, and my husband was in the Education Building, which was for the men and boys. There were 35 internees in each room of the Annex. It started to get even more crowded because more prisoners from the southern islands were being brought in. So we were allowed to build a shanty, which Jamiel did. It was located near the Main Gate on the right-hand side.

At that time the front gate was open, and if you had money, you could get materials to build a shack. When I returned to the camp after I had my second daughter, Beverly, I did not return from the hospital to the Annex. We joined my husband in the shanty.

We had an internee kitchen, but the food provided us kept getting less and less, and we had no protein. For the year and a half the gate was open you were able to buy things if you had money.

An internee government was established in the camp and committees were formed. Everyone had something to do. Still Japanese soldiers were everywhere. When you passed one, you had to bow from the waist down, with head down. One day I was walking from the hospital reading a book. I was not paying attention and I walked past a guard without bowing. I then felt a sharp bayonet against me. An internee rushed over and said, "For God's sake, bow!" So I did and turned and went on. When I got to the shack, Jimmy was furious. He had already been told about what had happened.

The last Christmas in the camp, 1944, Jimmy had paid two hundred fifty dollars for a duck. He knew a man who could get things done and get things for a price. So Jimmy got this duck and killed and cleaned it. Then I cooked it for Christmas dinner. We invited a friend over to dinner, Mr. Bert Silen [Bertrand Harold Silen] a radio reporter who was also in the camp. I stuffed the duck with rice, and Jimmy took a gallon can and made an oven for me. We put it over the charcoal. We cooked the duck and ate it—it was a fine dinner. I then put the children down for a nap. I had to walk a block and a half to go to the bathroom. The bathroom had one toilet and two showerheads for the women and the same thing for the men. It [the bathroom] was built by us, the plumbing committee of the camp.

When I went to use the bathroom, two women were showering. One, a very beautiful redhead, was saying to the other, "Oh, yes, we cooked it and had it and it tasted like chicken. It really was good." The other one said, "Yes, I have heard that is how it tastes." I opened the door and I said, "What did you cook?" And she said, "A cat!" I turned around and upchucked everything I had eaten right into the toilet, turned white as a sheet, and almost fainted. I went back to the shanty and Jimmy said to me, "What in the world is the matter with you?" I said, "I'm so sorry you paid so much money for that duck. Two women were talking about what they had for dinner today and it was a cat. I threw up all my dinner." When a cat disappeared in the camp we knew what had happened. Toward the end, nothing crawled or moved; anything that was alive was eaten.

A few days before our liberators came in through the Main Gate, we moved to the Main Building. At 6:00 p.m. that day, they announced we had 20 minutes to grab what we could and get in the Main Building. If we were not in the building by that time, we were told we would be shot. They had Japanese soldiers standing there making us hurry up. I grabbed diapers and bottles, and we ran, my husband carrying one child and I the other. We made it in the building okay.

My most memorable experience was our Liberation, the night of February 3, 1945, and seeing the tanks forge their way in—the United States Army, our saviors. This was heartrending. They raised the American flag on the Main Building. Then [came] the singing of the National Anthem. All the tears, cheers, and prayers were earth shattering to us. We were there when MacArthur came in. Were we ever there! I swear, I think I cried a bucket that day. Now, after all these years, I still cry when I think of that day. And now when they play the *Star Spangled Banner,* tears roll down my face. Nothing I can do about it. Wherever it is played, the memory just goes right back to that day. It will never be erased.

I think we were the last to leave the camp. They decided because I was pregnant, I couldn't fly home.[88] I would have to wait for a hospital ship. It was actually an Army transport that they made into a hospital ship. We gave away everything we could not pack: clothes, utensils, everything.

It was a long time before they were able to get a convoy together for the hospital ship, and we did not get home until May [1945]. It was the most horrendous trip of my life. We stopped many times because of weather and submarines; we were a month and a half on the ocean getting home. And this was to San Francisco, not even to New York. We were in a hold like the sailors. There was no place to sit—no chairs or anything. It was all steel—my two little children, my husband, and me, pregnant, with no space to lounge during the day. There were six of us in a cabin.

Manila was too devastated to return to with children, so in January 1946 Jamiel returned to Manila alone to rebuild and reestablish the clothing factory. We lived in our beautiful home in a lovely area of Brooklyn from 1950 to 1979. Four daughters were married in that house and our grandchildren loved it too. Jamiel retired in 1979 and we moved to Miami Beach in October 1979. Our children are Dianne Joyce and Beverly, both Santo Tomas internees, and Carolyn, Linda, and Patricia.

God Bless America and General Douglas MacArthur for saving us! Thanks to God for our freedom!

Sascha Jean Weinzheimer Jansen

Sascha Jansen was a young girl when she was taken into the camp. For many of the families who ended up in Santo Tomas the wives and children entered the camp after the men. That was the case with Sascha's family. One of the distinctive features of Sascha's story is how her memories come to life on the pages and how vividly she conveys the precious details of how things looked, sounded, smelled, and felt all around before, during, and after the internment.

I was born in the Philippines on a sugar plantation and was caught there during World War II when we were incarcerated in a prison camp with other Allied civilians. My family was in the sugar business in both Hawaii and the Philippines. Louis Weinzheimer, my grandfather, came from Germany to Hawaii in the 1800s as a Prussian officer on duty with the German Navy. He loved Hawaii and came back a few years later and married my Hawaiian grandmother and later they had my father. At this time he became interested in the sugar business, then in its zenith, and it became his lifelong interest. He rose fast in the sugar trade.

Years later Louis was wooed by the Adolph Spreckles Sugar conglomerate in San Francisco to become an equal partner of a conglomerate of several sugar and coconut plantation properties in the Philippines. At the same time they bought 2,000 acres of farmland in the San Joaquin Valley of California to experiment with sugar beets. This would become our home after the war.

My mother's parents—father German and mother Tahitian—were also from Hawaii where she was raised. My maternal grandfather was in shipping and import-export, also having to do with the sugar trade.

My parents met and married in the Philippines and had my sister, brother, and myself. We lived on a sugar plantation an hour south of Manila in Canlubang, Laguna. At eighteen months of age I contracted polio, and many times during my first ten years of life I had to go to San Francisco by ship for reconstructive surgeries on my legs, as well as new braces and new shoes.

I was due to go back for another session of surgeries in February of 1942, but the war had started two months prior, and I was unable to go as planned. So, I was three and a half years overdue going back to San Francisco for treatment. Later, when we were in prison, I outgrew my braces and special shoes. Without all the much needed support, I was in bad shape. I was eight years old when the war started and four days shy of my twelfth birthday when we were liberated from Santo Tomas.

When the war broke out, we were out on the plantation and we stayed there as long as we could. People did not exactly know what to do. We didn't know whether to stay put and get taken prisoners by the Japs or go and turn ourselves in. But when the Japs started bombing the railroad tracks on the plantation leading to the mill, that was the deciding factor for us in going to Manila. Because if we were by ourselves there was no telling what might happen to us.

We had a hell of a time going into Manila because Jap planes started strafing the roads. It usually took about one hour to drive into Manila, but we had to stop the car and hide in bushes and ditches each time planes strafed. When we got there we checked in the Bayview Hotel, right on Dewey Boulevard. A lot of people just like us—Scottish, British, Americans—were there for the same reasons and wanted to be with other people. We received many offers from friends to come stay with them in their apartments, but because their apartments were on the higher floors we did not want to risk the danger of being bombed. So we just decided to stay there at the hotel and wait it out until the Japanese came into Manila.

In the meantime, my father and some other men at the hotel were approached by the U.S. Army to see if they would help for three or four days taking men and supplies to the Bataan Peninsula. They were also asked to identify different bridges and railroad tracks that could be detonated so the Japs could not have access. My father left with these men and my mother was angry—she was "ticked." She had told him, "You have a family here to take care of! And here you are volunteering!" "It's my duty," he said. "If we can do something to help, let's do it!" So, he took off with the rest of the men who also had families at the Bayview Hotel.

When my father came back, days later, he brought some young GIs with him—eighteen, nineteen years old. They all were filthy dirty. They

139

were tired—looked like they had lost a lot of weight—and had had nothing to eat for a long time. My mother tried to get them to clean up, but they were too tired and hungry. My dad called one of the best restaurants in town and said, "Look, I am sending some guys over—give them a big steak and send the bill over to me." My mother told them, "You boys will be going home soon!" They answered, "Ma'am, we don't have a chance!" Then they took off. We never found out what had happened to them. We prayed they made it!

Japanese soldiers came into the city a couple days later. We were expecting massive numbers of tanks and trucks loaded with Japanese soldiers, but that was not the case. They were all so short. They were unkempt, unclean, with torn uniforms. They came by trucks, and most of them came in on bicycles—yes, bicycles. They took over the U.S. High Commissioner's office, which was directly across the street from the hotel. We watched as they took down the American flag and put up the Japanese flag. That was a sad day. That really hurt! It made us all cry! At the same time, they were rounding up people off the streets and taking people from their homes. So we just stayed put. Pretty soon, the Japs came into the hotel. They registered all of us who were staying in the hotel.

Good friends of ours, the Kneedler family, owned the Bayview Hotel. As soon as people started coming in from the country, the hotel owners said, "Look, this is no longer a hotel. I am not charging you folks anything to stay here. We are all in the same boat." "We will stay here just as long as we can and see what happens."

Soon after that, the Japanese came in and took over the hotel. They interviewed each family who was staying in the hotel. About five officers came in to our room with big, shiny boots. They first looked through our belongings. Then they looked at my little brother, who was only three months old, and said to my mother, "Your baby? Your baby?" My mother said, "Yes." Then the head Jap officer said, "Big girl and father go to prison! Everyone else stay here!" We, of course, did not want to be separated. My dad said, "What about the girl? She needs to stay with her mother! She has bad legs!" So they had me walk across the room with my braces—back and forth, back and forth—so they could see how I walked. The Jap officer said, "O.k., the girl can stay!" All the time they were sucking through their teeth.

In the meantime, Mr. Kneedler's wife, Dorothy, and five other women with children, including my mother, were ordered to go to the Kneedler's house, not far from the hotel. We were to live there until they decided what to do with us. So we said farewell to my dad and went to their house. We thought they were going to take him to Santo Tomas right away, because that is what we had been told. They put a sign in Japanese on the door of the house that said, "Do not bother these people," but the soldiers paid no attention to it. There were Japs bivouacking all over the place, on the street and right by the house. They got loud at night after drinking. We were scared.

My mother and all the women would take turns going to the market to buy food. They would always take a Filipino Amah (nursemaid) with them for protection. A couple of these women had been chased, caught, and slapped because they were white. One time, a Japanese soldier was hollering at my mother at the market and poking at her with his bayonet. So she took off running between the stalls of the market. She turned a corner and thought she had lost him. He was still running after her. She came up to a Filipino fishmonger who said, "Come! Come! Come!" She shoved my mother under the fish table and told her to hide. She covered my mother with burlap. They did not find her. This Filipino lady, Mrs. Abuig, and my mother became good friends. My mother would later become godmother for her child. In Manila in April 2001, after all these years I contacted the Abuig family. We did not know this, but while we were staying at the Kneedler's house, my father and the other daddies had been kept at the Bayview Hotel. My dad was an elevator boy. Another man we knew was running the kitchen. All of them were made to work for the Japanese. Later, when more Jap soldiers came to replace them, my dad and all the other men in the hotel were sent to Santo Tomas prison. At this time we were still in the Kneedlers' house.

The situation at the house got worse, with Jap soldiers coming drunk to the door and staying in the yard. My mother then went to the Assumption Convent. She asked the mother superior if we could come stay there for a while because it was too dangerous for us in the house where we were. My mother was told that the Japanese had shut the school and the nuns were going to be replaced with nuns from Japan. They said the Japanese knew exactly who was there, and they could not take anyone else in at that time. But she took my mother's name and address in case the situation changed. So my mother gave her the information. The mother superior said, "Are you related to Mr. Louis Weinzheimer?" "My mother said, "He is my father-in-law." "Oh, in that case you can come on in and stay until it is no longer possible. For the last ten years he has loaned the nuns his beach house for their retreats."

So because of that we were allowed to go to the convent and hide out there with the other women. This included all of us—five women and about eighteen kids. We all had one large room. It wasn't long until the Japanese nuns were moving into the convent so we were told we would have to leave. My mother went to the other convent, St. Paul's, to see if they could take us. She was told they could only take two women. By this time, the other women wanted to join their husbands in Santo Tomas Prison. We stayed on at St. Paul's as long as we could, but the Japanese had taken over the school at the convent as well. Things were getting pretty bad with the Japanese all over Manila. I watched them drown a small Filipino boy one day outside the building in an old bathtub and take his limp body away. The nuns were still teaching the classes at St. Paul's and I was allowed to come down to attend class about three times a week with the other children.

Last year (2001), I received an email from a man in Manila. He said, "I want to know if you have green eyes and braces on your legs and if you were in the third grade at St. Paul's Convent, because, if you were, I had a big crush on you." This was referring back to our days in Santo Tomas. His name is Jim Litton. I answered him and said, "Yes, that was me." The next time I went to Manila for a visit, he and his wife came to the hotel and we had a great reunion over dinner.

Toward the end of 1942, it became so dangerous at St. Paul's that we decided to go on into Santo Tomas Prison and be with my dad. We had to re-register at the Japanese office where we had registered before and put in our request. They approved this request, and we were allowed to take a few things like cooking utensils, a little food, and some personal things. Prior to this we had been visiting my dad every other month. We would know when something was wrong on those visiting days when we were not allowed to see him or to leave the food. Most of the time we went in and found him right away. One day shortly after we arrived they stopped the visits. Later they would not allow food to be brought in for anyone. We were glad to be reunited with my father.

I went to school with the other children out in the Father's Garden, near the seminary. After a while they switched it upstairs to the roof garden of the Main Building. That was not too easy for me because I had to climb all those stairs. We had teachers who were also prisoners who taught school. Eventually, without food, you couldn't think or function too well. So teachers had a hard time teaching and students had a hard time learning. Besides that, I had a hard time walking up and down those four flights of stairs. My mother didn't want my mind to get addled, so she had me write in a diary each day. I still have that. It's not in a traditional form because I had to write on anything I could. I tried to find small pieces of paper or anything I could write on. When we got to the States, we had it typed up so it was readable.

When we got into Santo Tomas, the women and children were put in an annex—a building way in the back of the campus. The men were in the Main Building, thirty or so in each room. They discouraged fraternizing between men and women. Over the years, they kept bringing in more and more prisoners until they were running out of room. Finally, they allowed us to build shacks. Our family shack was right up against the wall at first. Then they realized that Filipinos were throwing food over the wall for us. They threw over food like puto and bananas.[89] So, they made us move all the shacks back away from the wall. Then they built a big ditch between the wall and us.

They put rolls and rolls of barbed wire on the top of the wall. It was hard to locate material to build a shack, but all of us worked together and were able to build what we could. There had to be large open doors and windows so the Jap guards could see in at all times. At first, the women could only spend the days in the shacks and had to return to their quarters in the Annex at night. But because of overcrowding, they allowed families to stay together overnight, which was their only solution to the overcrowding. We were so glad to be together as a family.

We were kept busy all day. Everyone had a job. My father was in charge of sanitation in the Central Kitchen and also monitored to see that the prisoners did not steal food. Others worked at different jobs such as in the kitchen, where they were cooks or cleaners. They cooked lugao, rice gruel. They would put vegetables in hot water for soup, when they were available from the vegetable garden, where a lot of people worked daily. Women had to monitor toilet privileges by standing there handing out small pieces of toilet paper. Then the women had to scrub the toilets, scrub the showers, and do all the cleaning. Everybody had a duty to do. I used to go with my mom and help in the bathroom, which I hated.

One of the men we called "the exterminator" because his job was to keep track of rats. He was diligent in his duties until the prisoners ate the rats. Earlier we had garbage, but later on there was no garbage because we were *eating the garbage!*

My dad grew some large plants around our shack—elephant ears— and this worked out well. We could eat the roots, and they also shaded the shack and made it cooler. Toward the last days, when the bombing started, we could look up in the sky from this vantage point among the plants and see what was going on without being detected. Prisoners who were caught looking up at our U.S. planes would be taken to the front gate and tortured by looking up at the sun all day. The Jap guards were on the roofs of buildings looking for anyone watching the airplanes.

We also grew a banana tree but we never got to eat any bananas. We knew someone would steal them during the night if we let them get ripe. My mother, being Tahitian, knew you could take the cluster of blossoms when they were small, which had small bananas in them, and bake them in banana leaves in the makeshift palayok. It was delicious.

I got very ill with dengue fever. I got most all of the childhood diseases like whooping cough, measles, amoebic and basiliary dysentery because my best friends had them. We were all kept in isolation when sick. We had the Bataan nurses and civilian nurses to care for us.[90] We also had Dr. Fletcher, who was a wonderful person. We had Dr. Allen, who was a lady physician. These people took care of our families outside [of the camp] before the war. They were our unsung heroes. I had a very bad case of tonsillitis. It was so bad that my eyes were swollen shut. I had pus coming out of my eyes, nose, ears, and my mouth. Dr. Fletcher reported to the Japanese commandant that I was going to die if I didn't have proper treatment, and he requested I be taken to a hospital in Manila to have my tonsils removed, even with all this infection. The commandant approved it, and the following morning two Japanese sentries, the chauffeur, my mother, and Dr. Fletcher, in the commandant's car, took me to Mary Chiles Hospital. They took all my clothes off at the hospital and I put on a very short shirt and I walked down the halls with the two guards, my mother, and the doctor to the operating room. When I woke up after the surgery, they took me back to the prison camp and put me in the children's section of the camp hospital. I was so very sick. The bleeding from the surgery did not stop. They took me over to the main hospital where the Army nurses were. I was not doing at all well and had to sit up night after night to be cauterized. The priests were called in for the last rites. A miracle happened! During one night, the bleeding stopped and my fever went down. I began to get better and spent a whole week there convalescing.

My mother was nursing my little brother when the war started. She decided to keep on nursing him. She nursed him until he was three years old. Dr. Fletcher told her she couldn't do that any more because she did not have enough nourishment for herself. She weighed seventy-three pounds when we were liberated. She had beriberi and became bedfast because of malnutrition weakness. Dad and I had to turn her over in bed. She was so weak! My father designed a bedpan we could slip under her in bed.

My dad tried to figure out what he could do to help my mother. He did something he had never done before. Black-market! There was a man who would trade jewelry, watches, and things like that for food from the Jap guards. My dad thought some coffee, which we had not seen for a long time, would be a stimulant for Mom and help her. He got a kilo of rice and a pound of Hills Brothers coffee for an I.O.U for $350. My dad opened the can of coffee by my mother's bedside—he wanted her to smell the aroma that escapes when a can of coffee is opened. A broad smile came over her face, as she smelled this. He brewed a pot of coffee and brought it to her. It was amazing—she just perked right up. He gave all of us kids a cup of coffee. Four days later, we were liberated. We were able to share actual coffee with the GIs who came in to rescue us.

Four months earlier, in October 1944, when the bombing started, when the air raid sirens went off, we were supposed to run for the Main

Building. But I couldn't run too well at that point. So my dad asked for permission for me to sleep in the Main Building each night. My mother had a friend who made space available for me in a room. My dad would walk me over to the building every night after supper. That's where I was during the night of the Liberation.

While we were standing in the chow line for dinner on the afternoon of February 3rd, 1945, we saw a few small U.S. planes fly overhead at very low, treetop altitude. It startled us and excited everyone in line. No plane had ever come this low before. There was a sound of buzzing going through the whole camp. It was like throwing a rock at a beehive and having it come alive. One of the planes dropped a pilot's goggles in one of the chow lines that said, to the effect, "Roll out the barrel. Christmas will be here today or tomorrow!" Wow, what a treat that was!

Later on in the evening as it was beginning to get dark we could hear a rumbling off in the distance. Usually when this happened (we were used to the sound by now) the big bombers would appear overhead on the way to a bombing mission, always flying overhead over the camp. But this was different. The noise got louder but no planes appeared. The rumbling became unfamiliar. As my dad walked me to the Main Building for the night, people came out of their shanties asking each other, "Does that sound different to you? Have you heard that before?"

My dad left me in my room and went back to the shanty to the family. All of us in the room were hanging out the big windows straining to see something. The noise became louder, and there was a moon coming up in the horizon. The rumbling was so loud now we felt the ground shaking, a noise so unfamiliar to us. Flares started shooting upward outside the walls and we could hear a lot of metal on the streets gradually surrounding our camp. Someone shouted, "Tanks!" We ran to the front of the building jockeying for a spot at the windows. I was smaller than the women, so I squished myself through to a good spot. We were making a lot of noise now, excited and uncertain. "Are those Japs? Brits? Russians? Yanks?" We didn't know. Finally, we heard a lot of gunshots and explosions and crashing sounds as the front gate was knocked down by tanks of the 1st Cavalry. They came lumbering up the main driveway, searchlights blaring and foot soldiers behind each tank with guns cocked at the ever ready.

Someone got out of the first tank and yelled, "We're Americans!" The prisoners in the Main Building cheered and cried and rushed out into the plaza toward our boys. The first tank into camp was Battlin' Basic, and she was a sight for sore eyes.[91] Our Jap garrison commander, Lieutenant Abiko, came out of the Main Building into the crowd and was about to throw a grenade at the tank when one of the foot soldiers spotted his actions and felled him with his rifle. Some prisoners then dragged him into the Main Building. For the next day we filed past his dead body, which was stored under one of the stairwells. The prisoners had a chance to jeer, spit, or kick at him to satisfy their souls. Some just stared. The prisoners had him positioned with his boots facing the Rising Sun, which was a disgrace in their Japanese beliefs. It felt good.

I would like to tell you about my mother in prison. Before the war, my mother was very glamorous, as were most of the women her age. They had beautiful hair and lovely clothing and so forth. She had a figure that would never quit. But when everybody in the prison at this time was told that we would be there more than three days, the women started digging out small articles of "femininity" they had saved for "when our boys come back." My mother saved her lipstick. She would say, "Nobody touch this—this for when our 'boys' come in." I saved a hair ribbon. My sister saved a pair of socks that she had never worn. Once a month my mother, her sister-in-law, and her very best girlfriend would get together in our shanty and get some ginger flowers that were growing around the camp. They would put on some of my mother's lipstick, put rouge on their face, and have this beautiful ginger flower in their hair. They would sit there an hour and a half and talk about fashions before the war and what they did then. And what they were going to have for dinner in the States, and what they would do when they got home. And every once in a while they would pass around the little mirror so they could look and check on their femininity. These times were very important to them.

On February 3, Liberation night, my dad had run out toward the Main Gate. He didn't know what was happening but soon saw the U.S. Army. He just could not believe the "boys" were there. He ran back to the shanty and told Mother "Mom, they are here!" So when my dad tried to pick up my mom and take her to the main plaza, she said, "Wait! Wait! Get my lipstick. It's under the mattress." He said, "Oh, God, no! Not now!" She said, "No, I can't go see the 'boys' without lipstick on." So he grabbed the lipstick, sat her down on the bed, put it on her very carefully himself, and said, "Now are you happy? Can we go?" So he picked her up and ran out of the shanty with her. She was so happy, she didn't sleep at all that night. They saved her life. She died at age eighty-seven in Hawaii.

The next day we heard about the prisoners who were taken as hostages by the Jap soldiers in the Education Building. That was the men and boys building—the Santo Tomas Education Building. Several Jap soldiers held these 200 men and boys prisoners. Colonel Charles E. Brady negotiated with them all night for their release.[92] Finally it was agreed that the 1st Cavalry would give the Japanese safe conduct to the edge of Manila where they could join their other Japanese troops. The Japs insisted on taking all their firearms with them, but Brady insisted they each take only one firearm. They marched them out of camp a few days later and we did not see them anymore. We were later told that the Filipino guerrillas were waiting for them when they got to the edge of the town.

Because Manila had not been taken yet and cleared of Japs, we did not leave the prison camp until six weeks later. Manila was a bloodbath! When we left, we flew on a big plane to Leyte. There were about eight planes convoying us on the trip. We left from Nichols Field. Before we left on the trip there was a typhoon warning and when we got to Leyte, all the planes except ours turned around and went back. It was the end of March. It was raining when we landed, and the airstrip was a mud puddle in the middle of a lot of coconut trees. We got on trucks and went into the jungle. The men were left off at the men's camp and the women went on to Tacloban on the beach. We were at the Convalescent Hospital for a week for debriefing and physical examinations. Then we got on an LST and went out to the troop transport in the bay. Leyte had been wonderful because we got good food, and we would go to the movies every night with the GIs. We would sit on felled coconut trees and watch the movie under a full moon shining on the beach. I remember we watched the movie *Bambi,* which we had never heard of, and some war romance movies. The GIs loved having us kids around and spoiled us terribly.

The LSTs took us out to our troop transport waiting out on Leyte Bay. As we approached the ship we could see GIs hanging over the railing making whooping catcalls and whistles at us. Some of these guys hadn't seen a white woman in a couple of years. Regardless of what kind of shape we were all in, I guess we still looked pretty good to them.

We spotted our dad hanging over the railings waving, and were we glad to see him! We thought we would sail right away, but we sat out in the bay for a few days. It was hotter than anything and not a breeze blowing. The bay was filled with half-sunken and bombed-out enemy ships and planes sticking half out of the shallow waters. The Battle of Leyte Gulf was so much in evidence. It looked like it was a whopper of a battle. This ship, the *Admiral Capps,* was a troop transport carrying prisoners, GIs home on rotation, and the wounded soldiers. At this point we didn't know where we were going, as it was still wartime and everything was top secret and classified.

I remember the first night, going to the mess hall for supper. When we entered the dining room each table had beautiful white tablecloths, with pitchers of ice-cold milk and big red apples at each place. There were real plates to eat out of and glasses for our milk. It was amazing.

After our ship was joined with other destroyers, and escort ships to form a large convoy, we started on our way. While waiting to get under way we had to be briefed and re-briefed:

DO NOT TALK ABOUT OUR EXPERIENCES—Loose Lips Sinks Ships—either on the ship or when we get to our destination. The war was still on and we might hurt other prisoners still under capture by the Japs.

DO NOT THROW ANYTHING OVERBOARD—cigarettes, a piece of paper, etc. The enemy had submarines in the area, and these telltale articles floating in the water could alert them of our presence.

Everything was NOW HEAR THIS! NOW LAY DOWN TO THE DECKS! NOW LAY BELOW! NOW THROW HERE! (On secured waste baskets on deck) . . . We were always in blackout at night, and our convoy zigzagged during our whole trip. We were going twelve knots per hour.

Our first stop, for five hours only, was the Admiralty Islands at the North Bismark Sea. We didn't know where we were until we weighed anchor and took off. We could have the whole run of the ship, almost, but had to comply with strict rules, all for our safety, of course.

Our time was spent talking and visiting with the many wounded soldiers on their way home. Boy, what an awful time they had in the battlefields! We exchanged war stories and learned a lot from each other. They were allowed up on deck most of the days except for the guys suffering from shellshock. The GIs taught us how to play pedro, poker, and pinochle, which we all became pretty adept at. We enjoyed skunking these guys out of the few monies that they were betting with.

We had a jazz combo on board consisting of four Coast Guard fellows who played great music. We were taught all the hit parade songs of the day and the latest jitterbug dance steps. We were feeling good, and the cleansing sea air was such a treat. It was hard to believe there was a war on. We had to keep being reminded that we were sitting ducks in the middle of the ocean and, yes, there was a war on.

During our travels we were taught to look for mines in the water. We were all showed pictures and taught to identify the different kinds. Sure enough, quite a few of them showed up pretty close to our ship. They were promptly blown up by some of the crew [members] who were on watch on different shifts.

After a couple of weeks we saw land and still didn't know where we were. We weren't told anything, for obvious reasons. As we watched from our decks it was a familiar sight—Hawaii! We dropped anchor in the bay but weren't allowed in the harbor. We saw the Pearl Harbor devastation from afar, rotting hulls, and so forth.

We waited for quite a while until a tugboat pulled alongside our ship and released a few FBI men, who climbed on board. As soon as the tug pulled out we weighed anchor again, just as the ship's loudspeaker blared "California Here We Come!" We all screamed with joy!

The FBI came aboard to interrogate all the prisoners on the way to San Francisco. The adults were asked to relate their experiences during the war and to finger any atrocities that they personally knew of conducted by the Japs. They were very much interested in the quislings and turncoats of the prison camps. We also were asked to turn over any documents of the war that we had in our possession. They told us these things could be of great importance to the government. My diary stayed put, because it was just that—a kid's diary.

We watched a military burial at sea one day—one of the prisoners had died. Easter was spent on deck with some of the chaplains conducting different services all morning. This had a lot of meaning for us—a collective communion of sorts. Let freedom ring!

By the time we reached Hawaii we left behind all of our escort ships and just had a few transports with us on the way home. We still had to zigzag and go slow.

The morning we were to arrive in San Francisco we got up in the dark, had breakfast, and then took our stance up on deck. Boy, it was cold and foggy, and our ship slowed down a little bit more. Pretty soon it got lighter, and just as some of the sun started peeking out from behind the fog, we saw part of the Golden Gate Bridge rising in the mist. We cried for joy—she was our Statue of Liberty, our symbol of freedom, our Golden Gate Bridge. It was just a matter of minutes later that the sun popped up all the way, and the whole bridge and the backdrop of San Francisco was clear as crystal and welcoming us home.

When the *Admiral Capps* slid silently under the bridge we knew we were home. Fire boats were out to meet us spraying streams of water with all their might. About an hour later we were nudging up against the docks filled with yelling and screaming and waving relatives and friends. We were all together with our GIs and our wounded buddies, happy to be home but sad to part from one another. We all cried for many personal reasons. We watched and waved as they took the wounded off the ship first and loaded them into waiting military ambulances. Then it was our turn.

My grandmother and other relatives were there to meet us, and then they whisked us away to a hotel in town. We looked at these people as if we were in a trance, as they looked like a million dollars and we were in sloppy, ill-fitting GI khaki issue. The women had hats with veils on them and some with fur coats. They smelled clean and crisp, and their clothes looked impeccable.

President Roosevelt had died the day before our arrival, so all the stores were closed for the three days of mourning. We had to wait for haircuts and clothes shopping. In the meantime we went through a long debriefing by the Army and days of physical examinations.

The 2,000-acre ranch in the San Joaquin Valley was two hours away and became our home. I went to the Dominican Convent in San Rafael, California for a few years and went to Lodi High School to finish my upper class education before attending Stephens College in Columbia,

Missouri. After the war I had many more reconstructive surgeries on my legs and hip, way into my twenties. Rehabilitation was long and tedious but worthwhile.

I lived and worked in San Francisco as a young single adult. After marrying and raising three children, a divorce was in the making, and after quite a few years of being a single parent, I moved to Hawaii where I lived for nineteen years. Today I live near my children and grandchildren in Northern California, which I love.

Each February, I escort a group of ex-POWs from my prison camp and some of the liberators of the 1st Cav back to the Philippines from whence we came and met many years ago. I enjoy designing these trips and traveling with these wonderful people all of whom have such close friendships with each other. The "Battling Bastards of Bataan" are another extraordinary group I escort back in time and back in history. Freedom is wonderful!

Caroline Bailey Pratt

Caroline Bailey Pratt was a child during the Japanese occupation, interned in Santo Tomas with her father and mother. She provides her own recollections of time in the camp, no doubt supported by her parents' memories and the diary her father, who was involved in camp organization, kept while at the camp. As a child, she conveys her view of a child—ironically that she was allowed more "freedom" than before her internment. She thinks back on five key dates during that time—from the day she and her family were interned to the day they left the Santo Tomas for their return voyage to the U.S.

My father, Fay Cook Bailey, worked for the National City Bank of New York's Far Eastern Division. He had spent the 1920s in North China, and since 1929 my parents had made their home in the Philippines, except for two years (1934–1936) when my father was the manager of the branch in Canton, China. I was nine and one-half years old in December 1941. I recall that there was talk of war.

My father would bring home cases of food, especially evaporated milk, powdered milk, or KLIM, and liquor.[93] The assumption was that the Philippines would be blockaded and we would no longer be able to get supplies from the States. My mother went to classes organized by the American Emergency Committee to learn how to cook native vegetables on the native clay charcoal stoves. The American civilians living in the Philippines had great faith in their military and great disdain for the Japanese. Things did not turn out at all the way they expected!

My memories of World War II center around five dates: December 8, 1941, the day the war began on our side of the International Date Line; January 6, 1942, the day we entered Santo Tomas; September 21, 1944, the first U.S. air raid; February 3, 1945, LIBERATION; February 23, 1945, the day we left Santo Tomas and flew to Leyte and the beginning of our trip back to the States. Not a year has gone by when these dates come up that I don't recall the events that are associated with them, now more than half a century ago.

December 8, 1941, Manila, Philippine Islands. I was sitting in the fourth-grade classroom at the American School nursing a toothache and thinking about my dentist appointment with Dr. Doyle that afternoon. It was mid-morning. Twice, mothers had come to the class, and after a brief conversation with Mrs. Davis, our teacher, their children had been excused to go Christmas shopping. I was thinking that my mother would never take me out of school for that reason when she too showed up at the door! Her grim look did not suggest a shopping trip, and in the hall she said, "We are at war."

Nowadays, because of television, people know what war is like. But, in those days, we heard stories of what was happening in Europe, but the images weren't there to really bring it home. So I think we were very naive about what was going to happen. Because Manila was likely to be bombed, the bank staff arranged for their families to go forty miles south to the Canlubang Golf and Recreation Club, a comfortable facility maintained by the Calamba Sugar Estate for its managerial staff and their friends. The next day I had my tooth pulled by a petite Filipino dentist in the town of Calamba. The memory of that extraction supplanted all other recollections of the first days of the war. We returned to Manila Christmas Eve and waited for the Japanese to arrive. Although Manila had been declared an Open City, the Japanese continued to bomb the harbor and other sites. Two other bank families, whose homes were near airfields, moved in with us.

At the sound of the air raid siren, all the children would be hurried into the sandbag shelter that my father had had constructed at the far end of our garden, and one of the mothers would read to us until the "all clear" sounded. While awaiting the arrival of the Japanese, our parents and servants buried the stock of canned goods in the yard and consumed or poured down the drain their prized liquor supply.

January 6, 1942. Our waiting game ended at noon with the arrival of three Japanese, one interpreter in civilian clothes and two officers, each decked out in high top boots, jodhpurs, and a long sword. Our hopes of being able to remain in our home under house arrest were dashed. Instead, we were ordered to pack up food and clothing for three days and taken to Rizal Stadium to join hundreds of other "enemy aliens" to be registered. Hours later we were crammed onto the back of a truck heading for the University of Santo Tomas. We had gone only a few blocks when the truck became enveloped in smoke. One of the Americans had to show the Japanese driver how to release the brakes.

We unloaded in front of the Main Building and commenced a frantic search for floor space. Women with young children were supposed to go to the Annex, an elementary school behind the Main Building, but one look at the chaos in those rooms convinced our mothers to find a place in the Main Building. They were lucky to find a spot in the women's room next to the men's room their husbands were in. How we got through those first few days, I'm not sure. It is a total blur.

After several days our Filipino servants were able to bring us mattresses, more clothes, and other items, and, most essential of all, food. My mother and I shared a king-sized mattress with Mary Hamilton and her sons, David and Bill, for over a year—on the floor. Some of the women resented us children being in the room, especially David who was eight, so he eventually moved in with his father. Little did we realize that this was going to be our home for thirty-seven months, and that our situation was going to become progressively worse. As far as the kids were concerned, it was now an adventure, and, paradoxically, we had more freedom in camp than we had had in pre-war Manila. No longer did we have an amah (nanny) to follow us around and report on our behavior. Nor did we have to make special arrangements to play with friends. School was started within a few weeks, and numerous athletic activities kept the young people busy. The adults formed committees to handle all aspects of running the camp, and everyone was assigned a job.

It was a remarkable example of American and British organizational skills. The Japanese Military Administration had made no plans whatsoever to provide for the prisoners and for the first six months contributed nothing. All the food, bedding, kitchens, medical supplies, and food were contributed by the Philippine Red Cross–American National Red Cross and by the businessmen both in and out of camp and by the many loyal Filipinos, Chinese, and other foreigners. Even the Santo Tomas University site had been chosen by the American Emergency Committee as a potential internment camp for civilians should the Japanese decide to imprison the "enemy aliens." At the time, being only nine years old, these matters did not concern me. I knew that my mother cleaned vegetables for the camp kitchen and that my father worked in a room in the Main Building with Mr. Wolff, and that they had something to do with the Red Cross. It wasn't until I was preparing my father's diary for publication, a project I began in 1995 after a trip to the Philippines organized by Sascha Weinzheimer Jansen to commemorate the 50th anniversary of our liberation from Santo Tomas, that I became aware of the complexities of running the camp and my father's dual role as chief of the finance and supplies committee and as treasurer of the Philippine branch of the American National Red Cross (PR/ANRC).

In April 1942 the Japanese ordered the PR/ANRC dissolved and all its monies and properties turned over to a new Philippine Red Cross under Japanese control. The Red Cross funds that had been allocated to operate the camp would run out the end of June (1942), and the Japanese forbade further funding through the new Red Cross. The camp's executive committee urged the Japanese commandant to seek funds from the Japanese Military Authority (funds they should have been providing from the beginning of our imprisonment). From July 1, 1942, until February 1, 1944, when the Japanese Military Police took control of Santo Tomas Internment Camp and stopped the procedure, the camp operated on money provided by the Japanese at the rate of 70 centavos (35 cents U.S.) per capita daily. This amount was increased three times to a maximum of 1.50 pesos in January 1944, but by then its real value was well below that amount. Never during our thirty-seven months under their "protective custody" did the Japanese provide adequately for their prisoners. Keeping the books and distributing these funds for the purchase of food and other necessities was my father's responsibility.

The money to purchase supplementary food came from various sources, some openly from neutral organizations but most through secret transactions between internees and loyal friends and business associates on the outside—Filipinos, Chinese, and other foreign nationals. These transactions were carried out at great risk to the participants. For the first two years, the Japanese permitted members of the internee committees to go into the city of Manila on passes to conduct camp business, to purchase special supplies, to reimburse hospitals for the care of internees who were patients, and to distribute money to the Filipino families of interned husbands and fathers. Twice a month my father made a trip to the Bank of Taiwan to exchange the per diem allotment for cash in small denominations for the camp buyers to use at the market for the daily purchases of food. I remember that my mother was very worried when he was out on these trips.

As I now know, she had reason to be, because my father did sneak money into camp until it became too risky. For a time the money and messages flowed in and out of camp fairly easily, but as the war turned against the Japanese, they put more and more restrictions on the camp. They limited the number of people allowed out on passes and saddled them with guards, drastically curtailing their movements. Finally, in February 1944, the Military Police took over the management of Santo Tomas. All but the sickest patients in the outside hospitals were ordered into camp; with only a few exceptions, no one was allowed out on passes. The package line, which had operated since the first days of internment, was shut down. This had been a vital link between internees and their loyal friends on the outside who sent in food and other items to make life more comfortable. Packages were inspected by the guards, and communication between the parties was forbidden, but messages and money did slip through.

When the Military Police took over, they also stopped the per diem allotment and replaced the camp buyers, Mrs. Patricia Intengan, Juan Fernandez, and Guillermo Manalang, with a Japanese buyer. They [the three] had been part of the Red Cross team that had supplied the camp with food during the first six months and had continued as the camp's buyers, making daily trips to the Manila market. Mrs. Intengan also secretly carried messages to and from the internees. She was a vital link between the prisoners and the outside world. It was a great loss to the camp when her role as buyer was terminated. The food situation deteriorated rapidly under the new system. The Japanese trucked in rice, camotes, and perishables (vegetable greens and fish), which were often inedible. They reduced the amount of rice to 250 grams per person per day. The deficiencies were partially made up from the camp's reserves, which had been accumulated for emergencies, but camp officials feared they would run out. The camp was also spending P5,000 a day on supplemental food purchased by the Japanese buyer. The increasing scarcity and cost of food and the decreasing value of the Japanese Military Notes ("Mickey Mouse" money) made the situation even worse.

In April 1944, a top secret money and food smuggling operation to benefit the whole camp began with the daring assistance of Luis de Alcuaz, a young Filipino professor of physics at Santo Tomas University [before the war], and secretary to the rector of the Dominican Seminary. The seminary building was off limits to the internees, as was the side of the gymnasium in which Alcuaz had his office. A double wall separated his office from the side of the gym, which housed a men's dormitory. A hole in this wall served as the conduit through which promissory notes were smuggled out to Alcuaz, who then found merchants willing to exchange them for thousands of pesos, which he passed back through the hole. Alcuaz also purchased hundreds of pounds of beans and cases of canned goods, which he hid between the walls. The food was secreted to the kitchen in a small pushcart. The P5,000 and P10,000 promissory notes were issued by the interned executives of major companies, Standard-Vacuum Oil, General Motors Overseas Corp., Firestone Tire and Rubber, International Harvester, B. F. Goodrich Rubber, Asiatic Petroleum, and Tidewater Associated Oil. The repayment for these "Loans Negotiated for Cash" amounting to over P260,000 (Japanese Military Notes) was guaranteed by the American National Red Cross under the signature of T. J. Wolff, Chairman, and F. C. Bailey, Treasurer. Without these efforts to supplement the inadequate daily food ration provided by the Japanese, the internees would have been far worse off, but because of the need for secrecy the very people who had taken such great risks for the sake of the camp were criticized for not doing enough.

Under these starving conditions, more and more people turned to the black market. They were willing to pay outrageous prices and trade valuable jewelry for a paltry amount of beans, rice, sugar, a can of corned beef, or Klim. The Japanese authorities were aware that the internees had money in their possession, much to their disapproval. In August 1944 they ordered all money held by individuals and by the official camp committees turned in for safe keeping in the Bank of Taiwan. They claimed it was for the good of the internees, to curb gambling and frivolous spending, to protect against robbery, and to enable it to earn interest. Each adult would be allowed to withdraw P50 a month (children P25)—hardly enough to buy anything! My father was put in charge of collecting and dispensing this money. He notes in his diary that over one million pesos were collected and 1,660 accounts opened. The internee committee received over P200,000 in donations from the internees. Each month thereafter he would conduct bank days to enable people to withdraw their allotted sums. The Japanese promised dire punishment if anyone was found to have more money than allowed in their possession. Anyone caught holding pre-war Philippine pesos or U.S. dollars would be in even worse trouble. It was a risk some still took, but it had become more dangerous because the Japanese had increased their unannounced inspections throughout the camp.

September 21, 1944. I was searching for weeds between the talinum in the community vegetable garden with Ann Rockwell. At that time internees were still permitted to do this, but soon after, even the weeds were added to the communal soup, and private gleaning was prohibited. It was about 9:00 a.m. We were way out in the garden when we heard a most unfamiliar drone. Looking up we were stunned to see the sky filled with planes flying in small groups. As they flew over the camp heading for Manila Bay, each plane dropped out of the sky in a steep dive, one after another, dropping their bombs and soaring back up out of range of the very sporadic and ineffectual Japanese anti-aircraft fire. After thirty-three months of waiting and hoping for some sign that the American forces would return, we finally had our proof that we hadn't been forgotten. We were jubilant, but we were also terrified. We tore back to our shanties, Ann to find her son Jimmy and I to an empty shanty. My parents were both working in the Main Building and forbidden to leave. I crawled under my cot and spent the rest of the day listening to the wonderful new sounds. I must have snuck out for a look occasionally but was fearful of being spotted by a Japanese guard. From then on we looked forward each day for a repeat performance from the dive bombers and were terribly disappointed when there was a lull in the action. My father's diary records the dates of two other bombing events that I recall, the first sighting of the big land-based bombers (B-29 Superfortresses) on December 23, 1944, and on January 8, 1945, seeing one of them shot down. It was a terrible sight.

As our hopes continued to rise after September 21, 1944, our situation in camp continued to deteriorate. As I mentioned earlier, the sharp downturn had begun in February 1944 when the Japanese Military Police took over the management of the camp. By 1945 the "Mickey Mouse" currency was useless; inflation and scarcity of food and all other commodities had made life miserable on the outside as well as in camp. People were so hungry they were eating all sorts of plants not considered edible under normal conditions. The canna lily bulbs we tried we learned were poisonous. In December we ate the beans out of a bean bag frog that was to have been a Christmas present for Arthur MacArthur in 1941.[94] To add to internees' woes, the Japanese issued a continuous string of orders to disrupt their lives even further. We were ordered to stand for roll call twice a day, remaining in line for an hour at a time if there was a miscount. We had lessons on the proper way to bow from the waist. All kinds of electrical equipment had to be turned in. All shanties within twenty meters of the wall had to be removed. Our shanty was one of the ones that had to be relocated. The surprise searches by unpleasant guards made us fearful of how they might interpret what they found. They demanded heavy-duty work from internees for both camp and Japanese projects when we were living on barely over 1,000 calories a day. By February 3, 1945, we were getting less than 800 calories per day.

The death toll rose steadily after September 1944, from nine in September, to twelve in October, nineteen in November and also in December, and twenty-nine in January 1945. According to the camp records, 390 internees out of a total population of approximately 7,000 in the two camps, Santo Tomas and Los Banos, died. These figures do not include the deaths among the 500 civilian prisoners in Baguio who were transferred to Bilibid prison in Manila in December 1944. This, briefly, was the situation in Santo Tomas on February 3, 1945.

February 3, 1945. In the afternoon of that memorable day two planes—some say more—flew low over the camp, and one of the pilots dropped his goggles with a message, "Roll Out the Barrel!" My father records in his diary that he had just purchased 5 kilos of soybeans at $175 a kilo on his own check payable after the war. At dusk we heard rumbling sounds to the north that became progressively louder. A huge fire lit the sky. My father said it was probably a Chinese fireworks factory burning up. As it grew darker the sky was lit up by bright flares that seemed to hang up over the city to the north of us. My father insisted we go to bed about 7:00 p.m. This had been our routine to conserve our energy. His ankles were terribly swollen with beriberi, and he was very weak. The rumbling grew louder and louder, and the flares brighter and brighter. At 9:00 the sounds of heavy motor vehicles were coming from the front gate together with loud cheering. Someone came running past our shanty yelling, "They're here!" I was out of bed in a split second, dashing for the plaza in front of the Main Building, my father struggling behind. Mother stayed in the shanty to guard the precious soybeans we had just purchased. The scene on the plaza was awesome. Huge tanks, giant-sized soldiers, and ecstatic internees. The soldiers were as overwhelmed at seeing women and children as we were at seeing them. They gave us their K rations and everything else edible, which we consumed greedily. Later that night a lot of us were sick to our stomachs.

But there was a downside. The Japanese had fled to the Education Building and were holding hostage more than two hundred men and boys housed there. After exchanging gunfire, the risk to the internees seemed too great so the Americans held off. The next day negotiations took place for the release of the internees and the departure of the Japanese from camp under U.S. Army escort to the outskirts of the city. During the exchange of gunfire we remained in the Main Building because our shanty was right behind the Education Building. About 3:00 a.m. we returned to our shanty with our friends the Bunnells and cooked up our last bit of rice, which we topped with sugar! My mother also made parched soybean coffee. Later we had a second breakfast of really thick mush served by the camp kitchen. We were totally oblivious to the dangerous situation we were in, and, fortunately, the Japanese were ignorant of the number of troops that had rescued the camp. We were rescued by 700 men from the 1st Cavalry Division and the 44th Tank Battalion who raced 100 miles through enemy territory to reach Manila. It was two or three days before the rest of the army came in and the bloody battle for Manila was not won until March. Our happiness was cut short on February 7 when the Japanese began shelling the camp. Some very close friends were killed during those terrifying days. Fifteen internees lost their lives by enemy shelling, and also several soldiers and Filipino workers. Over ninety were wounded. I got very good at recognizing the sounds of shells going over. The ones from the American guns heading for the Walled City had a very different whine than the ones from Japanese mortars heading into Santo Tomas. The latter were silenced within a week.

February 23, 1945. This was my last memorable date and my last day in Santo Tomas Internment Camp, Manila, Philippines. The names of the first group of civilian internees to leave camp for the United States was read over the loudspeaker the evening before. We were told to report at 7:00 a.m. on the main plaza with one bag apiece. The Army nurses had gone out on February 12. My father, despite his weakened condition, was reluctant to leave because he still did not know what had happened to the bank staff that was in the Los Banos camp. We learned later that at the same time we were boarding trucks to leave Santo Tomas, the 11th Airborne Division was executing a spectacular rescue of the Los Banos prisoners. The trucks—personnel carriers I think is the correct term—took us to a stretch of highway north of the city which had been converted to an airstrip. We boarded a C-47 with bucket seats and only a couple of windows and took off down a bumpy runway heading for Leyte.

When we arrived in Tacloban we were hurried off the plane and onto trucks for the next stage of our adventure. There had been an enemy attack on the airfield that morning, which accounted for the hurry. The men spent one night on shore and boarded the ship, the USS *Jean Lafitte,* the next afternoon. The women and children were taken to the First Convalescent Hospital where we spent a delightful week sleeping and eating in large tents, playing on the beach, getting rides on the amazing vehicles that had been invented for amphibious warfare, and talking to the recuperating soldiers. They gave us the addresses of their families back home to contact when we got back, and we could only hope they would still be alive when we did get in touch with their families. We sailed from Leyte on March 4 in convoy until the Admiralty Islands. From there we zigzagged alone across the Pacific. It was a long and, fortunately, uneventful sea voyage home. We were reminded daily of the horrors of war because we shared passage with severely wounded amputees who were brought up on deck in basket-like stretchers each morning to escape the stifling atmosphere below deck. Our ordeal paled in comparison to theirs. We arrived in San Francisco on March 30, 1945, to face a totally different world than the one we had left behind.

Peter Robert Wygle and Robert Howard Wygle

This is another story of endurance by a family of four: Peter Robert Wygle; his father, Robert Howard Wygle; mother, Margaret Swartz Wygle;

and sister, Sarah Anne Wygle. Peter was only eleven when taken to Santo Tomas but has a vivid recollection of his childhood experiences. The father and son's recollections of their experiences in Santo Tomas are retold in Peter Wygle's book, Surviving a Japanese P.O.W. Camp.[95] *Peter's father died in 1961, and his contributions to the story are taken from his daily diary, letters, articles, and other sources, published in the book. Peter's father's story appears here in italics. Peter's story is taken both from his own account in the book and from my interviews with him. The first part of the story recounts how the Wygles ended up in Santo Tomas, and what was most memorable about their experiences there. The second part of this chapter focuses on the liberation from the camp. Here we have the personal recollections of Peter, the diary of Peter's father, and Peter's comments on his father's diary.*

Coming to the Philippines

My dad, Robert H. Wygle, served in the U.S. Cavalry on the Mexican border during World War I. After the war, he went to school at the Colorado School of Mines in Golden, Colorado, where he received a degree in mining engineering.

He had a job in the Phelps-Dodge Copper mines of Sonora, Old Mexico, which is where my sister Sarah and I were both born, she in 1928 and I in 1930. My dad held several other jobs during the depression. Two of the jobs I particularly remember. He was an engineers' "gopher" for the Boulder Dam project in Las Vegas in the early to mid-1930s; then he got a job in Reno as a bulk distributor for Texaco. While he was in Reno, in about 1938, he received an offer from a mining company in the

Philippines. He took them up on it and went to the Philippines while my mother, my sister, and I went to San Francisco for 1938 and 1939. We were there when the Golden Gate Bridge and the Bay Bridge were opened, even walking across the Golden Gate Bridge on opening day.

My dad sent most of his paychecks home to us until we finally saved up enough money for boat tickets to join him in the Philippines about New Year's Day in 1940. Through 1940 and 1941, we bounced around from mine to mine in the Philippines. The whole country is highly mineralized and Dad mined manganese, chromate, and several other things, ending up in the gold mines in Baguio in the northern section of the main island of Luzon.

Santo Tomas

On December 8, 1941, we got word of the attack on Pearl Harbor.[96] This did not worry us very much because we had no idea it would reach to the northern Philippines. I found out later that my parents were quite concerned about the probability of war with Japan, but we didn't have much reason to believe the Japanese would make a very effective enemy. The general attitude was that they were doing all right in China but we didn't think that they could stand up to us.

But, about nine o'clock that morning of 8 December 1941, the Jap planes came and bombed Baguio. With that the war was brought home to us rather forcibly. We still weren't too concerned, but the news was bad from the beginning. Around December 20, the mining company picked up the women and children in the company bus and took us to what they thought would be the relative safety of Manila. They left the men at the mines to keep them open if the Japanese didn't get there—or to destroy the mines and the fuel supplies if they did.

The Japanese did get to the mines, so Dad spiked the mines and blew up the fuel supplies. He did not want to be captured in Baguio. He could have just faded into the mountains, living in the jungle as long as the Japanese were on the island. He had been doing this for three or four of the years working in the rough mountain area since he had been in the islands. But he wanted to get to Manila where we were, so he walked, crawled, and tiptoed behind the Japanese lines from the mines in Baguio, through the mountains along the east side of the Central Valley of Luzon, all the way down to Manila. The mountains were extremely rugged, so this was quite a feat. He had to make time but he also had to stay out of sight.[97]

When he got to Manila, he knew we were or soon would be in Santo Tomas Prison camp. His task was to get himself captured without getting killed. He used his knowledge of Philippine politics to accomplish this. He knew that if he turned himself in to a Philippine politician asking for help, they would take him to the first Japanese that he came to—and the politician would know where they were. His plan worked, and Dad was put into camp.

Robert Wygle: *I was in Manila again and in a city supply yard when more Japs rolled in to the gasoline pump. Hiding in a small warehouse and watching through a crack in the building, I saw them loot the gasoline twenty feet away. After they left, the City Engineer drove up in his car. He seemed eager to help and offered me his telephone. I called a string of convents. At the Good Shepherd the sister lied like a gentleman. "No, she had no American Family there, never had!" Later I found out my family was there, and had been there for a week. She wasn't taking any chances.*

The city engineer offered to drop me at a convent along the way. When we got there, it was swarming with Japs who were collecting all the Americans in the place. My "friend" drove right in anyway and delivered me neatly to a Jap major. Having been a week without a change of clothes or shave, I must have looked pretty tough to the major. He motioned me out with his pistol and stood by while his boys searched me. They took my razor, knife, and bolo knife. The major took a fancy to the carved cane that I had with me. I had bought it for my brother and had sworn to deliver to him someday. I had used the cane as a pack-stick and didn't feel agreeable to losing it after all those miles—especially to a Jap. So as soon as he leaned it up against a tree, I collected it again.

I had been hearing that all Americans were being brought to Santo Tomas University. This raid on the convent told me that if my family wasn't there now, they would be soon. I had decided some days ago that I would turn myself in after my rounds of the convents if they showed nothing.

Instead of feeling apprehensive, I felt a sense of relief. I could quit playing hide and seek and ride right into Santo Tomas. As the gates there closed behind me and the rest of their load of Americans, I wondered if I'd ever get out again. That was January 8th, 1942, and the gates stayed closed until about February 8th, 1945. Three years and one month. About 1,125 days.

My mother, my sister, and I first got to Manila just before Christmas, December 22, 1941. We were supposed to have been put up in one of the hotels in Manila, but they were filled with refugees from China and other places, so a Catholic girls' convent took us in. The first place we were taken was to the north end of the city near the Grace Park Airfield. It got pretty hot because we were adjacent to the airfield, so we were moved back into the center of the city to another girls' convent just south of the Pasig River. I never knew exactly where this place was.

When the Japs came into the city, nobody knew what to do with us. It was obvious that we wouldn't be able to stay in this convent very long, but nobody knew how to go about getting us captured effectively. This was taken care of about a week later by a German priest at the convent who told the Japs who we were and where we were staying. They came in and got us on January 10, 1942. My dad had gotten put in the camp on the 8th of January, so he beat us to Santo Tomas by about two days. I was eleven years old at the time and my sister was thirteen.

Camp Organization

Nobody knew how prisoners of war were supposed to act, and the camp was growing very rapidly. The population began to hover in the 3,000 to 5,000 range. These were 3,000 to 5,000 people from all walks of life and from all the Allied nations, so we had Americans, Canadians, British, New Zealanders, Australians, Dutch, Free French, Norwegians, and so on. We had everyone in the camp from prostitutes to post-doctoral teachers and everywhere in between. So we had a real cross-section of humanity, not only of all persuasions and races, but also of all ages. When someone points to the fact that 800 people died while we were in this prison camp, you have to consider that a lot of those people would have died anyway in any three-year period. Some were 70 or 80 years old when they were put in the camp. So the mortality figures for the camp are a little bit deceptive. There are probably those who would say they all died of starvation. That is not true at all.

The first job in the camp was the social one of starting a community. The Japs went around and wanted to know who was in charge. Well, at that point nobody was in charge. Everybody was pointing to everyone else and a lot of people were pointing to a guy named Earl Carroll. He had been working with an American civilian group outside the camp. Fred Stevens talks about how the camp began.[98] A Central Committee was sort of appointed by the Japanese. I think the original committee was just arbitrarily chosen; another one—elected by the internees—took over very quickly. So we had a sort of self-governing situation in the camp. The Central Committee began to appoint other committees: Education, Medical, Public Safety, Sanitation, you name it. Pretty soon the jobs that were needed to keep the camp going were pretty much parceled out. So the camp started functioning.

Within the first few months we had a school system all the way from the first grade through several college courses. All of the children entered into this system. As a matter of fact, later I found out that one of my paleontology professors at the University of California was teaching in the camp, something I didn't know until after he was long deceased. I also had a job with the camp newspaper for a while, and I delivered messages for the Central Committee. People just did the things that needed to be done.

From Garbage Man . . .

Very early on Dad noticed that the garbage was being picked up but nothing was being done with it. It was all just being dumped in the backyard. The original estimates all the way up and down the line in the camp was that we were only going to be in camp for three days. It was obvious very soon that this would not be the case. That is when all these committees started coming into existence. But Dad decided unilaterally to take on the garbage game.

The first morning in camp I wandered to see what was there and to size it up for an escape—if necessary. The escape looked simple because, for the most part, weeds and cogon grass had grown on the grounds for years. When I wandered behind the Main Building, I saw an elderly man trying to burn some garbage. I went over to him and asked if he needed any help. "Good Lord, yes!" he said. "I've been here for two hours and they haven't sent any relief!" So I took his shovel and told him to quit, that I'd take over for a while. Well, no relief came for me until four months later. It was the camp's worst job. Since nobody wanted it, I was stuck. I'm the kind of sucker who sees what has to be done and does it—if nobody else will.

Dad went out in the backyard and dug some long ditches and started burning and burying the garbage. This was both good and bad. It was good that he was getting rid of the garbage by burying it. But it didn't occur to him that the camp was built on an old swamp filled in with sawdust from sawmills. When he burned the garbage, he set fire to the sawdust underground. It started to burn out away from the trenches and no one could put it out. Fortunately, this happened at the beginning of the rainy season and a big rain came and filled the trenches, putting out the fire. They thought about that for a while and did things to correct the situation like moving the garbage to a different location.

While Dad was doing this, being kind of a pack rat, he noticed people were throwing things away they had not intended to throw away, or things were being thrown away that someone else could make use of.

So he filtered the garbage and put all the reusable stuff on a table so that people could find the things they hadn't intended to throw away. Or if something had been there for a long while that another person thought they could use, Dad would just give it to them.

I buried all the camp garbage, for 4,000 people, alone. After a day or two, I began to be struck by people's wastefulness and foolishness. I was also amazed at the ignorance of my own people. I had always thought that Americans were clever and resourceful, but this garbage job convinced me that Americans were dumb—and that Englishmen were dumber! Soon I combined the garbage job with a salvage operation and supplied many people with things that others threw away. Silverware, jars, tableware, kindling, wire, nails, bottles, jugs, cartons, shoes, tin containers, wrapping paper, thermos bottles, spare parts, rags, clothes—all of this came my way, and I kept a "help yourself" pile in the shade under a tree. At first people were embarrassed about being seen carrying off salvage from the garbage dump. That changed. Seeds from kitchen garbage were in demand, onion settings, and other such things. My salvage supplied many a garden later. And a silver coin is still in one of my front teeth. The dentist had no silver, so he used a coin I had found in the dump.

... To Handyman

Dad's job then migrated to people bringing him things like wooden shoes that they might have thrown away but would now ask Dad to repair. He would tack them back together again and put rubber soles made out of old tires on them or do whatever it took to fix them. He began to take on this aura of a camp Handy Man, which he enjoyed much more than the garbage. When this happened, somebody else took over the garbage.

A lady came along to his handyman shop one day and told him she wanted him to make her some knitting needles. He said he didn't know anything about making knitting needles. She told him she would tell him everything he needed. He had a wire gauge card and asked the size she wanted. She wanted size #8 or something. She put the numbers on the wire gauge card. What Dad would do is take bamboo, leave the joint end on as the head, carve the bamboo to nearly the right size, run it through the wire gauge, strip the rest off, sand it, harden the point with fire, and put beeswax on the whole thing. That was how he made a knitting needle.

He gave this pair of knitting needles to the woman and made her promise faithfully that she would not tell anyone where she got them. That promise lasted maybe 10 minutes. Before that day was out, he had a line down the street of women wanting knitting needles. In the two and a half years he was there, he probably turned out three or four thousand sets of knitting needles of all sizes.

One thing that impressed me about the people in the camp was that they displayed so much talent. We had stage shows almost from the beginning. A fellow named Dave Hardy and some other people would put together stage and "radio" shows. They had a public address system that enabled them to present plays just like ones we had listened to on the radio before the war. Except for six or eight months of darker days toward the end of the camp, we were never devoid of entertainment.

We also developed a reasonably good hospital system. There were several doctors and nurses among the original internees, and about a dozen Navy nurses, from the Naval Hospital that was part of the Cavite

Naval Base complex, soon supplemented them. When Corregidor fell in May 1942, the Japanese captured the Army nurses who had been evacuated from Bataan in April. The Japanese had no idea what to do with them. They weren't soldiers, so the Japanese didn't want to keep them with the other military captives, which is where the nurses would have preferred to be, so they ended up connected to our camp. They were first housed in the Santa Scholastica Girls School, just outside the northeast wall of the camp. Gradually the Japanese put them in with the Santo Tomas population, though they maintained themselves as a separate group. Once they began working in a hospital treating internees, they were considered to be part of our camp. They started out in a convent just outside the northeast wall of the camp. The Committee made the girls' school in which the nurses had been staying into a hospital and moved the nurses into what we had been using as an isolation ward. It was one of the two buildings behind the Main Building, and during the days of the university it had been used as a mining engineering laboratory. The other building back there, the one we called the Annex, became a housing for women and small children just days after the beginning of the camp because it had its own kitchen. They put together a diet kitchen to prepare special diets for the children and moved the women and small children to the Annex. So, there was the Main Building, the Education Building (which became important during the liberation), a large gymnasium where the older men were housed, and these two buildings, the Annex and the Nurses Quarters. The nurses maintained the integrity of their own group, but they dedicated themselves completely to the care of the civilian internees. They were very good—if a little rough around the edges. Many of them had only treated the military for so long, but they had been through a lot themselves, even at the hands of their own military. Maude Davidson, the head nurse, had joined the Army in 1918 as a lieutenant, and in 1941, twenty-three years later, she was still a First Lieutenant. I believe she had just made Captain as the war started.

We had all the community functions. In addition to the stage-radio shows, we used to have hobby shows. The stuff in those shows was marvelous: elaborate beer mugs carved out of bamboo; chess sets made out of wooden thread spools; my dad's knitting needles—many things like that. We also had other artists who contributed to the hobby shows. A guy named Hardcastle (Charles Otterman Hardcastle), an old English merchant seaman, had somehow cornered a bunch of house paint. With that house paint and little pieces of board he turned out the most magnificent seascapes.

The Last Year in Santo Tomas

For the first year and a half, there weren't all that many hardships in camp. But then the war started going against the Japanese. Originally, the Japanese Diplomatic Service handled our camp. When the Japanese realized they were losing the war and there was no way out for them, they turned us over to the military. About half way through our time there, in late 1944, the camp was turned over to the Kempei Tai, the Japanese Military Police. At that time, we technically went from being "internees" to "prisoners of war" under the direct control of the Japanese Army.[99] That was when things began to get pretty tough. The regulations got much more strict and the rations began to fall off drastically. The place began to turn into what the American GIs saw when they got there: we were a pretty down-in-the-mouth bunch of people. Wet beriberi was rampant, there was a lot of dengue fever, various intestinal problems—and little medicine to take for these illnesses. People began to die from malnutrition-related problems. While they may not have starved to death, they were so weakened by lack of vitamins that their systems could not combat whatever else came along.

It got to the point where the internees were dying at a rate of five to eight a day. This, of course, does not compare with what happened to the military prisoners, when they were burying two or three hundred a day in the early days of internment.[100]

As new camps like Los Banos were opened, some of us occasionally were transferred. Los Banos was an agricultural extension campus of Santo Tomas University, which they simply improved with a bunch of barracks buildings. About twenty-seven hundred people were moved down here. Realize that the internment camp, and the camp experience, was itself kind of a living organism. It kept changing as time passed. The point at which the GIs came in and got us was as bad as things got.

You'll hear many stories about what the Japanese planned to do with us. There is the story of a mythical "kill order" out there someplace. I've seen a translation of this "kill order"—and believe it could be interpreted to mean practically anything. But in our camp I never saw evidence that the Japs were at all interested in killing us, except by starving us to death if we were left there long enough. And I was happy that MacArthur was able to convince Roosevelt not to follow the plan, proposed by Nimitz, to bypass the Philippines in favor of Formosa or Okinawa.

If the Japanese had seen that they were surrounded, cut off from Japan, I think things might have gotten considerably worse. It is one of those "breaks of the game" that the 1st Cavalry showed up and we got out.

The Liberation

Our U.S. Navy planes started bombing in September 1944. The raids were very spasmodic. Most of them occurred during the daytime, as it would have been difficult to pick out targets at night. The planes, for the most part, came from carrier aircraft: dive-bombers, fighters with aerial combat against Japanese aircraft, and that sort of thing. The Japanese made no effort to protect us from air raids, but the American planes apparently knew very well where we were. There were few Japanese military targets around the camp anyway, and the raids were concentrated in the port area of the bay and the area south of the Pasig River. The only real danger to us was the considerable amount of shrapnel falling from anti-aircraft fire. The shanty roofs were no protection from that. And the Japanese used the falling shrapnel as a reason to herd us all inside so we could not see and could not be seen. We were mostly inside the Main Building during the air raids. From what I remember, nobody was killed or seriously hurt from the air raids.

Just before Christmas (1944) I was in the backyard behind the shanty and heard airplanes, but the noise was entirely different. I looked up and here came a whole flight of B-24s. They had P-38s flying cover for them. This was one of the best sights I have ever seen in my life. We knew what these planes looked like and easily recognized them. Earlier during our time in the camp we had been able to buy balsa wood gliders. When the gliders were broken we would use the wooden parts to make P-38s.

The P-61 Black Widow was a surprise to me, though. I had never seen it before.

These planes would fly at about a thousand feet. The P-38s had nothing to do because they were fighter aircraft and no Japanese planes were in sight. In one of the later raids, they came in from the east. I don't recall hearing any anti-aircraft fire. One of the B-24 bombers moved over, away from the rest of the planes. Smoke was coming out of a right engine. When I first saw the plane coming in from the east, it was clear that it was in trouble. A little trail of smoke was coming from the number four engine, and a little east of the camp the plane started to move right, away from the rest of the planes in the formation.[101] What happened next was a little more dramatic than just bursting into flames. The whole thing blew up! It looked like a bunch of the people got out but I don't know.

In October (1944) we had heard about the landing at Leyte, but we hadn't seen anything. In December, the U.S. established an air base in Mindoro, which is where the B-24s were coming from. We knew something positive was happening, but we didn't know exactly what.

Something happened that had a tremendous effect on the likelihood of our survival as internees: General Yamashita, the Japanese army commander, decided not to defend Manila. He figured—correctly—that the American plan for the invasion of the island of Luzon would closely follow the Japanese plan at the beginning of the war: landings at Lingayen Gulf followed by a strike down the Central Valley to Manila. Yamashita evidently figured that if the Americans weren't stopped by his kamikazes at Lingayen, he would move to the mountains, let the Americans land, and hit them as they came down the valley. This plan should have left

Manila as an open city, as the Americans had left it three years earlier—and our camp wouldn't be dead in the center of 250,000 Japanese defending what was a surprisingly defendable city. (My use of the word "dead" here is carefully chosen.) All this was the good news.

As it turned out, the bad news was that the defense of Manila was left in the hands of one Admiral Iwabuchi and his band of Imperial Navy fanatics. Iwabuchi didn't feel that he was bound by Yamashita's plans for the city. He was going to fight for it, and he did.

Monday, January 1, 1945—In eight days I will begin my 4th year in dear old Santo Tomas University—the concentration camp of 4,000 Americans, British, etc., etc. under Jap rule.[102] *The first two years were none too good, but this third one has been worse day by day until I am down to 105 pounds.*

Breakfast was rice mush, and carefully rationed to one small dipper. Lunch was lucky! The kids and Mom worked all afternoon to collect and cook some crude gabi (a root of some kind) and camote peelings (a native sweet potato). They added a lot to the rationed dipper of soybean soup.

By this time our main preoccupation was food. We had survived without much of it for about a year, and that tends to color one's thought processes. We were pretty far down on the scale of physiological well being, though I don't remember being particularly concerned about it. Mom and Dad were slowing down considerably, and we made jokes about the beriberi.[103] We'd stick our fingertips into our water-filled ankles and watch the holes stay there for several minutes. Any infections we got would last forever, and we'd have to force ourselves to get up several times a night to go to the bathroom because we were so weak. Nobody ran anywhere. They didn't move very much at all if they didn't have to.

But this came on so slowly that I don't think we realized what was going on—at least the kids didn't. I guess that's how starvation works. One morning, instead of waking up, you're just dead.

Air raid siren at 10:00 a.m., but only four of our lads flew over. Just looking, I suppose.

Tues. Jan. 2—More of the same. Rumor has task forces and convoys all around the place, but rumor has had those for years. Just mush and Spanish rice this day. Too weak to carry on with anything else. Beriberi until my legs are rather paralyzed for the last few weeks.

Wed. Jan. 3—Rumor says Bataan is under Navy and air fire with many small landings. Boy, here's hoping.

Thurs. Jan 4—Rumor has a lot of landings south of here about 50 miles. Again, maybe. Planes were over and there were distant explosions. Well, we don't want the air boys here if they are busy on something like that. Glory to 'em.

Fri. Jan. 5—Nothing new today. The meals are poor as usual. There were no air raids or anything else of note.

Sat. Jan. 6—Camp was tied up under raid restrictions all day. Japs burning something vigorously until about 10 to 12 p.m. Rumor has it to be Jap office paper and that our dear "protectors" are all packed and ready to go. Oh, boy! Maybe it's true. I saw the fires under my window anyhow.

Sun. Jan. 7—What a day! Bombs all over the place. Japs pulling out of camp. Rumors wild. Food for two days here only. Well anyhow, those big four-motor planes weren't rumor. Counted those myself—28. Those dive-bombers weren't rumor either.[104]

Mon. Jan. 8—Only one raid today and that one not so nice. Clear sky, 9:00 a.m., and a flight of the big, four-motor planes came over. They dropped their pattern but were flying low enough that a Jap pom-pom (anti-aircraft) got to one of them. It burst into flame and rained destruction all over the country, starting big fires.

Oh, yes! Today is the third anniversary of my arrival to good ol' Santo Tomas. I'm a senior here now.

Tues. Jan. 9—Good air shows today, but we can't see much from here and the novelty has worn off considerably since that first raid on September 21 (1944).

The landings at Lingayen Gulf—about 100 miles north of us—occurred today without much organized resistance except for gawdawful kamikaze attacks against the shipping, which we heard about later.

Wed. Jan. 10—From the terrific air blasting around here today I figure that the boys are "just around the corner." How the big bombers and ground strafers did hit the Japs today! They blew Grace Park Field plumb into the sky, along with other things. The Japs have been adding to the general destruction by blowing up the place themselves. We suppose (rumor) that it is bridges and buildings. Well, come on boys. We hope you've got some food and that you get here while we are still able to at least cheer for you!

Thurs. Jan. 11—What a day! Steady air stuff. Planes flying at 50 feet. Two went right over here at about 300 feet and caused great excitement. Rumor has our general *** [perhaps a reference to MacArthur] in Lingayen along with big landings there (right for a change). But the main question in all our minds can't help but be "When do we eat?"

Fri. Jan. 12—Comparatively a quiet day. Not much to be seen, but considerable distant thumps and bumps to be heard. The boys were busy, all right. And the usual crop of rumors. Well, in this camp, rumors are always optimistic.

Sat. Jan. 13—Well, the boys didn't get here—but the rumors are wilder than ever (and all wrong). A few planes were over today, too, but the bombings were distant. It's pretty obvious that the Japs are licked. Come on USA!

Sun. Jan. 14—A dull day with even very few rumors. Some big explosions and fires, especially on the waterfront. Well, maybe the boys like Sunday off, too.

Mon. Jan. 15—Another dull day. Not much to go on but rumors. Not much to eat, either. No soup at noon. A dipper of mush at 8:30 a.m. and another one with some mushy greens at night isn't much. We haven't seen a Jap plane for a week. Are there any left!

Tues. Jan. 16—Red-letter day on eating. Mom and Sal made the camote peeling detail and got a good mess of peelings. The only thing we feel sure of is that the boys are getting close. Rumors have parachute troops at Malolos, 20 miles away.

Wed. Jan. 17—Another very quiet day except for the usual rumors. Not bad chow today. Camote stew and almost enough of it. One bird flew last night (escape) and friend Commandant Abiko is in an uproar. Threw Pace and Benny Stalker (I don't know who they were) into jail for 15 days (must have had something to do with escape).

Thurs. Jan. 18—Tried going back to work (Handyman). Got pretty tired, but felt pretty good to get back on the job. "Tinker Shop." Strange, isn't it, what queer things can happen to us in a lifetime. My shop grew from necessity and has been much value to the camp for two years. A few planes over but no action.

Fri. Jan. 19—Quiet day. Seems (rumor has it) the Japs have been licked in so many places that they are falling back into three lines of defense around Manila. Our lads are coming from the north and south (north, yes—south, not yet), and both sides are getting set for the showdown. Old General Watchamakaki said this himself in the daily news.

Sat. Jan. 20—A routine day, but the distant bombings seem to be getting steadier. Maybe help is "just around the corner."

Sun. Jan. 21—Sunday is always a dull day for news and so it is today. Four months ago today, our first bombing.

Mon. Jan. 22—Just another day. Worked at my shop as usual. No activity to speak of—only some distant booming that could have been most anything.

Tues. Jan. 23—A day of variation. Not much war, but quite a rain in the p.m.

Wed. Jan. 24—Plenty of war action but far off. Rumors have revived after having been knocked flat for a couple days.

Thurs. Jan. 25—No change today—not even in the rumors—so I'll talk about me. And I'm representative of us all. Beriberi we all have. My feet are badly swollen and my legs are about numb to the knees. I'm so weak I have to rest twice on each of three flights of stairs. My eyes have gone bad in here and I have a bad hernia.

This is all due to extreme weakness owing to a rice diet, and so little of it. Our muscles are so badly gone that our organs just can't function.

Fri. Jan. 26—The war is getting interesting again. Seems to be getting closer. The night and a.m. activity appeared to be field guns and the camp went pretty wild. I know we'll get out of here someday, but how and when depends on the strategy of the Army and Navy. I'll simply take what they do and get out on the day they arrive.

Sat. Jan. 27—Lots of distant booming today, and rumor calls it gun-

fire—but a boom can be just about anything today. Rumor says fighting at Antipolo, which is a little too strong for me, but glorious if true.

Sun. Jan. 28—Not much war to be seen, but a little to hear and plenty of rumors about it. The dope now has a ring around Manila that you could sail your hat over—if you had a hat. Big explosions in town and huge fires in Cavite (a former U.S. Navy base 10-15 miles southwest of Manila)—and that's no rumor. These you can see and hear. Perfect weather for wars, or anything else.

Mon. Jan. 29—Just another day with little to eat. Three dippers of water with some cereal in it. That's what they call three meals. People are dying at the rate of two or three a day now owing to the diet and to just plain starvation. No one can climb a set of stairs without resting on the way up. A lot of Jap demolition today. I wonder what the town will look like when they get through with it.

Tues. Jan. 30—Just another day, and people are tempted to go bugs. The waiting is tough. Five more (internees) died today.

American Rangers and Filipino guerrillas liberated the military POW camp at Cabanatuan—about 60 miles north of us today. This success gave MacArthur the idea for the flying column that led to our liberation.

Wed. Jan. 31—Routine again, with more sloppy stuff called food. More deaths—and what irony! To live and hope so fervently for three years, and then to die in the last few days. I don't bother with rumors much, but the artillery fire is now pretty definite to the north and south. But the wild joy we expected is not present. We wait only in a sort of desperate apathy.

A new operation was launched to the southwest, however, at Nasugbu Bay, about forty-five miles away. Another force was to cut across the top of the Bataan Peninsula to prevent the Japs from retreating down the penin-

sula and making a stand as the Americans had done three years earlier. The force was small, but the noise was big. This may have been what we heard in Manila.

Thurs. Feb. 1—More guns, and rumors of more landing nearby in Cavite (false), Bataan (true), but we are still here in the same old rut. My beriberi gets worse and worse although the rest of me seems to improve—or rather to hold its own. My feet and legs are as wooden as wood, and swollen to about double size.

Yesterday, General MacArthur visited the 1st Cavalry Division in its staging area at Guimba—about 70 miles north. MacArthur told its commander, General Mudge, that he was to mount up his troops and head for Manila. And he meant NOW!

MacArthur gave him some Marine airplanes to fly close air support and clear the roads on the way into town. It was apparently one of these planes that dropped the legendary "Roll Out the Barrel" message into the west patio of the Main Building. You couldn't prove it by me.

I wonder how many other people there were like MacArthur, to whom I probably owe my life.

Fri. Feb. 2—The war must be getting close. Not many planes but almost constant gunfire and blasts near and far. Also fires large and small, in town and out. Life here in camp is quiet enough, however I continue to work on wooden, beriberi legs.

Salvaged some caribou hooves from the Jap discard and cooked a broth out of them.

Sat. Feb. 3—BINGO! A dull day until about 6 p.m., when machine gun fire began popping to the north. At about 4:00 p.m. eight of our planes flew slow and low over camp. We suspected something then, but we only hoped.

But later, the evening brought the ground fire, and then tanks began rolling on Rizal Ave. At 9:00 p.m. they rolled in the gate! The big day at last!

Ever since we had been put into the camp, everyone kept saying "Wait 'til the Marines get here!" You can probably imagine what Dad's smirk was like when the Army—and better yet, his old cavalry buddies—came rolling through the wall. He was always proud of that.[105]

No sleep tonight. Too much fighting. Too many huge fires and explosions. Too much excitement. THIS, my friend, after 37 months, IS IT! The Jap Commandant (Abiko) was killed near the front door. We were sorry about that because we wanted to stamp his face in personally. The rest of the Japs are caught in the Education Building, but are holding some of our men as hostages and hiding among them. We hope to see them dead in the morning. No sleep tonight.

We had been hearing explosions in the distance for quite a while. We knew that the Japanese resistance in the city had fallen way off. Nothing indicated that something like the battle for Manila was ahead.

I was up early on the 3rd. Some planes came over very low. One SBD came from the north, and when he got over the back wall, he dropped lower into the garden. He was flying along between the shanties and me. I doubt if he was 10 feet in the air. I waved at him, and he waved back at me. His gunner, in the back of the plane, was waving too. This was quite an experience. I felt the day had finally come.

About midday that same day it was becoming more obvious that something unusual was happening, though we didn't know what. Sunset came between 7:00 and 8:00 p.m., and we began to see parachute flares and ricochets of tracer bullets off to the north. And then at about 9:00 p.m., there was commotion out at the front gate. I didn't hear it at first, but my mother and sister did. The news began to spread rapidly. My dad and I lived in a room on the third floor of the Main Building facing the Education Building. My mother and sister were on the same floor in the same building in the corner opposite us. They were looking right down the road toward the Main Gate. I wanted to see whatever was happening, so I went over to their room. We watched from their window, and I saw searchlights coming up, just off the road, on the right side. There was concern about whose tanks these belonged to. They had a white star on them, just as did the Japanese tanks. We could see tall guys walking beside the tanks. We weren't sure who these people were. By now they were just inside the gate approaching the plaza area in front of the Main Building. Some thought these might be tall Koreans or somebody working with the Japanese. I figured whoever they were, I wanted a piece of it, so I went downstairs and out the front door. I got over to the corner of the plaza about the time the tank reached it. One of the Japanese officers, Lieutenant Abiko, had also come out of the building. I walked over and met the lead tank.[106] I shook hands with one of the soldiers and went back into the building holding my hand up. I swore I would never wash it again. Abiko had already been shot when I went out the front door. He was on the ground, 30 to 40 feet in front and to the right of the front door of the Main building. Some people were already around him, kicking him. He was in bad shape—alive but bleeding from the mouth and nose. He must have been shot in the chest because he was exhaling blood. I kind of lost track of what was happening here—I had other things on my mind such as talking to the soldiers.

I later learned some of the internees took him into the clinic room, which was just off the front lobby of the Main Building and had been used as an emergency clinic. After they took him in this little long room, a few of the 1st Cavalry troopers went to get Dr. Stevenson out of jail to treat him. Dr. Stevenson, the head doctor in the camp, had been locked up in jail a few days before for refusing to change the cause of death on the many internees' death certificates. He put the cause as "malnutrition." The Japs didn't like that and told him to change it. He said, "Go to hell—go directly to hell!" Dr. Stevenson tried as hard as he could to save Abiko's life but couldn't. Abiko was beyond saving.

Then the fight started over at the Education Building. The tanks had been told that the Japanese had gone over there. That's where their offices were. They took the tanks over there and lined them up in front of the building. They started to shoot the bottom floor from under the building. Then the Japanese started moving up to the second floor. Some of the men and boy internees were on the second floor, but most of them were on the third floor. I went back to my room and could see clearly all the shooting going on. The troopers mounted a 50-caliber on the fourth floor of the Main Building, directly above us. It was the noisiest thing I have ever heard in my life. I could see all these tracers going into the windows of the Education Building and ricocheting down the halls. Then, everybody stopped shooting. Some guy, an internee, got up in the corner window and explained the prisoner situation to the Army troopers. Apparently, when they started shooting, they did not realize the internees were in the building. Eventually they made a deal with the Japanese soldiers and took them back "toward" their own lines at the edge of the city.[107]

MacArthur came into the camp the morning of February 7 before the shelling of the campus started. I got a glimpse of him, but there was a large crowd around him. He was there only about an hour and left.

We were eating out in the hallway of the Main Building when the shelling started. They hit the Main Building many times. The building had been built to be earthquake-proof, so the damage could have been much worse. And many of the internees were packed into the hallway on the bottom floor, away from the direction of the shelling. We didn't join them. Instead we stayed in our room on the third floor.

During this shelling the kids were always looking for shrapnel.[108] At some point, another kid, Bob Cadwallader, and I were walking along the side of the Main Building toward the incoming shelling. We thought we were pretty safe. We got fifteen to twenty feet from the corner of the building when several shells hit the room on the corner. I turned around and ran back to the back of the building toward the chow line where people were standing. I forgot about Bob. About a month later, I got blood poisoning in my leg and they put me in the camp hospital. I was wandering around, and, sure enough, there was Bob Cadwallader. He had gotten a piece of shrapnel in his foot, which damaged his leg. He had been in the hospital from the time of the shelling. I expect the shelling was interesting to me because I never got hurt. Despite getting close to several of the explosions, I never got a scratch.

During the shelling, they put the bodies of the internees killed in the lobby of the Main Building, which then served as a temporary morgue. That was pretty awful. The wounded people were at an aid station in the Education Building.

We were left in the camp, and many more people were brought in. The water supply had been cut because of the fear that it had been poisoned. The sanitary facilities were terrible without any water. During February and into March we were processed to go home.

Then, on March 9, 1945, we were evacuated to Leyte. A couple weeks later, we sailed on the USS *Admiral Capps* for San Francisco with stops at the island of Manus in the Admiralties, just north of New Guinea, and at Pearl Harbor. The *Admiral Capps* was a troop ship—we were stacked six bunks high, though some of the women were given officer staterooms. At Pearl Harbor we picked up some FBI people who debriefed the adult internees on the way home.

Everyone had to list a "home of record." Ours was at my mother's parents' home in Keokuk, Iowa.

When arrived in San Francisco we were put up at the Drake Wilshire hotel for several days. We had been given some kind of voucher book to buy meals and clothing. One day my dad went into a grocery store and got a full basket of groceries. The cashier asked him for his "ration book." He said, "Ration book? What's a ration book? I have no ration book." She said, "Well yes, don't you know a war is going on?"

After about a week in San Francisco, my mother, sister, and myself boarded a train for Keokuk. People were just hanging on the train to get on it. We were surprised to receive a compartment, and we never found out how we got it. Dad stayed on the coast to find a job. He found one at a sugar factory in Santa Maria, California, and we joined him there after about seven months in Iowa. Ever since, I have called California my home.

Dad died in 1961 from smoking, though I suspect his constitution was weakened from his time in Santo Tomas. Mom died several years later in her seventies, and my sister Sally later married and had two children. She died in her forties.

Mary Jane (Brooks) Morse

Mary Jane (Brooks) Morse was just a year old when the Japanese attacked Manila, and four when she and her family were released. Her own recollections of living in the camp are obviously amply supplemented with those of her parents, Robert "Brooksie" Brooks and Pacita Brooks. A chief concern for the internees was getting adequate food. Her father was not well off and found creative ways to supplement his family's diet. Along with descriptions of Japanese cruelty, Mary Jane [Brooks] Morse also tells of the empathetic Japanese soldier who befriended her and would bring food to her family in the middle of the night.

I was born in Manila, Philippines. My parents were also born in Manila. But because my father's father was an American, my father held an American passport. Although he had never been to the United States and his mother was Chinese originally from Shanghai, it was very ingrained in him that he was an American and all of his children were going to be American. My mother is of Spanish and Filipino heritage.

The Japanese started bombing the Philippines on December 8, 1941. They were bombing Clark Air Force Base and Nicholas Field, the army airport near Manila, and Cavite, a naval station across Manila Bay several hours after the Pearl Harbor attack. It [the attack on the Philippines], too, was a surprise attack, and the Japanese bombers destroyed most of the American airplanes before they could even get off the ground.

When the bombing raid came over Manila, everything for a few moments came to a halt in disbelief that this could truly be happening. After all, we had been reassured by General MacArthur that the American armed forces were prepared for any possible Japanese conflict and could protect the Philippine Archipelago. Then everybody started running and confusion broke out. At the time my mother was at work at the Philippine Long Distance Company. She said that everybody left what they had been doing and started pouring out of the building in an attempt to get home to their families. The transit systems stopped in their tracks, leaving the crowd to walk or run home. It took my mother several hours to walk home amid the panicked confusion and the continuing air raid.

The bombing raids continued on for days without opposition. All the ships in Manila Bay and the Pasig River were bombed. At night Manila was in total blackout except for the light from fires that were still burning. Manila was declared an "open city" while the American military forces withdrew and headed for Bataan. There were rumors that the Japanese had landed and would be entering the city of Manila by January 2, 1942.

Young as I was, I can still remember, like a recurring dream (or were they memories of what my parents had told me since I had just turned one?), when the Japanese came into the city. I remember the noise of their marching, the sound of their boots hitting the pavement in unison. Everything in Manila was pitch black at night for many nights. The windows and shutters were closed tightly and we all huddled together. When we peeked out, we could see all these Japanese soldiers with their shiny bayonets and convoy of trucks and tanks all coming down the street. I remember my aunts and cousins screaming at us, "Don't go near the windows! They might shoot us!"

In the daytime, if you were outside and you saw the Japanese coming, you had to bow. If you didn't, they would hit you with their rifle. My mom made sure that from an early age I knew how to bow.

Soon after the Japanese arrived, it was learned that all foreign nationals, especially Americans, would have to register and that they would probably be taken to a concentration camp. It was decided that all of our extended family would move to my aunt's house because it was prudent to all be together to help each other out—safety in numbers. Besides, she had a large home and could use some company because her husband who was captain of a ship belonging to Everett Shipping Lines was at sea.

There were four families, my maternal grandmother, and a young unmarried aunt living together.

The Japanese came into the provinces first. My father and his brother-in-law, my Uncle Albert, an ex-Army man from the U.S., tried to join some of the American armed forces that were retreating to Bataan and Corregidor. Every man counted in the fight against the Japanese. My dad was twenty-four years old and was ready to fight. Unfortunately the Japanese rounded them up and took them to the Army-Navy Club. The men were placed against a wall and told to take everything out of their pockets. They had to put their hands against the wall and remain in that position. They thought they were going to be killed. They stood that way against the wall all night. The next day a convoy truck came and took them to Santo Tomas Prison Camp. That was January 4, 1942.

My mother and I were able to go see my dad, but we were not allowed to see him very often—maybe once or twice a month, and only for an hour or two. We could, however, see him from outside through the iron gate. My dad was not from a wealthy family and had to depend on what we were able to send in. We did his laundry and sent in food. At the gate, the Japanese had a table, and we would hand in a package with my father's name on it. They would check it, and if it was okay, pass it over the table to him. At the beginning, he would put his laundry in a sack, my mother would pick it up, take it home and wash it, and bring it back to him through the Japanese guards. They would very carefully inspect everything.

But then things started to get more difficult. There was a turn in the tide of the war. There were rumors that the Japanese were going to close the gates to Santo Tomas and that there would be no further communications at all—in or out. When it became known that the gate was going to be closed and no one would be allowed to visit, my dad and Uncle Albert went to Carroll Grinnell, Executive Chairman of the Internees, and requested they be allowed to bring their families in. Things were really getting bad on the outside as well as on the inside, and they felt if we were all going to die, we should be together. Grinnell then went to the Japanese commandant and asked if we could come in. It was allowed, as it was for other families in similar situations.

My grandmother (my mother's mother) was opposed to us going in, and asked my mother, "Why do you want to take a two-year-old child into a prison camp?" She [the grandmother] wanted all of us to stay together. Not just us, but Uncle Albert's family also. But my mother and my aunt were young and in love and wanted the family to be together. So in spite of my grandmother's opposition, my mother and I went into camp in January 1943.

When we went in, all the men and boys over about twelve years old were in the Education Building. The Japanese did not allow the families to be together or, more specifically, they did not want husbands and wives together. They did not want to have any babies born in camp, which would mean more mouths to feed.

The women and children were put in the Main Building of the camp.

In one classroom were thirty women and all their children. The room was divided up in imaginary squares, and we took the last open square available. In that square was a wooden slatted cot, which my mother and I both slept on. All we brought with us was a small suitcase with a few personal belongings, mostly clothing. The bathroom was down the hall and was shared by women and children housed in several classrooms. The lineup was long and you had to wait your turn no matter what. This presented a very difficult situation, especially for children.

We were given food tickets and had to line up for food. We would receive only whatever they wanted to give us. The Japanese were never very concerned about feeding us properly. It was only through the auspices of the Red Cross that we got food in the camp.

My dad was young and entrepreneurial, but had very little money. But there were many people in the camp who did have money. They had Philippine currency or would give I.O.U. notes for anything they needed that was available. So my dad and my mother's sister, who was now a widow and owned the house that we all lived in outside the camp, started a Chinese Lunch Box business. My dad would take orders for food from the people in the camp who wanted to buy a good hot meal. He would give the orders to my aunt at the iron gate, and she and my other aunts would cook it [the food] at their home, put the names of the people who had ordered it, and bring it to the camp. This got to be fifty or sixty orders a day. Of course the Japanese guards would inspect it and would have to be given some, but it worked well. My mother's cousin would deliver all these lunches on a calesa (horse and carriage). This is how my dad made it possible for us to survive for the first year we were in the camp and at the same time help my aunt's family on the outside. With the money we were able to buy food for ourselves and other necessities such as soap, candles, matches, and so forth.

All day there were messages blaring over the loudspeakers. But they also played music over them. We would be awakened by the Andrews Sisters some mornings and would have to go out in the main yard at 7:00 a.m. for roll call and in the evening at 7:30 p.m. report to our rooms for roll call again. No matter how young or how old, you had to be present for roll call. At 9:30 p.m. the lights would be turned completely out. You had to stay in your room all night. Sometimes the Japanese would come in and have a roll call at 10:00 p.m. or later or when they suspected something was happening. When some internees tried to escape we would have to stand by our cots and be counted. There was constant commotion and confusion. Also there were many fights, squabbles, and people who didn't get along with each other.

Each room had a monitor who had to deal daily with the numerous problems that arose from overcrowded conditions. My mother was chief monitor of Room 30A. Monitors were also held responsible for any internees that went missing from their room, were drunk, or tried to escape. The Japanese would discipline them harshly.

During the day, we could walk around the camp, stand in the line, and eat in the mess hall with my dad. The camp was well organized by the Americans and British, which kept down the conflicts with the Japanese. There were plays presented and other types of entertainment. The first movie I ever saw in my life was in the camp. It was an Al Jolson movie—I remember "Se-wanee—how I love ya."

Later the Japanese allowed the families to build shanties and live together. The families had to be able to get the supplies to build the shanties themselves. Each shanty area was given a name. We lived in Froggy Bottom because there were a lot of frogs around, especially after the typhoon rains. My dad built a one-room "lean-to" hut with a narrow porch in front and open on two sides so the Japanese could see in at any time. The shanty was made out of Filipino palm and bamboo. There was just enough room for a bed for my parents and a crib for me. We had one shelf for our utensils and supplies. Dad was also able to get a Filipino charol, which is a charcoal and ceramic cooker. That is how we cooked our meals when we had anything to cook.

Soon after, we planted a vegetable garden around the shanty to supplement our meager meals from the chow line. Actually the Japanese requested that we do this individually and on a larger scale to relieve them from the burden of supplying food.

We planted several native vegetables, but the one I remember most fondly was opo, a Filipino squash. This squash grew on vines, which quickly grew up the walls of the shanty onto the roof and through the roof so it hung from the ceiling of our lean-to hut. When the squash grew to full size it looked like a huge light green zucchini and it would dangle from the ceiling just above my crib. It made a great mobile, and I would swing it back and forth just before I went to sleep.

It was so wonderful to be together again with my dad and mother after such a long time living separately. There was not much privacy because you could not close off the shanty so the Japanese could not see in.

When the gates [were] closed, the lunch box trade stopped, and in a short time we had no money to get anything. Things really got bad after a while. For breakfast we stood in line for what was called lugao: water and little bits of rice and greens, plus a few dead bugs. So my dad continued to barter and trade with different people. He was on the garbage detail—everyone except young children had a job to do in the camp—and was able to get things people would throw away. Also his job provided a way he could communicate with the outside. The Filipinos on the outside would come and pick up the garbage. He could send out notes and get information back in, like whether the Americans were coming and other war news. Most people in the camp thought the Americans would come sooner than they did, so news was very important.

Because my dad was trading and bargaining, he could get in food from the outside. The Japanese had ruled that you weren't supposed to have any kind of money. The only money allowed was Japanese issue, which we called "Mickey Mouse" money. At one point, the Japanese somehow suspected my dad of having some contraband money. One day my mother and I were in our shanty and three or four Japanese soldiers raided our shanty, screaming and yelling with bayonets drawn. We had less than a nine-foot shanty, and they were screaming and tearing everything apart. I was about four years old at the time. I cried and cried, and my mother picked me up and sat on the bed with me on her lap. We had no other furniture. I was screaming so loud the Japanese did not make her stand up. They looked under the mattress on one end and then on the other end. Lucky for us, they found nothing. I found out later that my mother was sitting on I.O.U. notes and the other money my dad had received in trading. It was hidden under the mattress right where she was sitting.

My dad had been warned by his friends not to go back to the shanty right away because we were being raided. They found him anyway—

there was no place to hide in the camp—and they put him in jail for about a week. They also suspected my dad was involved in having a radio transmitter. He was not directly involved but did know about it.

While my dad, who was known in the camp as Brooksie, was in jail, my mother took food to the jail for my dad—one or two tins of tuna or Spam and asked the guard there to give it to him. The guard was not a Japanese soldier but an American internee. The committee had organized a small police force to take care of our own problems and to keep the Japanese from killing the people in jail. When my dad came out, Mom asked if he got the food she brought every day. He said he never did receive anything. The guard probably had hungry kids too and he gave it to them. Mom went looking for this American guard and when she found him, she really chewed him out. My mother is a very demure woman but she really let him have it and told everybody about it, but he did not give them the food back.

Like us, there were Japanese soldiers who didn't want to be there. I happened to be very fortunate that one Japanese soldier befriended me as a child, towards the end of our internment. We kids were always outside in the yard playing, usually in front of the Main Building. There were kids of all ages. One of the Japanese guards standing on the roof of the main entrance to the building had two packages of Wrigley's chewing gum—ten sticks. He would throw them up in the air and then catch them himself. Finally, he threw all ten sticks of gum down to the kids. All of the kids scrambled to get a piece. I was only four, so did not get one. I was crying—really crying. A Japanese soldier watching nearby walked over when my mom and dad came to get me and said, "Don't worry. I bring something for little girl tonight."

At 2:00 a.m. that night, my dad was awakened in the shanty and looked out and saw a Japanese guard. He thought—they're here to get him again. But it was the Japanese soldier. He had brought sugar and meat for me. He told my dad he had a little daughter at home the same age, and I reminded him of her. My mom had cut my hair in bangs like his daughter probably had. He came back many times and brought us food and continued to do so, always in the wee hours of the night, until the Americans came.

For months before the Americans came to the camp, there were many air raids. I remember all the confusion, the airplanes and bombing. We would all have to stop what we were doing and run. Wherever we were, we tried to run into a building or air raid shelter or something. Air alerts and actual air raids were constant throughout the day. Even to this date, when I hear a plane making a similar sound, I can remember that time. It was a scary time—we didn't know what was happening. You always heard a lot of confusion outside the camp—people running, shelling, and all sorts of noises.

The day I remember the most was the last day, February 3, 1945. Everyone was running around—there was a lot of commotion. People just didn't understand what was happening. I remember we were running from our shanty towards the building. When the Americans were approaching, the Japanese were also scurrying around—trying to get out of there.

My mom and I were not with my dad as we ran from our shanty towards the Educational Building looking for him. The Japanese guards pushed us into the Educational Building. A lot of male internees were trying to get in the building because that's where a lot of them stayed.

Everyone thought the bombs would be dropping on the campus shortly and we would be safer in a building.

The Japanese would not let the men go in the Educational Building but were pushing the women and children into the building. I was in my mother's arms and remember my mom begging the Japanese guard, "No, No! We have to go look for my husband! Please let us go!" And to me she kept saying, "Mary, we have got to get out of here. We can't stay here." But he would not let us go out of the building. As they were closing the big doors to the building, two of the guards were distracted by all of the bombing and strafing outside and turned their backs to us. As they pushed the others in, we ran out the door. We took a chance of being shot. We ran back to the shanty and on the way found my dad who was running back yelling, "The Americans are here—the Americans are here! The tanks are breaking through the gates."

We hid until the Americans came in after dark and later learned the Japanese were holding hostages in the Educational Building—64 Japanese soldiers were holding 221 internees hostage. The Americans started firing into the building until they learned what the situation was. They negotiated almost two days before the hostages were released. My mom and I came that close to being part of the hostage group.

Later that first night (February 3, 1945), everybody was just going crazy. My dad, like many others, saw the Japanese Major Abiko killed when the American soldiers thought he was going for his gun and shot him. Actually, we later learned he had a hand grenade in his jacket. Many of the internees pounced on him while he was down and hacked away at him until he was taken away. In the following days, the Japanese continued to shell Santo Tomas Internment Camp. Several internees were killed and many were wounded. The west side of the Main Building was badly wrecked by shelling. The Education Building, which was turned into a hospital, was hit by shelling, and some were wounded. We could still hear guns firing and yet some of the internees were just running around, paying no attention to it whatsoever.

After we were rescued and before we left the camp, we learned that the retreating Japanese were burning and destroying the city of Manila and killing thousands of Filipinos. And, as it turned out, it was safer for us to be in camp than on the outside. The Japanese were massacring everyone—Spanish, Filipinos, Swiss, and even Germans. One of my cousins was in Mabini, a part of Manila not far from Manila Bay, an area where the Japanese were retreating. My cousin (a young boy at the time), his mother, and his brother went into an air raid shelter, which was kind of a dugout. There were many other Filipino civilians with them in this shelter. A Japanese soldier found them in there and threw a hand grenade in the air raid shelter. All were killed except for my cousin, who survived because his mother shielded him with her body, but he was critically wounded. It took him a day to crawl back to my grandmother's house.

We were there about another month before we left Santo Tomas. When we left we were put on Army convoy trucks to be shipped out. We had been given warm Army clothing because we had little clothing of any kind. We were sent to the U.S. on a Navy ship, the USS *Eberle.* There were very many of us, probably in the thousands. Men and women were separated. We were in a hold—five bunks high. My mother was seasick the whole trip—twenty-five or thirty days. Most of the children had lice. All of the children were told to report to a room and were sprayed. We never found out what they were spraying us with, but it got better.

On the trip back to the States, Japanese submarines were spotted and we thought we were all going to be killed. The war was not over, even though it seemed like it was to us. We knew the Japanese submarine would not care if these were civilians on board or not, nor would they know since we were on a Navy ship. After several hours they left with nothing happening, but this was a time when we thought that was it.

Most people do not realize that the U.S. Armed Forces, Far East, at the time the Japanese came to take the Philippines, were made up mostly of Filipinos and also members of the Reserve Officers Training Corps of the Philippines. My mother lost her brother because he was in the Army and was killed on the Bataan march. He was only nineteen and part of the Army Reserve Training Corps. So many people were hurt and suffered and died during the war in the Philippines, not just those in the camps. When the Japanese came into the Philippines, my uncle went to my grandmother and told her he had to go. She begged him not to go. He had only received a few weeks training in the ROTC, but he knew he had no choice—he had to go. And he died.

In closing, we would like to express our deepest gratitude to you, Robert Holland, the First Cavalry Division, and all those who risked their lives to set us free. During the darkest days, we lived in fear that our captors would kill us all. Later through military intelligence interception, General MacArthur learned that the Japanese did in fact plan to kill all prisoners of war in internment camps throughout the Philippines. Thanks to all of you, this did not come to pass.

Lieutenant Colonel Madeline Ullom
United States Army Nurses Corps, Rtd.
January 1, 1911–October 3, 2001

I don't consider myself a hero. None of us do. But even though women were not supposed to be on the front line, on the front lines we were. Women were not supposed to be interned either, but it happened to us. People should know what we can endure.

—Lt. Col. Madeline Ullom, USA, NC (Ret.)[109]

Madeline Ullom endured a lot. She was a nurse at Bataan and Corregidor, working under dangerous and incredibly trying conditions, unsure if she would even live through the war. She came to Santo Tomas relatively late in the war. There she again showed her strength and courage, caring for the internees in the camp with her fellow nurses.

I joined the Army on April 6, 1938. I graduated from Thomas Jefferson Hospital in Philadelphia and stayed on the staff at Jefferson for about a year. I had to pass the State Boards because you had to be a registered nurse to go into the Army. After I passed, I was sworn into the Army at the Quartermaster Depot in Philadelphia. I was told I would be stationed at Walter Reed Hospital in Washington, D.C.

I liked the Army very much at Walter Reed. I went to work in the operating room. When I told them I wanted to take care of patients, I was assigned to patient care on wards and in the operation room, where I was also a scrub nurse. I worked with another nurse there, an anesthetist. Her name was Ann Mealor from Alabama. Ann later went to the Philippines. Before she left I told everyone that if I had surgery of any kind, Ann had to give me the anesthetic. Then after she left, I said I couldn't have my appendix out because she was gone!

About six months after Ann left, the chief nurse called me in and asked if I still wanted to go to the Philippines. I said yes. I told her I was happy at Walter Reed, but I did want to go. She said I would probably go in June 1940, and I did.

We sailed on the USS *Republic,* a ship that had been a German luxury ship before World War I. The route was through the Panama Canal. There were four nurses from Walter Reed who went together. Two of them were Pennsylvania nurses, Adele Foreman and Clara Mueller. Since there were seven nurses on board the ship instead of the usual five, they took everything alphabetically. Juanita Redmond and I ate with two colonel's daughters. The ship was full of lieutenants who had just graduated from West Point and married. Every evening when they had "happy hour" these young couples would invite us to join them. My friend Ethel Thor and I were in a room just down the corridor, so we knew many of these young people.

We couldn't get off at Guam when we arrived because there was a case of measles, which for them was a deadly disease. A day out of Guam, we were initiated into the King Rex "Order of the Deep" when we passed the International Date Line. That was an all-day affair. The day before we arrived at the Philippines, we received a radiogram welcoming us. We received another radiogram saying all five of us would be assigned to Sternberg Hospital in Manila, which was the Army Headquarters Hospital in the Philippines. Another hospital was located on Corregidor and one at McKinley and Fort Statsenberg.

When we arrived at Manila, a band was playing, and Miss Messiner, the chief of the Filipino Department and Sternberg nursing, was there to greet us. She said, "The first thing we are going to do is to take you to the Army-Navy Club and you will meet many Army personnel." So they whisked us off in a limousine to the Army-Navy Club. When we arrived there, everyone was offering us a drink and we didn't know who these people were. We all said, "No thank you. Not right now."

Someone told us, "Listen, you will be paying part of the bill for drinks; next time you might as well take one." We spent about five hours visiting. Then, they took us to our nurses' quarters, which were at the corner of Conception and Arrocares streets in Manila. It was across the street from the government complex of the Philippines. They were constructing the Legislative Building at that time. When we were taken to our rooms, our baggage was already there. Each one of us had a "sponsor" to help us. They arranged everything for us. A lavendora was assigned to each individual who would put our clothes in the closet and dresser drawers. The light in the closet burned all the time to keep away moldiness on account of the dampness. We were placed at the last table in the dining room because everything went according to rank.

We went on duty the next day and found out what we were supposed to do. Many of the doctors had been at Walter Reed Hospital when we were stationed there. So it was really "Walter Reed Hospital at Sternberg." Sternberg had nine wards; Miss Messner rotated the nurses from one ward to another. It was very hot in the tropics with no air conditioning, only ceiling fans.

I was assigned in the Officers' Ward at Sternberg. When General MacArthur took over, he had his staff working eighteen and twenty hours a day. I had several of his aids who came in the hospital as patients because they were sick from working long hours under pressure. Every morning, Colonel Southerland would come in at eight o'clock and give the aides their work for the day even though they were patients in the hospital. Major Gillespie was trying to get these patients well. Yet they were given all this work to do. As the bombing by the Japs increased, the nurses were working almost around the clock.

By the end of December 1941, almost everybody had departed from Sternberg in Manila to Bataan and Corregidor. About twenty Americans and ten nurses remained in Manila. Manila had been declared an "open city." About 2:00 a.m. on December 29, 1941, I was called and told to bring my musette bag and go down to the living room of the nurses' quarters. I heard rumbles of tanks going by. I proceeded to the porch to see what was going on. The chief nurse came out and shouted, "You get back in here! You don't know whose tanks they are!" I went back in. Later I was told to get into an ambulance without lights on, and we all headed out, dodging bomb craters in the dark. We reached the dock. A Navy officer there, Ensign Beale, was supervising the loading of documents on a submarine. Another Navy officer was supervising the refueling of the submarine. He was the officer who soon would order that many tanks and other storage places throughout the area be blown up. One of these officers yelled at us, "Get on that little boat, immediately!" We dashed onto the boat. After we were on the boat, a shell hit that dock where we had been standing and blew it to bits.

Manila had been bombed, bombed, bombed. There were many sunken ships in the harbor. It was a deep harbor, and the ship came right up to the dock. So the captain of this little boat hid us behind the shadows of these big sunken ships. We stayed right there until five o'clock the next morning. The Japs tried to get to us but they couldn't. After 5:00 a.m., we went through the minefields in the water on over to Corregidor.

When we reached Corregidor, there was an air raid on. Someone shouted, "Get off that boat, quick!" A big truck came by—didn't even stop. The soldiers just reached down and grabbed us and put us up on the truck. The driver said, "We're taking you to Malinta Tunnel."

We had heard about Malinta Tunnel and we knew it was restricted and top secret.

The truck drove into the tunnel. There were railroad tracks in both directions. Because of the air attack going on then, they had received many casualties. I went in right straight to the operating room. My friend Ann Mealor was giving the anesthetics, and I was the scrub nurse, just like old times at Walter Reed. This was my first day over there on Corregidor.

The Japs shelled us morning, noon, and night. General MacArthur and his group; Sayer, who was the high commissioner, and his group; and President Quezon and his group had left Manila Christmas Eve and gone over to Corregidor. The Corregidor hospital on topside was bombed on December 29. These three groups had just moved their offices down to Malinta Tunnel. Here we nurses were, right in the middle of all these activities.

President Quezon's term was running out, and he had been re-elected, so they held the inauguration in the tunnel. They found an old, antique organ they brought in. They had the inauguration in the tunnel. I went to the inauguration. All the band instruments had been blown up. They played the Presidential March on this old organ. President Quezon spoke and pledged his support to the Americans. General MacArthur acknowledged President Quezon very briefly. He said we had our freedom, and it meant so much to us. And that we would work together with the Filipinos.

The Quezons lived in one of the laterals, and the Sayers lived in another lateral.[110] There were hardly any bathroom facilities. The bathroom was in a lateral, and we all had to use the same one. They would not bother the nurses early in the morning, knowing we had to go on duty. In the beginning we did not have toilets. We just had big cans, which they emptied daily. Later they put in better bathroom facilities.

We were assigned beds in a lateral. When you went into the lateral, there was not a door but only a sheet hung over the opening to the room. Miss Davison, the chief nurse, had a little desk inside the lateral next to her bed. We were very lucky to have Miss Davison as chief nurse. She had been a World War I nurse and had a great deal of wisdom and daring. She was staunch, and her word was law. In the lateral, our beds were head to toe, head to toe. In the hospital a lateral was assigned for post-operative patients and one for medical patients.

The Japs would bomb us every day. They would start at about ten o'clock in the morning because about 8:00 a.m., "photo Joe" would fly over and photograph places they had hit or would look to find gun emplacements and places like that. I used to go on duty early in the morning. I would give baths first thing in the morning. About ten, I would eat lunch. By that time, "photo Joe" would have had time to develop his pictures, so they would start bombing about then. So then they would need extra help in the operating room.

Little Arthur MacArthur was about four years old at that time.[111] He would come to the mess hall and sit across from me and eat his lunch. He was real cute. His amah took care of him and would bring him in. He wore a little overseas cap and he would play soldier and walk up and down the lateral.

I continued to work in the operating room all the time. Maybe I would get supper at 6:00 p.m. or maybe ten at night, depending on whether I was needed in the operating room. After dark, it usually was quiet and Carl Mydans and all the correspondents would gather in the mess hall.[112] They used to talk about what was going to be broadcast on the news to the States. They always broadcast from Corregidor. The announcers would always end with, "Corregidor still stands!" When the Japs took over later, one of the troopers said, "Yes, Corregidor still stands, but under new management." They broadcast back to the States about nine o'clock at night. Everything that went out on the news, General MacArthur had reviewed ahead of time. MacArthur's headquarters were just down the hall in another lateral next to the Navy tunnel and the Army tunnel.

The walls in all the laterals were bashed out. Because of the very sharp granite, it was real dangerous to be near these walls. During bombing and shelling, the dust coming in through these walls was terrible. We took wet gauze and put it over the nose and mouth of the patients to breathe through.

"We were bombed the night before, we were bombed today and we're going to be bombed like we've never been bombed before. They're over us! They're over us! One little hole for the four of us. Thanks be to God there are no more of us, or they'd get the whole damn [crew]." We would chant, "We are the battling bastards of Bataan. No Father, no Mother, no

Uncle Sam. No guns, no artillery pieces, no supplies and nobody cares a damn."

One day, Major "Pick" Legrande Diller, who later became a general, said to me, "What's new today?" I said, "Well, there's a new poem out, but I don't think I ought to tell it to you." "Why?" he asked. "Because, it's kinda bad," I said. "Tell me anyway," he said. So I recited the poem [above]. He laughed and said, "That's great! We'll put it on the air tonight to the States."

The Japanese kept closing in on us. There was barge after barge— barges filled with Japanese everywhere. Everybody was out fighting— even patients got out of bed who could hardly walk, to fight them off. The Marines had been assigned to General MacArthur. They had barricaded the entrances to Corregidor with barbed wire and everything they could find to ward off the enemy. The Marines were out there fighting.

There weren't too many Marines, but they seemed to be everywhere. It was hand-to-hand fighting. It really was. [Madeline cried as she recounted this.] The Japs kept coming. General Wainwright was there. The casualties were being brought in. We were working day and night. We couldn't handle all the patients. The engineers had welded the beds together, double-deck beds and then triple-deck beds. All the beds were filled.

Finally, the Japs' demolition troops penetrated Malinda Tunnel. General Wainwright said, "This is it!" It still went on all night and into the next morning. One of the corpsmen bringing in a casualty said, "They took out the white flag!" General Wainwright was going to broadcast the surrender the next day at ten o'clock. Captain Richardson, a dentist, had a radio, so we all gathered around the radio to hear the surrender broadcast. Everyone was crying [Madeline was crying as she said this]. The troops had fought so gallantly. They fought when they had no ammunition. We didn't have food. We didn't have anything. We were destitute.

The Japs sent a colonel to accept the surrender. Then General Wainwright had to go over the next day and meet with Japanese General Homma. They wanted all the Philippines; all the islands. General Wainwright told them he was only the commander of Luzon. The Jap General told him, "You have to get the Southern Islands and the Northern Islands, and they have a general in charge there who must agree to the surrender." They had to send emissaries out to those places to agree that we had surrendered all of the Philippines. All of them agreed to it.

The Japs said, "You are now entering the era of greater East Asia—co-prosperity." In another breath they added, "Every offense against the Japanese is punishable by the death penalty. Not only the offender but ten members of his same unit will also be executed for the offense."

A few days later, there was a large group of Jap Army generals and Navy admirals that came through Malinda Tunnel, about twenty of them. As they came through, they arrived at the nurses' lateral. The leader started to pull open the sheet, which covered the entrance to the nurses' lateral. Captain Davidson was instantly on her feet. She said, "Halt! You cannot come in here without permission!" And "Halt" they did! They looked at her standing in the entrance and turned on their heels and walked away. Instantly, she realized what she had done—that we were Japanese captives. She ran down to our commander's office, Colonel Wibb Cooper, and told him what she had done. For the next three hours, we wondered what offense she had done to the Japanese, let alone telling them to halt! And we wondered who would be the other ten who would be executed with her. After that, a Japanese soldier brought a large white sign with black Jap characters on it and put it up by our door. Nobody, nobody again ever attempted to come into the nurses' quarters.

It appeared that everyone—nurses, doctors, and patients—were simply being relocated to a hospital on Luzon in Manila. The next morning at the dock, the women were put on small boats and ferried out to the freighter. There was no gangway or hull ramp; we had to climb a long rope ladder to the deck.

The Japanese took us over to the Santa Catalina Girls Dormitory, which was across the road from Santo Tomas. They put us in two rooms. One was an eating room, and one was a sleeping room upstairs. We were not allowed to see any other of the prisoners.

The Japs thought we were very dangerous people because we had volunteered to be in the Army. Not only that, we had been taking care of restoring the health of the people who were fighting their efforts. The Navy nurses, with the exception of Bernatitus, who was a surgical nurse, had stayed in Manila all that time. So we were considered very dangerous people. So when the internees brought the food for us to eat downstairs, after we finished we had to go back upstairs. Then the internees would come back and clean up. We could not be there when other internees were in the room.

We were in the Santa Catalina dormitory seven weeks in just these two rooms. It gave us a chance to rest up from what we had been through on Corregidor and not do any nursing. A couple weeks later they let a chaplain come in with his wife and she brought some old magazines, pencils and paper, and so forth.

They had special guards around us. A garden with a Hibiscus hedge fence around it was in the back. We asked them if we couldn't get out-doors and walk in that little garden. They finally said yes, but with ad-ditional guards when we were there. They let us walk one hour in the morning and one hour in the afternoon. Every morning and afternoon, these big Jap guards would stand all around the garden. One of the Jap guards decided to be friendly to a nurse. She was inside the fence and he was outside. He said to her, "O-hi-o" like saying "hello" in English. You are supposed to reply "O-hi-o Guayamu. The nurse said, "Oh yes, yes, Cincinnati!" They looked at each other, and neither knew what the other was talking about.

Ann Mealor had a class every day on etiquette. We had to do some-thing. Ann made us all do exercises. In the morning we had our "finish-ing school," which is what we called the class on etiquette.[113] Ann taught us "Army etiquette." Many of these nurses had arrived in the Philippines in November 1941. Most of them had just finished training when they came. Ann also taught them "Army etiquette." We all graduated from the fitness school.

After seven weeks, we moved over to Santo Tomas. We went into the School of Mines Building. After we left the School of Mines Build-ing, it was made into a hospital for communicable diseases. Then it was changed to an isolation hospital for communicable diseases for all pa-tients. We moved to the Main Building. The first assigned housing put us in kind of a corridor. There was no ventilation. It was awful. We went to the Relief Office, and they provided each one of us with a little bed with five slats about four inches wide. It also had a kind of mattress that was filled with weeds and stuff. And that is what we slept on. Then they put us in four rooms on the second floor, front and center of the Main

Building. I was in room 41. It was directly opposite the guardhouse of the Japs.

One night we were in our room and the one light we had burned out. What you had to do is find a Manila Gas and Electric man. That man would get a bulb and he would come and replace the burned out one. We had a little table inside the door of the room. When the man took the burned light bulb out, he didn't throw it away, thank goodness. He put it on this little table. The light had gone out about a quarter of eight. We were all lying in our beds in the dark. After he replaced the bulb and left, someone said, "Does anyone want this light on?" We had to have it out by nine o'clock anyway, so we said to turn it off. We were all very tired. Because of such hard work, we always slept very deeply. About five minutes after nine, the light came on in our room. The room was full of Jap guards pointing their guns with shiny bayonets at us saying, "We know who you are! We know you are Army officers. We know what you're doing. Who are you contacting? What are you saying? What are you telling them? Where are they?" We all sat up in bed. We were so sleepy that for a minute we didn't realize what they were saying. One of the girls finally had the presence of mind to say, "The light went out, and we had to get the man to change it." "We know what you are doing! What are you telling our enemies?" They went on and on. The girl said, pointing, "There it is! There is the burned out bulb." The leader finally decided that was all it was. He picked up the bulb and they marched out with it. We couldn't go back to sleep that night. We never knew when we were going to meet our Maker.

The hospital where we worked was about a block from the Main Building. There was a road there, and they closed it off at both ends. The hospital was in a convent. The nuns were there on the other side of the wall next to us. There was also a chapel there. We stayed and worked under these conditions for a total of thirty-three months at Santo Tomas, the oldest university under the American Flag, established 1611.

On February 3, 1945, Rosemary and I were on afternoon duty. We came off at 7:00 p.m.

As we walked along the road to our quarters, we looked at each other and said, "Do you hear what I hear?" "Those are our guns that are firing!" We ran to our room and said to the girls there, "The Americans are out there! We heard their guns!" "We can tell by the firing." We heard the ground rumbling from the tanks. We were in total darkness. Back by the bathroom, the only light in the building was a little can of coconut oil burning. Each of us was going to the bathroom three or four times a night because of our diet. So when you came back to the room from the bathroom, you counted the room. There were over forty people in most rooms. We would get in our bed and someone would say, "Get out of my bed! You're in my bed!"

Lieutenant Abiko, the head of the Jap guards, came out. We all hated him because he was so mean to us. The executive officer of the 1st Cavalry was here. He hadn't taken his eyes off Lieutenant Abiko. Abiko reached inside his shirt to get a grenade. He wanted to kill everyone around there. We hadn't been dying fast enough for him. Major Gerhard put a shot right through Abiko's neck. He fell down. He didn't die instantly but bled furiously. But later, he did die. Dr. Stevenson, who had been in charge of our hospital, looked down at Abiko.

Dr. Stevenson had told us that a few weeks earlier, seven men died in the hospital in a few hours. He had to make out the death certificate and he put for cause of death, "Died from malnutrition and starvation." The Japanese doctor had told him he had to change it. Dr. Stevenson said he could not—he had taken the Hippocratic oath. "I cannot change that diagnosis on their death certificate." The Japanese said they would put him in jail if he didn't change them. The Japs had a special jail for men and women prisoners. So they had put Dr. Stevenson in jail, and he was there until that night when the 1st Cavalry released him.

I was walking around near the front of the Main Building, and I saw a 1st Cavalry officer with his leg hurt and limping badly. I walked up to him and said, "What's the matter with you? How did you get that?" He said, "Oh, it's nothing. Just got hit by a grenade." I said, "I am a nurse. Come go with me and I will put a bandage on it." I took him over to the hospital and dressed his wound. When I got finished treating his wound, I realized I had to make out an emergency medical treatment form. I grabbed the form and a pencil and asked, "Name please!" He said, "Conner, H. L., Lt. Colonel." I said, "Conner, H. L., Lt. Colonel?" He looked at me as much as to say, "I just told you that." I said, "Are you any relation to Colonel Haskett Lynch Conner of the Army Medical Corps?" He said, "That's my dad."

His dad was the president of the Physical Evaluation Board in Philadelphia when I had the physical to join the Army. He had told me when I joined, "Now we don't want any mistakes in all this. When you get your orders, come down to Grays Ferry Avenue and to the Quartermaster Corps. I will take you over to Captain Jones's office and he will swear you in.

I talked with this Colonel Conner as long as he could stay. Of course, he was delighted to give his parents' address to me. I wrote to them for a long time. Not only was his father an Army doctor, his mother was an Army nurse. I continue to correspond with the younger Colonel Conner and had a letter from him about a month ago.

There was quite a skirmish at the Main Gate. Some of the Japs were trying to force their way out on trucks. And some of the Japs with machine guns took over the Education Building with many male internee hostages. A great deal of activity was in progress, and we worked in the operating room until 3:00 or 4:00 a.m.

In a few days the Japs began shelling Santo Tomas and hit the Main Building. The main water tank was destroyed. The operating room was moved back in the library of the Main Building. General MacArthur had already been there early that day (February 7) and left. During this shelling, which started February 7, we had 117 injured and 17 died.

A very famous lawyer was operated on that night. He was supposed to be the most brilliant lawyer in the Philippines. He was hit in the head by a shell fragment and had surgery. Unfortunately, he was one of those who died. His name was McFee.

At the beginning of the war, all the Allied ships at sea at that time in the Far East were ordered to the Port of Manila. They had on these ships many educators, scientists, consultants—professional men of all kinds. The people from these ships were located in Santo Tomas with us. There were many high-ranking people there. This lawyer, McFee, was one of the last ones we operated on that night. We finally finished about 2:00 a.m. and I said to Ann, "There's a little alcove here by the library. I'm going to lay a blanket on the floor and rest there for a while. But I'll be right by the door if I am needed." She said that was fine. So I went asleep in this room.

All of a sudden I began to wake up. It was getting [to be] daylight. I was conscious of movement going on all around me and smelled a different odor. As I lay there, I saw two men take a body out. Then all around me I saw several others, also carrying out bodies. They were the people we had operated on who had died during the night. They had temporarily stored these bodies in this little room for the rest of the night. Here I was, sleeping with all the bodies around me. When I realized what was happening, I sat up quickly before they grabbed my blanket and carried me out.

The internees being held by the Japanese in the Education Building were released on February 5. The Japanese were marched out of the camp. In STIC, there were about 600 children. They kept shouting to the U.S. troops.

On February 7, General MacArthur came and there was a great celebration. That afternoon, after he had left, the Japanese had regrouped and started shelling the camp. It was constant; they were shelling us all the time. One of the shells hit the roof of one of the buildings where there was a big water tank, which was our emergency supply of water. We lost something like 4,000 gallons of emergency water in that tank. We lost it all. That had a terrible effect in the sanitation in the camp. It was really bad before they could get enough water to replenish what had been lost in the shelling. Of course, many were killed or injured, and we were taking care of the casualties. We were still in the Main Building although most of the time those of us who worked in the operating room slept in the operating room because we were constantly being called. It was a terrible time.

On February 11, a field hospital arrived. Willa Hook, who had been with us and was one of the "angels," was the chief nurse of this field hospital. On February 12, the next day, early in the morning we were suddenly told to be ready to leave immediately—quick!

We were told to take our musette bags with us, and we were loaded on several trucks. We didn't have time to say good-bye to anybody. These fellows would just take our musette bags and help us up on the trucks. We were just crammed onto these trucks. First thing we knew, we were speeding down Dewey Boulevard. There was a plane waiting for us. They shoved all of us on the plane. The plane was terribly overloaded and had a lot of trouble taking off the ground because of the number of people on it. They finally squeezed all of us in and the plane took off. The Japanese fired some shots at us but we kept on going up. We were on our way to Leyte. On the way, we stopped at Mindora. We were then put on two planes because we were so crowded. Then we went to Leyte.

When we reached Leyte, everybody was out to see us. They had a table there where all the nurses stationed there put all their lipsticks and cosmetics for us to help ourselves. They also gave us a garment. We thanked them for it. We were in the Army hospital there on Leyte. They had all of us located in one ward.

The next morning, they said to us, "We see you have your old uniforms on." We had put back on our khaki skirts and shirts. "What do you think of the new uniforms?" they asked. We said, "Well, we don't know. We haven't seen them." They looked rather puzzled and said, "But we gave you each one of the uniforms last night." "Oh, that garment you gave us," we replied. "Yes," they said, "that's the new uniform." "OK," we said. "We thought the Army got very sensible, and we thought those were bathrobes because they are seersucker." "We took a shower and then we put them on." We had no idea that was the new uniform we were wearing.

We listened to all the conversations going on around us at the time. We heard them saying, "Well, today is the day that the wax arrives." "Oh, we will be so happy when the wax gets here." "We need wax so badly." "Yes, there is a whole shipload of wax coming." It will be good to have more wax." Finally, we summoned enough courage to ask, "Would you mind telling us; what in the world are you going to do with all this wax that is coming?" "You need wax so badly that you have a whole shipload coming?" "What do you do with this wax?" They looked at each other and then us and said, "Guess you don't know!" "No," we said. "We don't know, but all we have been hearing about is all this wax." "Well," they said, "WACS are Women's Army Corps. That's what they are, W - A - C - S!" "Oh, we thought it was wax, like you put on the floor," we said. We realized then we had a lot to learn.

Army Public Relations and Intelligence and all of those specialties interviewed us. Everybody was pushing in to talk with us. A place down on the beach was set up for interviewing where we could be interviewed in seclusion. People couldn't just come around anytime to talk with us. They had to make arrangements to do so. Then they gave us physicals and the dentists examined our teeth. That went on for a couple days. In the meantime, we were eating very well and resting. We had been moved to little pup tents and were enjoying the seclusion.

Eleven of our nurses were quite ill. They were going to send them home on a hospital plane because they were all getting IVs [intravenous fluids] and were quite sick. The rest of us were going to go back home to the States in two different planes. The reason for two planes was that they were going to take out the division between the two seats so we could lie down.

We started off from Leyte—early in the morning. The first place we stopped was Johnson Island. The men there had not seen a woman in over a year. When we arrived there, we went to have breakfast. And here were all these fellows; just sitting around the mess hall walls, watching every move we made. We had breakfast, including ice cream. It was so good! The first ice cream I'd had in many years. And they had lots of fruit of every kind: apples, oranges, bananas, and so forth. They had bowls of fruit around in the mess hall. We told them, "We appreciate the fine breakfast, but would you mind if we took an orange or apple with us to eat later?" They said, "Yes, we would mind, but you just wait right here." About fifteen minutes later, here they came with bags of fruit. They gave each one of us a bag of fruit to take with us on the plane.

The next place we stopped was Kwajalein. When we arrived at Kwajalein, we were taken to the officers' quarters. The officer quarters were called "Hells Belles." So we went to Hells Belles. We went in the dining room, and they had a table with all kinds of cakes, cookies, and candy. We helped ourselves and put some in our pockets to take with us. We had our lunch at Hells Belles and soon after left for Honolulu.

When we landed at Honolulu, they wanted to have a big parade and a lot of things like that. But the decision was that would be too strenuous for us. They did take us on a sightseeing trip around the island. No one bothered us or watched us. The next day, they took us to the PX (Post Exchange). They gave each of us $50 of our traveling money, and we could spend it any way we wanted. We could buy a suitcase, or a pair of nylons, or anything we wanted.

We had a good time in Hawaii. They cut our hair, polished our fingernails, gave us presents, and did all these nice acts for us. General Richardson was living in one of the movie actresses' homes. He had a dinner for us. It was a gorgeous place. The food was awfully good. By that time we were eating very well.

After about a week in Honolulu, we flew to California. We arrived at Letterman Hospital in San Francisco, and they assigned us to a ward where each of us had separate rooms. We were there only about fifteen minutes when an Army finance officer came and paid each one of us in full for past salary. We had a lot of money. We had another complete physical. We were at Letterman about ten days. After that, all of us who wanted to stay there a little longer could. They started issuing our orders to go home. We could stay home as long as we wanted to. Most of us thought a month would be long enough. We could determine that later. No specific return date was on our orders.

Omar Kahyam decided he would have a dinner in San Francisco for us.[114] Long before then, about a year and a half earlier, we nurses had made a promise to each other. We made a promise that after we came back that if any person served rice to us, we would throw it back at them. That was our solemn promise. Well, it came the night of this very special dinner. Omar Kahyam had closed his restaurant that night just for us. He had the restaurant beautifully decorated. Everything was wonderful. There was a tremendous menu. I remember they had "rose petal" ice cream. We were all seated at our tables. The cooks came out of the kitchen with big trays of roasted turkeys. They paraded around the dining room showing the turkeys to us. Then they sliced the turkeys and served each of us with a big plate filled with choice food. We looked, and on the plate was white and dark turkey meat, stuffing and gravy, vegetables, and much more. The plates were just loaded down with food. We looked and there was rice. How could we throw rice at Omar Kayham? Then we looked more closely. It was "wild" rice. Wild rice is not rice. We ate the special wild rice and enjoyed a luscious dinner.

Omar Kahyam invited us up to his penthouse. It overlooked the Golden Gate Bridge. We stayed until midnight, talking and visiting.

People in San Francisco wanted to interview us, but they were not allowed to because they said that it would be too traumatizing. They sort of continued our isolation. We did go on a tour of San Francisco. All the people we saw were all dressed up and they looked like they were in the movies. They were all going different places. They all had hats on. It looked for all the world like we were watching a movie.

I went home to Nebraska (O'Neill, Nebraska). I stayed about a month and then I thought I had been home long enough. They had a big "to do" for me and gave me all kinds of gifts. They asked me to speak in the public school and the students gave me gifts and things they had made.

I decided I had to go back and go to rehabilitation. Colonel Mary Gen Phillips, Assistant Chief of the Army Nurse Corps, had recommended it to me so that is where I went. After that, I was given several choices but decided on Foster General Hospital in Jackson, Mississippi. Colonel Augusta Short was chief nurse there, and I had known her at Walter Reed Hospital. I asked to be put on a hospital ward and let me just do general duty. I had never heard of penicillin. I didn't know any of these new medications. I didn't even know what they would do. After a week on the ward there, I was made head nurse.

I was chosen to go to the state of Alabama to sell war bonds. We made $100,000 over our quota, and I received a commendation from the U.S. Treasury for making so much money. While in Alabama, I was promoted to captain. I then reported back to Foster General Hospital in Jackson.

Later, I was given the opportunity to go back to school, so I went to Columbia University for a year and then to Catholic University in Washington, D.C., where I received my masters degree. I made lieutenant colonel in 1958 and retired at Fitzsimmons Hospital in Denver, Colorado, in 1964. And that's it!

Lieutenant Colonel Madeline Ullom was awarded two Bronze Stars and three Presidential Unit Citations for her performance in the face of the enemy. She was Honorary Past National President of the American Defenders of Bataan and Corregidor. On May 30, 2001, she was one of the first 50 veterans inducted into the Arizona Veterans Hall of Fame in Phoenix, Arizona. She passed away in a Tucson Hospital on October 3, 2001.

Epilogue

The Rape of Manila

Manila had been known around the world for many years before World War II as the "Pearl of the Orient." A few days after we arrived in Manila on February 3, 1945, the city was completely destroyed. It was estimated that as many as 100,000 men, women, and children were horribly massacred and murdered during this one month. Lieutenant General Yamashita, commander of Japanese Forces in Luzon at the time, had ordered all military to retreat from Manila and all of central Luzon. Some 230,000 had retreated to the mountains in northern and eastern Luzon. General Yamashita's Shobu group of 110,000 was in the northern mountains, with his headquarters in the Baguio area. The balance was in

General Yokoyama's Shimbu group, scattered in the southeastern mountains. However, Admiral Iwabuci, commander of 18,000 Japanese naval forces who had left their sunken ships in Manila Bay, had ordered his sailors and 1,600 remaining Jap infantry to kill all Filipinos on sight. This killing of innocent men, women, and children continued from February 17 through March 3, 1945.[115]

Many Americans, as well as others who had lived and worked in Manila, such as General Douglas MacArthur, loved Manila more than any other city in the world. General MacArthur's love for the city was borne out by his insistence all the way to the top with President Roosevelt, face to face, that the Philippines be retaken before attacking Formosa.[116] No one could have anticipated the ravaging of the Filipino people by the Japanese military as they retreated from the city. The streets were littered with the bodies of Filipino men, women, and children, even small babies. Every type of building was blown up or burned to the ground. As Santo Tomas internee Edgar Kneedler explains in his story (see chapter 5), the Japs placed drums of gasoline in the buildings and fired into them with cannons to blow them up and set the buildings on fire.

The carnage was incomprehensible. Between January 9, 1945, when we landed at Lingayen Gulf, to the end of the war in August 1945, on Luzon 255,795 Japanese military were killed or committed suicide and 125,755 surrendered. Among Americans, 10,380 ground troops were killed during the same period and 36,550 were wounded.[117]

Lest We Forget

After VJ Day and the official surrender of the Japanese, most of us in the military knew we would be discharged and sent home soon. And the government wasted little time doing just that. We went to our respective homes to forget and to start new lives. There were few jobs, and people who had worked at home in the war effort were in the same situation. They had nowhere to go. We all floundered around for several months and finally planned something of a future. For the most part, the internees at Santo Tomas also returned to their homes. A few who considered the Philippines home stayed around there, only to find out there was nothing left and that rebuilding was almost an impossible task. Many of them eventually returned to the United States.

I slowly began to work toward a future. In 1947, I met and married a wonderful girl, and we had three wonderful children. With my background in electronics in the Marine Corps, I worked for the government for the first several years. In all that time, I recall only one incident in which the subject of my Marine Corps experience in the Philippines came up. Shortly after the war, I went to work at Mare Island Naval Shipyard in Vallejo, California, on the north side of San Francisco Bay. I worked there as a radio and radar technician, repairing radar systems on ships and submarines. One day, after about three years on that job, another radio technician, Al Naftaly, who had become a good friend, was working with me on a ship's radar system. We went out on the main deck, sat down, and leaned back on the bulkhead to have our lunch. As we opened our metal lunch boxes, Al asked me what I did during the war. I told him I was in the Marine Corps and spent two years in the South Pacific and was with a group who rescued American prisoners of war. I could see his eyes light up. "What prison was it?" he asked. I said, "A prison camp at Santo Tomas University in Manila." Al then said to me, "I was one of the prisoners—you rescued me!"

I could not believe it. His whole family was in Santo Tomas Internment Camp, listed in Steven's book *Santo Tomas Internment Camp* as William Sidney, Albert Lester (Al), Anne Louise, David, Harry Abraham, Joseph Lyon, and Maurice, all Naftalys.[118]

When I started this project, I tried desperately to find Al during my research. Finally I found his brother, Maurice, who lived in Watsonville, California. He told me that Al had passed away years ago. Maurice, whom I never did get to meet, also passed away just a few months after I talked with him. A friend of his called me to tell me this.

Now most of us who lived that history are gone. I recently heard a U.S. senator say that World War II veterans are dying at a rate of 1,500 every day. Most of my World War II friends are gone. While much has been written on World War II, it as been done to recount the major events of the war and the decisions of great leaders. In large part, the stories of those of us who were there have never been told or have been forgotten. My hope is that this book is a contribution to their being told and remembered.

Appendix A

Captain John Abbot Titcomb, USMCR
October 27, 1910–March 1, 1945

John Abbot Titcomb was born October 27, 1910, in Newton, Massachusetts, the elder son of Harold and Ethel Titcomb. His father was a native of Brooklyn, New York; his mother, Ethel Brignall, was born in Norwood, Surrey, England, and lived in England until her marriage on July 8, 1908. From 1911 to 1919, John (known as "Jack" to his family and friends) lived in England. His father worked as consulting mining engineer in London. In 1919, Jack's father was demobilized from the Royal Air Force, and the entire family returned to Farmington, Maine, where Jack entered the Model School.

Jack then returned to London to attend the Westminster School, which he attended from 1925 to 1929. He then returned to the U.S. and entered Dartmouth College, where he received his A.B. degree in 1932, *summa cum laude,* and was also elected to Phi Beta Kappa. A postgraduate in Theyer School, Dartmouth, in 1933, he received the C.E. degree. Jack worked in the engineering department with the Trepea Mines, Ltd., Avecan Yugoslavia from 1933 to 1934. Then, after taking graduate courses in geology at Yale University, he worked as a mining engineer, geologist, field manager, and mine superintendent for Nemont Mining Corporation of New York.

Jack Titcomb married Janet Stanwood Foote on February 3, 1940. A daughter, Marian, was born to them in Grass Valley, July 11, 1942, and a son, Peter Abbot, on May 9, 1944, at Brookline, Massachusetts.

In December 1942, Jack resigned from Newmont Corporation and volunteered for the U.S. Marine Corps. He was commissioned first lieutenant on March 11, 1943. After extensive Marine training, he took courses in radar at Harvard and the Massachusetts Institute of Technology, was promoted to captain in August 1944, and sailed for the Pacific the following month.

When Captain Titcomb joined Marine Air Group 24, First Marine Air Wing, on the island of Bougainville, in the northern Solomon Islands, he was made group communications officer. This job was an awesome job in that he was responsible for the repair, servicing, and maintenance of all the aircraft communications in Marine Air Group on two airstrips on the island (Piva North and Piva South). In addition to that, he was involved in the operation and planning for providing close air support for ground troops in the Philippines.

Captain Titcomb played a significant role in the "Flying Column," the operation that resulted in the recapture on February 3, 1945, of the 3,700 internees held at Santo Tomas University Internment Camp in Manila. Captain Titcomb was one of the seven Marines assigned to the 1st Cavalry Division, which raced to Manila. Captain Titcomb, Staff Sergeant A. A. Byers, and Staff Sergeant P. J. Miller were with the MAG-24 Hallicrafter Radio Truck with Major General Verne D. Mudge, Commanding General of the 1st Cavalry Division and this operation. Captain Francis B. (Frisco) Godolphin and I (the author) were with General Hugh Hoffman and the 2nd Brigade, and Captain Samuel E. McAloney and Corporal P. E. Armstrong were with General William C. Chase and the 1st Brigade, which was in the front of the column.[119]

Captain Titcomb, the victim of a Japanese sniper's bullet, died on Luzon Island in the Philippines, March 1, 1945, after the internees were liberated.

Captain Ned Thomas, USMCR, Public Relations officer with the First Marine Aircraft Wing, paid tribute to Jack Titcomb and provided some insights into his personality and motivation:

Jack Titcomb wasn't the only Marine to die on Luzon, but he was one of the best.

Captain Titcomb was a cultured, mild-mannered gentleman—not the kind you'd expect to be eager for front-line fighting. But he was. A Jap sniper got him through the head.

Jack took the war as a personal thing. He had lived and gone to Westminster School in London much of the time until he was 19—his adolescent, impressionable years.

He hated the Nazis for the pasting they gave England early in the war. And while the Marines all along have fought exclusively against the Jap in the Pacific, his grudge against the Japs was just as intense, because they were a common enemy. He could hardly wait to get at them.

He was killed doing one of the most dramatic jobs of the Philippines liberation campaign. With the Filipino Army Guerrillas, he was directing strikes of Army and Marine planes, helping them in their drive on San Fernando La Union.[120]

War Diary of Captain John Abbott (Jack) Titcomb, MAG-24

Captain Jack Titcomb kept his War Diary in a few little spiral note-books small enough to fit in his shirt pocket. In it he recounted his experiences from January 25, 1945, after we had landed at Lingayen Gulf, Luzon, in the Philippines to March 1, 1945, the day he was killed by a Jap sniper's bullet. His mother, Ethel Titcomb, copied the diary, and included a few notes as well. The diary, reprinted here with permission of the Titcomb family, provides a battlefield-level firsthand account of the war while it was being fought. Captain Jack Titcomb, who appears in the text of this book, was the one from among the Bougainville crew providing close air support who did not make it back.

Jan. 25 Nip flew wing on a P-47 and strafed the strip.

Jan. 26 [no entry]

Jan. 28 Nip power dived at 1000' [1,000 feet] over us in moonlight and dropped 5 100 pounders [dropped 5 each 100 pound bombs] mile away.

Jan. 29 Went up to Reg. OP [Regimental Operations] and watch SBDs paste hell out of the Japs 2 miles away.

Jan. 30 [no entry]

Jan. 31 Started South for Guimba at 1730 [5:30 p.m.] Lovely sunset crossing AGNO river. Stayed at Guimba waiting to jump off for the drive on Manila! Slept a couple of hours.

Feb. 1 Drive started at 0001. We left Guimba about 0400. I was running the 299 truck with S/S Miller's help. Tanks & guns & trucks as we moved on ominously in the night. Heard distant gunfire. Went slowly over bad roads and through rivers. About 4 p.m. arrived at area to spend the night.

A few Jap shells landed _ to _ mile away as we heard M.G. [machine gun] fire. Worked late on the radio. Slept on my air mattress with loaded pistol and carbine beside me!

Feb. 2 Up at 0500 [5 a.m.], had some K-Ration and went to work on the radio [meaning talking to home base]. Started off about 1000 like a bat out of hell on concrete highway for Manila.

Crossed river at CABANATUAN. Evidence of fighting—overturned burning Jap trucks and cars full of bullet holes and a few dead Japs, but did not see 'em. Too busy! One burning truck with ammo [ammunition] exploding. Several dead Japs, but I was busy with the radio and didn't see 'em. Drove far and fast to within 25 miles of Manila!

Joyful people making "V" for Victory signs and throwing flowers.

Occasional shell holes & bomb craters & overturned trucks, but on the whole not much evidence of fighting. Slept in a field. Heard a lot of Mortars—M.G.s [machine guns] blasting a pocket of 400 Japs a mile or two away.

Feb. 3 Busy as hell all day with the radios sending planes on missions. Moved on toward Manila through Baliang east of Santa Maria. Our "K-Rations 1" [truck call sign] had to stay behind the convoy to transmit.

As we were going alone across the countryside, radio reports came in of 300 mounted Jap Cavalry last seen 3 miles to our left! "Oh hell," we said, "we are three Marines and one good Army man so we should worry!"

Never saw the Cavalry as our planes couldn't find 'em, but it sure was a relief when we caught up with Army trucks and tanks.

Had a "hellish" river crossing—A "cat" [Caterpillar tractor] finally pulled us [through]. Could see fires down towards Manila.

Drove on in pitch darkness.[121]

On the dash to Manila, had to get pulled through streams and at night after dark, apart from convoy, providing own protection with tommy guns and rifles. Terrific fight at filter plant! Jap artillery—Jap diaries admit planes prevented counter attack.

Feb. 4 Stopped finally about 3 a.m. and tried to sleep a little sitting in the truck. Woke at 5:30 [a.m.]. Fires and considerable shooting down towards Manila. This was the most rugged day so far. We stopped in one place and an excited Filipino rushed up & said there was a Jap nearby.

About 7 of us went over and flushed him. (He had only a pistol.)

We fired a volley but my Carbine misfired! We went on up and found the Jap dead. Heard a lot of shooting nearby. Apparently numerous Japs around. Saw blasted trucks and occasional dead Japs by the road. General MacArthur drove by twice in a jeep. A huge explo-

sion occurred about _ mile from our bivouac area at NORZAGA-
RAY. A small ammunition dump exploded and killed and injured
quite a few (our men). Our truck furnished power for lights in
the hospital tent so the medics could work on the poor devils. We
worked 'til 1 a.m. getting out messages. Lots of shooting around
us—mortars, rifles, & M.G. nearby, all ours. Was awakened by
a helluva volley which sounded only 100 yards or so away. We
grabbed our helmets and carbines but it died down.

Feb. 5 Crossed river at Monagaray & proceeded to Manila outskirts.
Pockets of resistance ahead slowed us up. Stopped a while at Grace
Park. Lots of destroyed Jap aircraft were dispersed around the area.
Could see big columns of smoke from Manila. We are now run-
ning on Jap gas!

Feb. 6 Had about 2 hours sleep only for 2 nights but last night we *really*
slept.

Shaved and washed and feel like a new man. Still considerable opposition between us here at Grace Park & our troops in Manila. The
1st Cavalry Division is a real outfit—more like a Marine Division!
Stayed at Grace Park all day. Our shells from a nearby battery were
whistling overhead quite frequently during the night.

Feb. 7 Went into Santo Tomas University. It was pathetic to see the poor
people. They were terribly undernourished. The kids looked in
better shape than the grownups. They were just overcome with
emotions after being released after three long years. Poor Gordon
Bettles [Gordon Meldrum Bettles] died in the Philippine General
Hospital on June 14, 1943. They believe he died of diabetes—not
malnutrition or mistreatment. They think he is buried in the Ca-

thedral of St. John, but Japs still hold that area, so could not go there. Duggleby, taken away January 5, 1945—presumably to Ft. Santiago & now probably at Los Banos or Muntiniiupa. He was ok when last seen.[122] Found the Kneebones[123] in Bilibid prison right near Santo Tomas. It was a wonderful experience to find them. I brought them some canned lobster & K-Rations, etc. I was the first person they had seen from Grass Valley. Poor Gene had been given the works by the Japs for a week several times and was HUNG UP BY HIS THUMBS with his hands behind his back by the yellow bastards. They have two cute kids, Kay, age 7, and Terrance, age 2 (born during the internment).

Went back to Santo Tomas. Jap 5" [5-inch guns] were shelling it. Trying to kill the civilians I guess. They got three direct hits on the Main building while I was there & about six shells landed between me and the building—about 100 yards away. It isn't a bit frightening—don't know why. What a horrible tragedy if some of those poor people are killed after three desperate years of waiting half starved. The "K-Rations 2" Jeep had real adventures (Capt. McAloney and PFC Armstrong). They went right into Manila on Feb. 5. Jap trucks with M.G.s would dash out of side roads into their columns. They really used their Tommy gun. The General's Jeep [General Chase] just behind them had bullet holes in it.

[Later, Feb. 6 or 7] When we, Capt. MacAloney and I, got to Bilibid Prison, a guy grabbed us and said "You're Marines—come here—there's a girl been waiting 3 years for you and I promised I'd bring her the first two Marines I could find!" So we went up to the gal—she gave us each a hug and a kiss and had tears in her eyes. It was really touching! I think I was the fifth or sixth Marine to get to Manila!

Feb. 8 Move our G. P. Before we moved a shell landed one or two hundred yards away and a guy handed me a piece of hot shrapnel from it!

During the night, I was wakened by firing and could see tracers ricocheting overhead. They were being fired at us! Our artillery pounded all night and the shell whistled and fluttered right over us and we could see the glow and flames of Manila burning about 4 miles away. Had a busy day of radio operations. Our planes seem to be doing more and more. We are well settled now and sit at a table for mess! Real luxury after a week of K-Rations.

Feb. 9 Violent bursts of Tommy gun and rifle fire about 100 yards away in the night. I jumped up, slammed on my helmet, and loaded pistol, carbine, and tommy gun within a few seconds. I had such an arsenal that I couldn't help laughing. Nothing more happened.

Feb. 10, 11, 12 Three fairly routine days of radio operations. Two SBDs were hit but managed to get in to the strip near our G. P. It was darned interesting to talk to the Pilots we had been directing!

Mail arrived on Feb. 12—Hooray! A wonderful letter from Jan written Jan. 8th.

Feb. 13 Went to absolute front lines! At forward O. P. Artillery and mortars were shelling a dozen Japs out near the Marikina airstrip. We could see Japs through field glasses. There was a dead Jap at the O. P. that they hadn't had time to bury yet. I picked up a clip of Jap 25 Cal. Ammo and a Jap sun helmet.

Feb. 14 Again right in the front lines! Drove miles through the southern devastated part of Manila to the 5th Cavalry O. P. right on a knoll. We were shelling Japs and Jap positions about 1 mile away near the Manila Officers Club. Am sitting here watching the bursts and hearing our shells going overhead. We are near the Manila Officers Club and have two radio jeeps with us.

We directed our planes (25 of them) in on the target about 1 mile away. Huge explosives and black smoke as the bombs landed. One hit a gasoline dump and soon a huge fire was roaring and a great column of black smoke went up to the sky.

The people in South Manila are not waving and shouting. War is too grim and close for them. Large areas are flattened and you see wounded civilians being carried on carts and stretchers. Poor people.

[There are no entries for Feb. 15-18.]

Feb. 19 Yesterday, the Army boys ran a telephone line for us to their forward observation Post. A bare knoll with a marvelous view to the East of the whole Marakina Valley which is East of Manila. This O.P. is about 1 mile by trail forward of our main front line at the filter plant.

Six men were delegated to take me out there because snipers infiltrate the area quite often. Reached the O.P. and got out my field glasses, maps, and aerial photos ready to direct the planes in on some prearranged targets. Had been sitting there about an hour with four or five other Army men when suddenly some shooting started. The sound had the nasty sharp crack of shots that are "coming" instead of going! I dropped flat on my belly where I was and felt a slight pain in my leg where a bullet just nicked me.

Boy, did I hug that ground keeping my heels flat and my nose down in the dirt! The Jap machine gun gave another burst and there was an interval and a few more shots and then quiet.

I raised my nose and could see no-one—all the other lads had got into their foxholes, and it was a mighty lovely feeling to be the only guy on top of the ground!

At any moment, I thought the M. G. [machine gun] might start up again.

I could see the feet of one poor chap about ten feet away who was hit and killed just as he dived for the foxhole. It's lucky for me I flattened out and didn't try to get to a foxhole.

Fortunately the poor fellow died quickly and he was not married. After about 5 or 10 minutes lying there, a medic crawled over to see if he could help the chap who was hit, but it was too late.

Then I made a violent Swan dive into the nearest foxhole and boy did it seem safe and cozy and comfortable!

The Army fired mortars all around to our left for a while in case there were more Japs there. Patrols were circling the area.

When all was calm again, we found out that that three Japs had sneaked up on an adjoining knoll in the night with two light machine guns.

They fired two bursts and then all three Japs ran back away from their guns sneaking into our Patrol that was behind 'em!

Thank God they are such darn fools—they could have put up quite a fight with those two M.G.s.

The bullets had killed one man, made a tiny nick in my leg that one Band Aid more than covered! Busted a beautiful can of apricots, smashed a bottle in front of the guy's nose, and put a hole in a canteen cup.

The Army boys sure kidded me about being the most lightly wounded man in the War. "The only Marine up at the front and then you get the Purple Heart that easy!"

They're a great bunch, this First Cavalry Division. They have spirit and pride and drive just like the Marines! Spent the rest of the day on the O.P. phoning back instructions to our planes which were sent over the air by the radio jeep.

Feb. 20 Returned to Mangalden Airfield [where MAG-24 is] in a TBF. It was a lovely day with white fluffy clouds. I sat in the ball turret and got a superb view of everything. Clark Field was an amazing sight. The whole area littered with the wreckage of hundreds of Jap planes.

[No entries for Feb. 21-23]

Feb. 24 Down to 121st Gun. Reg. Advanced G. P. Crossed river on tiny bridge and into mysterious area of houses under trees. Men around flickering fire.

Feb. 25 Real close air support. 9 A-20s and about 18 SBDs. The guerrillas advanced 2,000 yards.[124]

Feb. 20 Flew up in a TBF to guerrilla headquarters for all of Northern Luzon! (Col. Volckmann, U.S. Army headquarters). We were behind the Jap lines, but you'd never have known it. It was on a pretty sandy bar. H.Q. was in a school building. Typewriters were clicking and everything very G.I.

Lt. Col. Volckmann was C. O. of staff of Lt. Col. Calvert, Ch. of Staff and Lt. Col. Murphy, Ch. of Intell. Officer. They were swell guys who said "to Hell with the surrendering business" when the Philippines fell four years ago. Most of the other officers were well educated

Filipinos. The organizations of U.S.A.FIP—United States Army Forces in the Philippines (Northern Luzon).

Flew back to our base. The TBF stuck in the sand of the runway and we had quite a time taking off. The pilot had to bounce her over a truck at the end of the runway.

Feb. 22 Put our 299 radio truck on one LCM (Landing Craft Mechanized) and a radio jeep on another and had a lovely six-hour trip up the east coast of Lingayen Gulf to U.S.A.F.I.P. Headquarters. Stayed that night in a nice bamboo hut right on the sandy beach. Waves breaking gently on the beach, a bright moon overhead, and the distant roar of surf on the coral reef—and Janet ten thousand miles away—Ah me!

Feb. 23 Routine radio operations. Directed a strike of 36 A-20 bombers in on their target. Met some amazingly interesting people. One was Lt. Col. Blackburn, Commander of a regiment up north. He has fought here for years with 200 rifles for his 2,000 men, and only 100 rounds of ammunitions for each rifle! Of course they had some captured Jap weapons as well—but it staggers you to think of what these people have done with so little. He told me many, many tales of the Japs torturing people in various horrible ways. I doubt if the average person can or ever will realize the utter remorseless cruelty and sadism of the Japs.

Feb. 25 4 mi. N.E. of San F [Fernando]. Real close support assault following 9 A-20s and 18 SBDs bombing and strafing 2,000 yards advance during day.

Feb. 26 With C.O. of 3rd Bat. Of 121 Infantry. Guerrilla troops at river just No. of San Fernando. Got Jap flag—brought in wrapped around captured Jap soap! Col. Barnett gave the flag to me. Watched the assault 400-500 yards in front after our planes pounded Reservoir Hill. Several wounded brought in. Man with dum dum through his right wrist—a nasty wound—said to his C.O., "I'm sorry sir, but I cannot salute." The Filipinos are wonderful people.

We can hear the crack of a sniper's rifle now shooting in our direction from across the river 500 yds. away. I'm glad they're lousy shots!

Feb. 27 Back to Col. Volckmann's headquarters at Darigayas Point. What a lovely place. We stay in a pretty bamboo hut right on the sandy beach. I'm sleeping in a jungle hammock out in the moonlight and in the morning I fall out of the hammock and have a swim before breakfast. These people are awful hard working. The Colonels and many of their Filipino officers and men work till midnight or later every night and are going again next morning.

They are all doing such a marvelous job with so little equipment and so few men.

Feb. 28 Spent most of the day trouble shooting our 299 Radio transmitter (in the truck). We finally found a bad condenser shorted, but one side had only 300 ohms resistance to ground.

March 1 I'm in a foxhole about 300 yards from the Japs.[125] Had an exciting night. Went to the advance command post of the 121st (Guerrilla) Infantry. Went through dark trails amid moonlight and shadows. We then got 8 Bolomen[126] to carry our portable 284 radios, and with (dirt from a sniper's bullet hitting the edge of the foxhole just spattered over this diary!) 8 guerrilla soldiers to guard us, we started a three-mile hike up a long ridge just west of San Fernando. It was lovely in the moonlight with the 9,000-foot mountain range to our left and the China Sea on our right. One chap said the whole thing had an Arabian Night feeling climbing silently up with the guerrillas knowing that the Japs held the other end of the ridge.

We arrived about midnight at the tiny bamboo hut hidden in a clump of trees, and slept there till 6 a.m. Heard quite a bit of rifle and machine gun fire in the night.

This morning we moved about 2,000 yards south along the ridge to the front lines. This foxhole is a bomb crater that has been dug out some more—it's a dandy. The knoll, which is the Jap front line, is about 300 yards in front of us. The Japs are dug in and we can't see them, but an occasional bullet zinging overhead is a good reminder that they are there!

A-20s just made very close strafing and bombing runs on the ridge in front of us, while we directed them with our radio.

Our front lines were marked with white panels and the strafing bullets started landing about 200 yards ahead, and swept the ridge. The A-20s also dropped bombs about 1,000 yards along the ridge from us. When they strafe it, it's quite exciting as their machine guns open up about a quarter of a mile behind you (and you hope they're not aiming at you!) and then the planes roar overhead at 100 or 200 feet with all guns blazing and the tracers spraying its scenery ahead.

Our guerrilla troops are now advancing across the open in front of us. It's pretty tough, as they can't see that darn sniper.

Lt. Sid Taylor is here in the foxhole with me. He said, "This would be the greatest and most exciting experience of my life, if it wasn't the saddest time." His little daughter, aged 2 _ (Molly's age) has just died. He got a dispatch, which gave no details, and he's terribly worried about his wife, as of course he hasn't seen or heard from her. I said, "Do you have any other children?" And his answer was, "I had a son, but he is dead too." It seems terrible that such sadness can come to one family. Sid is a grand guy and is doing a wonderful job here in spite of his grief.[127]

The following account of Jack Titcomb's death is taken from a pamphlet prepared by his father in tribute to his son in 1945.

It happened at 11:30 on the morning of March 1, in a shallow foxhole on an exposed ridge from which the guerrillas were launching an attack against the strongly dug-in Japs. Jack had been behind the front lines until the night before. His job as communications officer for the Marine Support Air Party (SAP) put him in charge of the crew operating a radio truck and a radio jeep. The truck was the nerve center through which air strikes were coordinated, and it was in constant touch with both planes overhead and Marine observers in the front lines calling targets.

It was the same setup he had had when his SAP (then called ALP) worked with the First Cavalry Division during its famous armored dash down the central plains and into Manila. He (Jack) had been nicked in the calf of his left leg by machine gun fire on the outskirts of Manila, and his commanding officer had recommended him for the Purple Heart. He had felt pretty guilty over the prospect of being decorated for what he called a scratch.

That night, he had talked with Captain Samuel McAloney, who was in command of the Marine SAP, into trading places with him (directing air cover using the jeep radio), so he "could get up front and have a personal hand in walloping the Japs."

While he was eating K rations with Lieutenant Taylor, a signal came over their radio. Jack had reached over the edge of the foxhole he was in and picked up the hand-set with the antenna, which drew fire every time the Japs spotted it. In his well-modulated voice, he spoke into the microphone:

"Blank, Blank, this is . . ."

Those four words were the last he uttered. He slumped back into Taylor's arms, blood oozing from a small hole in the left side of his forehead. The 31-caliber bullet, fired from a distance of 300 yards, had gone completely through his helmeted head. He never regained consciousness, but his breathing and pulse kept on for an hour.

Taylor did all he could. He poured sulfa powder on the wound and emptied the precious contents to his canteen trying in vain to get Jack to swallow a sulfa pill. He called the forward command post and told them to have a doctor ready. He had to stay there to direct the incoming strike, so Master Technical Sergeant George Ascuena crawled in and took over the job of getting Jack out.

Ascuena did a masterful job of snaking his captain out under submachine gun and rifle fire. With Titcomb flat on the ground, face up, Ascuena got on his hands and knees over him and dragged him back to some Filipino bolomen who carried him to the protected forward command post on a stretcher fashioned from two bamboo poles, part of a blanket, a scarf, and Taylor's dungaree jacket. The way was jagged and steep but the sure-footed Filipinos bore him gently to the command post, where the doctor and intern were waiting. He died there, a mile from the foxhole.

He was taken to the hospital at Guerrilla headquarters. His wound was bathed and bandaged. His clothes were cleaned and put back on him neatly. Covered by a new Army blanket, he lay in state on a cot in a tent lit by candles. A guard of honor of four Guerrilla soldiers stood over him all night long, on orders of Lieutenant Colonel Russell W. Volckmann, U.S. Army officer and West Pointer who commanded all Guerrilla forces in northern Luzon.

"Captain Titcomb did a great job for us, and we will always remember him," said Colonel Volckmann. Lieutenant Colonel George M. Barnett, commanding officer of the regiment with which Jack was working when death caught up with him, added his tribute: "He was a swell fellow, a fine gentleman, and a competent and brave officer."

Perhaps the most touching comment was made by a bashful Filipino woman who had done his laundry while he was with the Guerrillas: "Captain Titcomb fine man. He wanted to pay me, but I no accept. He do so much for my people."

From Mindanao, Philippine Islands, in the latter part of May (1945) came the announcement that an airstrip captured by Filipino guerrillas and now used by elements of a Marine Air Group had been named Titcomb Field in honor of Captain Jack A. Titcomb.[128]

The last time I saw Captain Titcomb was when General MacArthur was standing around watching what we were doing. Seven Marines attracted a lot of attention around almost a thousand 1st Cavalry Army

GIs. Over the many years, I have referred to Captain Titcomb as my "best friend" while I was in the Pacific. We met when he arrived on Bougainville to get ready for the Philippines. Seldom it happens that you meet a person you just "click" with and you know right away you can relate to. He and I just saw things the same way. I guess this was because we both realized we were getting ready for something real big that was to happen in the Philippines. We didn't know when; we didn't know for whom; and, we didn't know exactly where; but we knew we had to be ready when the time came. And we were. That was our common connection that made us friends as well as fellow Marines.

Jack's mother, Ethel, after she had transcribed Jack's entire diary, added a poem that most eloquently sums up this man's life.

Epitaph

There was an epitaph
I read . . .
"Beloved and unafraid,"
Was all it said,
I never heard
A finer tribute paid
In simple word . . .
What man could
Ask for more?

Here is the very core

Of character

And manhood—

Brave and good!

To exit, with a line

So brief, so fine - -

"Beloved and unafraid!"

(Abigail Cresson, New York Tribune, *January 1947)*

Appendix B

Captain Francis Richard Borroum, (Frisco) Godolphin, USMCR

Captain "Frisco" Godolphin has not left us a record of his time in the war as detailed as that of the war diary of Captain Jack Titcomb, but he did leave letters he sent to friends during the war that give us a sense of how he saw his experiences in the Philippines. And, unlike Jack Titcomb, he lived to see the end of the war and was able to return to his life in the States, a life now shaped by his wartime experiences. A sketch of this life before, during, and after the war is provided in this appendix. It is illustrative of one of the many of those individuals who served in the war and made important contributions to the war effort. About his time in the Pacific he said, "Experiences pile up in a hurry and you live a long time in a very brief period." "Frisco" Godolphin lived a long time in a long life as well.

I remember Captain Godolphin well. He was the kind of person who made an impression, and was the only person I ever met in the Marine Corps that acted as if he had no boss. He did his own thing the way he thought it should be done, without any advance approval. When there was a serious problem, he would simply say, "I will take care of it!" He would not offer any explanation of how he would take care of it but he did it. Everyone who worked with him looked up to him, in part because he was a master organizer. He laid out what had to be done and who had the responsibility to do it, and it would be done, or the person assigned the task was in real trouble. He said "good morning" to you each day with authority. You did not question what he had taken as a position. Why? Because you knew he had to be right. Few men have I admired and respected more than Captain Frisco Godolphin.

Francis Richard Borroum Godolphin was born at Del Rio, Texas, on April 8, 1903, to Reverend and Mrs. F. B. Godolphin. He would later graduate from Oak Park High School, Oak Park, Illinois, where his father was rector of the Grace Episcopal Church for twenty years. He entered Princeton as an undergraduate in the fall of 1920. He received his A.B. degree in 1924 and graduated *magna cum laude.* From 1924 to 1926 he carried on graduate study and served as an instructor at New York University and received his M.A. degree there. In 1925, he married Isabelle Simmons of Oak Park, Illinois. They had two children, Katherine Jeanne and Thomas Simmons. During the years 1926-27, he taught at the New Jersey College for Women and started study at Princeton for his Ph.D.

in the Classics, which he received in 1929. He served as an instructor at Princeton from 1927 to 1930; he was assistant professor from 1930 to 1940, when he became Associate Professor and then, in 1942, full professor. In 1941-1942, he was acting chairman of Classics.

In October 1942, he applied for a Reserve Commission in Combat Intelligence with the U.S. Marine Corps. In a letter of recommendation written on October 28, 1942, a fellow Princeton University professor, Mr. Radcliffe Hermance, said: "He not only is an excellent administrative officer [of Princeton University] he also possesses personal qualifications which inspire both friendship and respect. He will be a great loss to this University, but in a time like this his loyalty to this country prompts him to offer his services. As an Infantry Officer in the last war (WWI) I trained hundreds of men and I know the high standards for the Marine Corps. Godolphin will meet them."

Associate Professor Francis R. B. (Frisco) Godolphin, chairman of the Department of Classics, left Princeton University on February 10, 1943, on a military leave of absence to begin training as a First Lieutenant in the United States Marine Corps Reserve. He was ordered to report to the U.S. Marine Station at Quantico, Virginia.

During World War II, Godolphin served in the Pacific and participated in the Marine invasions of Kwajalein, Tinian, Saipan, and Luzon. In the first three landings, he was air liaison officer with the Fourth Marine Division, and in Luzon, in the Philippines, he was attached to the U.S. Army 1st Cavalry Division. He received the Bronze Star Medal following the recapture of the Philippines.

After the Kwajalein, Tinian, and Saipan campaigns, Captain Godolphin wrote to a friend:

"After being with an assault battalion in the Marshalls, on Saipan and Tinian, I think I can match dirt, sweat, heat, and thirst with most members of my class. Willing to enter the exhaustion derby too. Now at the rest base, I'm even thinking of golf and tennis, though not so long ago the presence of feet beneath my boondockers was only an assumption.

"I've been very fortunate in drawing an interesting job where it's easy to feel that you are accomplishing something. Experiences pile up in a hurry and you live a long time in a very brief period. I'll probably be a sucker for any unprepared freshman with a gift for asking questions about the war. Then again, there may not be as much variety as I think. I am pretty sure that I understand some things, and especially some passages in Homer, as I never did before.

"When night comes you know that before you can see daylight again Japs are going to infiltrate and that they are going to throw hand grenades. Ajax's pleas to die in the light if he must die hits pretty hard. Our outfit did a beautiful job of nailing them but one night a whole group rushed in strewing grenades with both hands. Like roses, and I don't care to see a second performance.

"Toe-dancing through a mine field is interesting too; sorry there are no movies of it. But mostly you dig foxholes and curl up in the mud with a good weapon."

Shortly after that, he wrote another classmate:

"I have certainly drawn the most interesting and exciting of assignments. It's terrible to be able to feel that one is actually a veteran of front line action.

A somewhat less exposed assignment would be nice but you can't help feeling that it would be foolish and wasteful to put someone green in when you know how it is and what to do. After all, the Marines' theory is to get them on the run, keep them on the run, never let up. I only lost fifteen pounds during it this time."

In a letter dated December 4, 1944, to President Dodds at Princeton, Captain Godolphin wrote the following:

"Despite a very considerable change of activity from my previous duty, I continue to have most interesting assignments, ranging from a great deal of lecturing and teaching based on previous experience to strafing and bombing of line targets.[129] According to my calculations, I haven't missed much but submarines. One really couldn't cram much more into the experience. Very well and healthy withal."

On December 11, 1944, Marine Air Group 24, to which Captain Godolphin had been assigned, embarked from Bougainville Island in the Solomons, where we had been several months, for Luzon in the Philippines aboard the USS *John T. McMillan*. MAG-24 landed and debarked at Lingayen Gulf on January 22, 1944. On January 31, 1944, two radio jeeps and a radio van joined up with the U.S. Army 1st Cavalry Division at Guimba, 35 miles from Lingayen. Captain Godolphin and I were assigned on one of the jeeps to General Hugh Hoffman of the 2nd Brigade, 1st Cavalry Division.

After Captain Godolphin had completed thirty-eight days of continuous combat in Luzon and after the total recapture of the Philippines was ensured, he was ordered to return to the home base at MAGSDAGUPAN in northern Luzon. The 1st Cavalry Division awarded him the Bronze Star for his outstanding service during this campaign. At his home base, he received orders from his commanding officer to return to the United States for R&R. In his mail at MAGSDAGUPAN was a letter to him from President Dodds of Princeton University, which read in part:

"Dear Frisco:

I have been conspiring with your wife about your early return to Princeton. She agrees with me that it would be a fine thing for the University.

We have a program for returned servicemen under an administrative committee. We have a strong feeling that some member of the faculty who has seen active service is the best one for this post. You qualify on any count and I should like to name you to it.

I feel that the post we have in mind for you is distinctly in the public service, fully justifying an application for retirement, which application I should support in the strongest language I can command.

I await your reply eagerly, with advice as to what I can do at this end to facilitate your return. Harold W. Dodds, President"

President Dodds' letter did not request Captain Godolphin's approval to take this action, but simply advised him of what he was going to do. After a short time in the United States, Captain Godolphin was placed on in-active status by the Marine Corps and after a period of rest, reported to Princeton University on September 15, 1945, as Director of the Princeton Program for Returning Servicemen. Specifically, his role there was "to direct the admission of guidance programs for the servicemen who are expected to return to their studies in increasing numbers as demobilization proceeds."[130]

A Japanese battle flag decorated Captain Godolphin's office wall after he returned to Princeton. His office was located in the historic Nassau Hall, the hall itself a veteran of the American Revolutionary War. Captain Godolphin had served in the full sense in World War II. He was one of the oldest men to see front-line service with the Marine Corps. Captain Godolphin, even in his early forties, stormed ashore with the landing waves in four major landings. On his return to Princeton, he was in charge of a special program concerned with the adjustment of returning veterans to the college campus and in October 1945 was named Dean of the College.

In 1955, Dean Godolphin returned to full-time teaching, research, and writing. In 1964 his wife Isabelle died; in the next year he married Catherine Vanderpool Clark of Princeton. He held the Musgrave Professorship of Latin from 1956 until he retired in 1970. He died at his home in Tucson, Arizona, on December 29, 1974, at the age of 71.

Information concerning Captain Godolphin, in particular concerning his personal life outside the U.S. Marine Corps, came from the Faculty file of the Seeley G. Mudd Manuscript Library at Princeton University, Princeton, New Jersey.

Notes

1. Captain John C. Chapin, USMCR, . . . *And a Few Marines: Marines in the Liberation of the Philippines*, World War II Commemorative Series, 50th Anniversary (Washington, D.C.: U.S. Marine Corps Historical Center, 1997).

2. Ibid., p. 13.

3. Frederick H. Stevens, *Santo Tomas Internment Camp* (Stratford House 1946), pp. 487-97.

4. Tom Brokaw, *The Greatest Generation* (New York: Random House, 1998), dust jacket and p. 15.

5. William J. Dunn, *Pacific Microphone* (College Station: Texas A&M University Press, 1988), Preface.

6. Lord Louis Mountbatten of the British Navy had been appointed British Commander of the Southeast Asia Command by the Queen, but was actually chosen by Winston Churchill. He was on his way at this time to work with General MacArthur at his SW Pacific Headquarters in Brisbane, Australia (Douglas A. MacArthur, *Reminiscences* [New York: McGraw-Hill, 1964], p. 219). Many years later this successor to the throne of Great Britain was assassinated in the Northern Ireland religious dispute.

7. George W. Garand and Truman R. Strobridge, *Western Pacific Operations—History of U.S. Marine Corps Operations in World War II*, vol. IV (Washington, D.C.: Government Printing Office, 1971), p. 769.

8. Captain John C. Chapin, USMCR, *Top of the Ladder: Marine Operations in the Northern Solomons*, World War II Commemorative Series (Washington, D.C., Marine Corps Historical Center, 1997), pp. 1-3.

9. *Marine Corps Gazette*, September 1946.

10. Account of Goodman reported in Robert Sherrod, *History of Marine Corps Aviation in World War II* (Baltimore: Nautical and Aviation Publishing Company of America, 1987), p. 190.

11. John A. DeChant, *Devilbirds: The Story of United States Marine Corps Aviation in World War II* (New York: Harper & Brothers, 1947), p. 123.

12. Ibid.

13. Sherrod, *History of Marine Corps Aviation in World War II*, p. 190.

14. Chapin, *Top of the Ladder*, p. 30.

15. Ibid., p. 32.

16. Sherrod, *History of Marine Corps Aviation in World War II*, p. 193.

17. Chapin, *And a Few Marines*, p. 9.

18. Charles W. Boggs, *Marine Aviation in the Philippines* (Washington, D.C.: Historical Division, Headquarters, U.S. Marine Corps, 1951), p. 61.

19. The SBD dive-bomber has a pilot and gunner.

20. Chapin, *And a Few Marines*, p. 9.

21. National Archives records indicate this was not a commissioned ship of the U.S. Navy.

22. MacArthur, *Reminiscences*, p. 214.

23. Ibid., p. 217.

24. Dunn, *Pacific Microphone*, p. 276.

25. Boggs, *Marine Aviation in the Philippines*, p. 66.

26. Account of the building of the airstrip is taken from Sherrod, *History of Marine Corps Aviation in World War II*, pp. 298-99.

27. About every two weeks we could draw from the paymaster some spending money, a portion of our pay. The only things available to spend it on were some toiletries at a makeshift PX. The guys who played poker at night sometimes drew on their money, but I didn't—because I knew I'd just lose it.

28. Boggs, *Marine Aviation in the Philippines*, p. 68.

29. Garand and Strobridge, *Western Pacific Operations*, p. 342.

30. On January 28, Lt. Gordon R. Lewis, USMC, and his gunner, Cpl. Samuel P. Melish, USMC, of VMSB-153 were shot down by Jap anti-aircraft guns. They were the first MAGSDAGUPAN Marine casualties.

31. Major General McCutcheon was Commanding General, 1st Marine Air Wing in Vietnam. He received many awards and was later nominated to be assistant commandant of the U.S. Marine Corps. A serious illness prevented him from accepting this post; however, Congress promoted him to four-star general on July 1, 1971. He died twelve days later. Chapin, *And a Few Marines*, p. 9.

32. Sherrod, *History of Marine Corps Aviation in World War II*, p. 300.

33. DeChant, *Devilbirds*, p. 156.

34. There are many accounts of the rescue at Cabanatuan in the literature. This one is based on "The Rescue at Cabanatuan," *Life*, February 26, 1945, pp.

34-40.

35. Ibid., pp. 34-35.

36. Ibid., p. 37.

37. Si Dunn, *The First Team, 1st Cavalry Division, A Historical Overview—1921-1983* (Dallas: Taylor Publishing Company, 1984), p. 85.

38. Ibid.

39. Garand and Strobridge, *Western Pacific Operations*, p. 344.

40. Dunn, *The First Team, 1st Cavalry Division*, p. 85.

41. U.S. Army, XIV, *After Action Report, M-1 Operation*, chap. VII (Manila, National Archives, College Park, Md., n.d.). These were the Japanese military responsible for almost all of the destruction of Manila and the murder of many Filipino men, women, and children. It was General Yamashita, Commander of the Japanese military in the Philippines, when he moved his Army troops to northern and eastern Luzon, who ordered that "the City of Manila was to be left outside the zone of battle." Aubrey Saint Kenworthy, *The Tiger of Manila* (New York: Exposition Press, 1953), p. 18.

42. Major B. C. Wright, 1st Cavalry Division Historian. *The Luzon Campaign, The 1st Cavalry Division in World War II* (actual author unidentified, n.p., n.d.), p. 126.

43. He was posthumously awarded the Silver Star.

44. Garand and Strobridge, *Western Pacific Operations*, p. 347.

45. White phosphorous shells were fired from the 1st Cavalry artillery howitzers to mark the targets. Mortars and sometimes, if we were close enough, phosphorous hand grenades in different colors, which we had used on Bougainville, were also used.

46. DeChant, *Devilbirds*, pp. 186-87.

47. Ibid., p. 187.

48. Wright, *The Luzon Campaign*, p. 127.

49. Sherrod, *History of Marine Corps Aviation in World War II*, p. 301.

50. Lieutenant Sutton was later awarded the Distinguished Service Cross for his heroic action.

51. Heading the forward echelon of the 1st Cavalry Division entering Manila was the 44th Tank Battalion Sherman tank *Yankee*, with the crew of St. Donald J. McDonald, Sgt. Lawrence, Corporal Bernardo, and PFC Malmfelt. 44th Tank Battalion, *Tank Tracks: Tennessee to Tokyo* (Tokyo, Japan: Dai Nippon Printing Co. Ltd., 1945), p. 33.

52. The following description of the rescue of the internees was taken from the 1st Cavalry Division official report, found in the National Archives, College Park, Md. The writer of this particular report was not identified.

53. No one seems to know what happened to these goggles, but several of the internees at the time saw and read the note. Over the years, the story has been told that the goggles were dropped from the backseat of one of the SDB

planes by a Marine machine gunner who had a brother, Frank Joseph McSorley, who was an internee in Santo Tomas at the time.

54. The Battlin' Basic's crew was Captain Jesse L. Walters, Sgt. Alfonso R. Trujillo, Cpl. John C. Henke, and Pfc. Peter B. Dillon (44th Tank Battalion, *Tank Tracks: Tennessee to Tokyo*).

55. Army Nurse Madeline Ullom treated Conner's wound, as she recounted and which is recorded in chapter 5 of this book.

56. Dunn, *Pacific Microphone*, pp. 299-300.

57. U.S. Army, 1st Cavalry Division, 5th Cavalry, Part 1 *Lingayen to Manila—27 January to 7 February 1945* (College Park, Md.: National Archives, n.d.).

58. Eva Anna Nixon, *Delayed, Manila—1941-1945* (self-published, 1981), p. 86. Eva Anna Nixon was an internee in Santo Tomas Internment Camp for three and one-half years. On December 8, 1941, she was one of 200 passengers including 15 other missionaries on board the ship SS *President Grant,* docked in Manila harbor, on their way to India. Since the ship could not leave port, she and the others were taken to a hotel in Manila and later incarcerated in Santo Tomas. Her book is available from the Friends Foreign Missionary Society, Evangelical Friends Church, Eastern Region, 1201 30th Street NW, Canton, Ohio 44709.

59. Richard Connaughton, John Pimlott, and Duncan Anderson, *The Battle for Manila* (Novato, Calif.: Presidio Press, 1995), pp. 41, 42, 92-95. It has never been confirmed that Stanley was an agent of the United States or Great Britain—or whether he was working with representatives of General MacArthur or anyone else outside the camp. Maurice Frances of Worcester, England, read about Stanley's negotiating the release of the 200 internees held hostage at Santo Tomas and was so intrigued, he decided to research the story. In an article in the *Worcester* (England) *Evening News* (March 9, 2001), Frances reported that Stanley at age 21 went to a religious college in Lincolnshire, England, and trained to be a missionary. He moved to California in 1928 where he stayed for two years before traveling to Japan as a missionary, where he became fluent in Japanese. In June 1941, he went to the Philippines to continue his work in the Manila area. With the capture of the Philippines by the Japanese, Stanley was confined in Santo Tomas Internment Camp. Frances further says, "Because of his talent for languages, he was used by the Japanese as an interpreter, although this didn't go down well with many of his fellow inmates, who considered him a collaborator. It was a view reinforced by the special treatment he received, being allowed to live on his own, away from the main body of internees. . . . Perhaps gilding the lily somewhat, those same news reports referred to Stanley as 'a British intelligence officer' or 'a special agent working for the Americans.' More likely, he was just a peaceful religious man who could speak Japanese."

60. While strolling in front of the Main Building when I stepped in front of a 1st Cav guy taking a picture of some young internees and other guys. He asked

me to get in the picture, so I did. This picture appeared in "The 50th Anniversary Commemorative Album" column, with an article written by Sgt. Gerard H. Daley, Division Headquarters, 7th Recon. Squadron. It is an official U.S. Army picture taken by PFC Thomas Kates.

61. As reported in Stevens, *Santo Tomas Internment Camp,* but later reports were that more than 21 had been killed in the shelling.

62. Nixon, *Delayed, Manila,* pp. 87-92. Reprinted with permission from the author.

63. In most records this is referred to as the Balera Water-filter plant. It is located about five miles south of Novaliches Lake Reservoir.

64. The Marine Corps Fiftieth Anniversary pamphlet, *And a Few Marines,* describes it this way: "The rocket attack began at midnight. Captain Godolphin went to the roof of the plant with a sextant to determine the azimuth of the rocket position. Six enemy rockets landed within 40 yards of the CP, but Captain 'Frisco' got out alive with enough data to pinpoint the target for the SBDs the next morning."

65. In Wright, *The Luzon Campaign,* p. 133.

66. An article by Kenji Hall, titled "Wartime Documents Set Record Straight," sheds new light concerning the Japanese World War II nuclear project and their race to develop the Atom Bomb before the United States did. The article states, "Japan's own efforts to build a bomb are difficult for many here to accept because of the bombings of Hiroshima and Nagasaki, and the widespread feeling that Japan would never have even considered such a brutal attack." The *Japan Times* (March 7, 2003).

67. This plane was the same as the DC-3.

68. Garand and Strobridge, *Western Pacific Operations,* p. 354.

69. Ibid., p. 348.

70. Ibid., p. 349.

71. Ibid., p. 351.

72. Ibid.

73. Chapin, *And a Few Marines.*

74. Garand and Strobridge, *Western Pacific Operations,* p. 347.

75. Ibid.

76. Ibid.

77. Ibid., p. 354.

78. Ibid., p. 357.

79. DeChant, *Devilbirds,* p. 173.

80. Ibid.

81. Garand and Strobridge, *Western Pacific Operations,* p. 390.

82. DeChant, *Devilbirds,* p. 174.

83. Chapin, *And a Few Marines,* p. 28.

84. All Americans living in the Philippines had to register with the Japanese

military government.

85. Dorothy Howie did not remember his last name.

86. These three internees included Carrol G. Grinnel, Chairman of the STIC Internee Committee, whose body was found February 20, 1945, after the liberation. The next day, fourteen bodies were found wired together, including Alfred F. Duggleby and Clifford L. Larsen, both also members of the STIC Internee Committee. In Stevens, *Santo Tomas Internment Camp*, p. 71.

87. Beverly was born on August 17, 1943.

88. This time with her third child.

89. Puto is like a bread pudding made from rice.

90. The "Bataan nurses" were U.S. Army nurses who served in Bataan—one of whom was an internee, Madeline Ullom, who tells her own story in this chapter.

91. A note from Sascha: "Fifty-five years later, on February 3, 2000, at Santo Tomas in Manila a group of prisoners and some of the liberators of the 1st Cavalry's Flying Column met for a reunion. The machine gunner of the Battlin' Basic, John Hencke, was with us, and for the first time we got to thank him and learn much about that night of Liberation many years ago. I now have a small wooden box with an image painted on it of Battlin' Basic, from John Hencke, that simply says, 'Someone From Texas Loves You!' It is so dear to me."

92. Colonel Brady negotiated 36 continuous hours before agreeing to march the Jap soldiers to the city limits and release the Japs in exchange for the prisoners they were holding.

93. Powdered milk.

94. Arthur MacArthur was General Douglas MacArthur's son.

95. Published by Pathfinder Publishing, Ventura, California, 1991. Much of the material in this chapter is taken from the book and is used with permission of the copyright holder, Peter Wygle.

96. December 7 in the U.S.

97. See enclosed map of Robert Wygle's travel to Manila in the Image Section of this book.

98. In the introduction to his book *Santo Tomas Internment Camp*.

99. The military camps (like Cabanatuan) that were under control of the Japanese Army from the beginning started out bad—Santo Tomas did not.

100. In Bataan, for example.

101. The right outboard engine.

102. Chapter 16 of *Surviving a Japanese P.O.W. Camp* is titled "Hope and Rescue" and includes his dad's diary of the last days before and during their rescue. Excerpts from this chapter, with some of Peter's comments, follow.

103. A condition that causes fluid retention in the lower extremities.

104. The Marines were there, all seven of us—with our SBD dive bombers overhead.

105. February 3, 1945.

106. The tank Battlin' Basic, which had broken down the front gate.

107. This happened on the morning of February 5, 1945. The story is recounted in more detail in chapter 5.

108. The shelling lasted six days.

109. Evelyn M. Monahan and Rosemary Neidel-Greenlee, *All This Hell* (Lexington: University Press of Kentucky, 2000), p. 112.

110. Laterals were tunnels that were built perpendicular to the main tunnel.

111. Arthur MacArthur, General Douglas MacArthur's son.

112. Carl Mydans is the photographer for *Life* magazine who is mentioned elsewhere in this book.

113. Madeline described this instruction as learning to be a lady as well as a soldier.

114. A famous San Francisco restaurant.

115. Frances B. Cogan, *Captured: The Japanese Internment of American Civilians in World War II, 1941-1945* (Athens: University of Georgia Press, 2000), pp. 119, 263.

116. Connaughton, Pimlott, and Anderson, *The Battle for Manila*, pp. 80-81.

117. These statistics are taken from Connaughton, Pimlott, and Anderson, *The Battle for Manila*, p. 205.

118. Stevens, *Santo Tomas Internment Camp*. Stevens lists the names of the camp prisoners.

119. Garand and Strobridge, *Western Pacific Operations*, p. 344.

120. One of many letters provided by the brother of Capt. Titcomb, Andrew, and his wife, Gloria, along with a pamphlet of tributes to Capt. Titcomb prepared by his father, Harold, in 1945.

121. A note was inserted in the diary here, apparently by his father, Harold, on Cornell Club of New York letterhead: "Beyer [meaning Sgt. Byers] enlisted man with Jack, and Bones Holland, Tech. Sgt. Worked with Jack" (underlined by Captain Titcomb's father). Captain Titcomb called me "Bones" because, like the other men, I seldom wore a shirt on Bougainville and weighed about 130 pounds. He asked me and the other enlisted men to call him "Pappy." He did not want us shouting out "Captain" in jungle fighting.

122. He did not realize that the Japs had executed Duggleby, one of the three Santo Tomas highest leaders of the Internees Management Committee, presumably because they heard rumors that someone had a radio on the campus. No one at the camp knew what had happened. Three of them were just taken away and later found buried.

123. Eugene J. and Katherine Mary Kneebone.

124. His mother notes here (Feb. 22, 1947) that this is where the diary entries in the first notebook end. They are continued in second notebook. He starts

the second notebook with his name, Capt. John A. Titcomb, USMCR, Hq. Sq., MAG-24, and labels it "WAR DIARY." Apparently he rewrote some of his observations about Feb. 20 through 25 in the second notebook, where it repeats information in the first.

125. March 1 was his last day, a day he wrote four pages.

126. "Bolomen" were guerrillas without a rifle. This term comes from the weapon the guerrilla did carry, a bolo knife.

127. Jack's diary ends here with the note: written 1 March 1945. Copied by E. T. (Ethel Titcomb, Jack's mother) Feb. 1, 1947.

128. I learned of Captain Titcomb's death soon after he was killed, from Staff Sergeant Byers, who wrote to me just after I left for the U.S. But it was only on July 12, 2000, fifty-five years later, when I received the small pamphlet from Joanna Titcomb, the wife of Captain Titcomb's brother Andrew, that I learned the story of how he died. Captain Titcomb had given me his wife Janet's address in Farmington, Maine. I wrote her immediately but was still moving around in the Marine Corps and never received an answer. I had looked for information on how he died for years but only vigorously when I decided to write this book. I was elated when I received the pamphlet and called Joanna to thank her. Their son Jonathon answered the phone. He seemed eager to talk to someone who had known "Uncle Jack" in the Pacific. I asked Jonathon, "Did anyone ever call Captain Titcomb 'Pappy'?" He said, "Yes, as a matter of fact, they have. MT Sgt. George Ascuena referred to him as that." I told him, "Well, he asked us to call him 'Pappy.' Snipers would look for officers to shoot first. He didn't want anyone hollering at him 'Captain!' All his officer friends called him 'Jack.'"

129. Here Godolphin is referring to teaching us close air support.

130. *Princeton University Bulletin*, September 21, 1945.

Bibliography

44th Tank Battalion. *Tank Tracks: Tennessee to Tokyo.* Tokyo, Japan: Dai Nippon Printing Co. Ltd., 1945.

Boggs, Major Charles W., USMC. *Marine Aviation in the Philippines.* Washington, D.C.: Historical Division, Headquarters, U.S. Marine Corps, 1951.
Brokaw, Tom. *The Greatest Generation.* New York: Random House, 1998.

Chapin, Captain John C., USMCR, Rtd. . . . *And a Few Marines: Marines in the Liberation of the Philippines,* World War II Commemorative Series (50th Anniversary). Washington, D.C.: U.S. Marine Corps Historical Center, 1997.
Chapin, Captain John C., USMCR, Rtd. *Top of the Ladder: Marine Operations in the Northern Solomons,* World War II Commemorative Series (50th Anniversary). Washington, D.C.: U.S. Marine Corps Historical Center, 1997.
Cogan, Frances B. *Captured: The Japanese Internment of American Civilians in World War II, 1941-1945.* Athens: University of Georgia Press, 2000.
Connaughton, Richard, John Pimlott, and Duncan Anderson. *The Battle for Manila.* Novato, Calif.: Presidio Press, 1995.
Contey-Aiello, Rose. *The 50th Anniversary Commemorative Album of the Flying Column, 1945-1995.* Tarpon Springs, Fla.: Marrakech Express, 1994.

DeChant, John A. *Devilbirds: The Story of United States Marine Corps Aviation in World War II.* New York: Harper & Brothers, 1947.

Bibliography

Dunn, Si. *The First Team, 1st Cavalry Division, A Historical Overview—1921-1983*. Dallas, Tex.: Taylor Publishing Company, 1984.
Dunn, William J. *Pacific Microphone*. College Station: Texas A&M University Press, 1988.

Garand, George W., and Truman R. Strobridge. *Western Pacific Operations—History of U.S. Marine Corps Operations in World War II*, Volume IV. Washington, D.C.: Superintendent of Documents, Government Printing Office, 1971.
Godolphin, Frances R. B. (file). Princeton, N.J.: Mudd Library, Princeton University.

Hoffman, Major John T., USMCR. *From Makin to Bougainville: Marine Corps Raiders in the Pacific War*, WWII Commemorative Series (50th Anniversary). Washington, D.C.: U.S. Marine Corps Historical Center, 1995.

Jansen, Sascha Jean, Margaret Sams, Jane Wills, and Karen Lewis. *Interrupted Lives*. Ed. Lily Nova and Iven Lourie. Artemis Books, 1995.

Kenworthy, Aubrey Saint, Lt. Col. U.S. Army. *The Tiger of Malaya*. New York: Exposition Press, 1953.

MacArthur, Douglas A. *Reminiscences*. New York: McGraw-Hill, 1964.
Marine Corps Gazette. Quantico, Va.: Marine Corps Association.
Monahan, Evelyn M., and Rosemary Neidel-Greenlee. *All This Hell*. Lexington: University Press of Kentucky, 2000.
Mydans, Carl (photographer). *Life* magazine. New York: Time-Life. Issues dated February 19, February 26, and March 5, 1945.

Nixon, Eva Anna. *Delayed, Manila—1941-1945*. Self-published, 1981. Murdock Learning Research Center, George Fox University, Newberg, OR 97132.
Norman, Elizabeth M. *We Band of Angels*. New York: Pocket Books, (reprint), 2000.

Parade Magazine. New York: Parade Publications. June 17, 2001.

Sherrod, Robert. *History of Marine Corps Aviation in World War II*. Baltimore: Nautical and Aviation Publishing Company of America, 1987.
Stevens, Frederic H. *Santo Tomas Internment Camp*. Stratford House, 1946.

Titcomb, Captain John A., USMCR. Personal Diary, January–March, 1945.

U.S. Army. *XIV Corps–After Action Report, M–1 Operation, Chapter VII.* Manila. College Park, Md.: National Archives, n.d.

U.S. Army, 1st Cavalry Division. *Headquarters, 1st Cavalry Brigade–S-2 Periodic Report.* College Park, Md.: National Archives, n.d.

U.S. Army, 1st Division. *The Luzon Campaign.* From original typed copy, author not identified. College Park, Md.: National Archives, n.d.

U.S. Army, 1st Cavalry Division, 1st Cavalry Brigade. *B. Narrative Operation.* College Park, Md.: National Archives, n.d.

U.S. Army, 1st Cavalry Division, 1st Cavalry Division. "Unit Journal Messages." College Park, Md.: National Archives, n.d.

U.S. Army, 1st Cavalry Division, 5th Cavalry. Part One *Lingayen to Manila—27 January to 7 February 1945.* College Park, Md.: National Archives, n.d.

Van Sickle, Emily. *The Iron Gates of Santo Tomas.* Academy Chicago Publishers, 1992.

Wright, B. C., Major, 1st Cavalry Division Historian. *The Luzon Campaign, The 1st Cavalry Division in World War II.* Actual author unknown, n.d.

Wygle, Peter. *Surviving a Japanese P.O.W. Camp: Father and Son Endure Internment in Manila.* Ventura, Calif.: Pathfinder Publishing of California, 1991.

Index

Printed in the USA
CPSIA information can be obtained
at www.ICGtesting.com
JSHW082152140824
68134JS00014B/202